C000184472

MOSSAD

Also by Ronald Payne

Private Spies
The Carlos Complex
The Cruellest Night
The Terrorists
Counterattack
The Falklands Conflict
The Dictionary of Espionage
War Without End

MOSSAD

ISRAEL'S MOST SECRET SERVICE

RONALD PAYNE

BANTAM PRESS

LONDON · NEW YORK · TORONTO · SYDNEY · AUCKLAND

TRANSWORLD PUBLISHERS LTD
61–63 Uxbridge Road, London W5 5SA

TRANSWORLD PUBLISHERS (AUSTRALIA) PTY LTD
15–23 Helles Avenue, Moorebank, NSW 2170

TRANSWORLD PUBLISHERS (NZ) LTD
Cnr Moselle and Waipareira Aves,
Henderson, Auckland

Published 1990 by Bantam Press
a division of Transworld Publishers Ltd
Copyright © Ronald Payne 1990

The right of Ronald Payne to be identified
as author of this work has been asserted in accordance
with sections 77 and 78 of the Copyright Designs and
Patents Act 1988.

British Library Cataloguing in Publication Data
Payne, Ronald, *1926–*
  Mossad.
  1. Intelligence services, Israeli. Israel : Sherut ha –
  bita hon ha – kelali
  I. Title
  327.12095694

ISBN 0–593–01443–X

All rights reserved. No part of this publication may
be reproduced, stored in a retrieval system, or
transmitted in any form or by any means,
electronic, mechanical, photocopying, recording,
or otherwise, without the prior permission of
the publishers.

Printed in Great Britain
by Mackays of Chatham, plc, Chatham, Kent

Contents

Part IV: Violence of Lebanon

Part V: Allies

Part VI: Mossad Goes Nuclear

Part VII: London End

Part I
The Spyocracy

1. The Institute

Of all the world's intelligence services, the most intriguing is Mossad. Its full title – the Institute for Intelligence and Special Services – sets the tone. The CIA is an agency and calls itself the 'company'; the British SIS is a service and calls itself the 'firm'. Mossad is an institute, academic and scientific, combined with the firepower backup of special services. Clever man-tough man is the game it is best fitted to play.

The fact that Mossad operates on behalf of a country surrounded by avowed enemy states in which every citizen is conscious of the continual threat of war makes it a secret service quite unlike any other. Even inside Israel's disputed borders there is now constant hostility from the Arab population in the occupied territories, and life is no longer 'normal' in the sense in which that word is used in European countries. In addition, the long shadow of the Holocaust in which 6 million Jews perished – going, as the younger generation in Israel is constantly reminded, 'like lambs to the slaughter' – touches every family in the new homeland. Pride in being Jewish and determination to prove that never again will they let their defences down has its effect upon everybody in the service, from the youngest recruit to the most experienced veteran. For such reasons, the men and women of the Israeli intelligence community are more dedicated than their equally patriotic colleagues who work in the same line of business in other countries on behalf of the CIA, KGB or MI6. The external threat to Israel is much more tangible, much more apparent than that to the superpowers. In 1953 the acting head of Israeli intelligence issued an order of the day to mark the foundation of the service: 'For our state which since its creation has been under siege by its enemies intelligence constitutes the first line of defence. Located as we are in the heart of the Middle East with its upheavals and shocks, we must learn well how to recognize what is going on around us.'

In the world of secrets where they discuss the rise and fall of intelligence services, Mossad, and Aman military intelligence, enjoy an enviable reputation for devotion and efficiency. 'The best intelligence service in the world', was the judgement of the CIA in a report upon them. To their friends – and there were many – their exploits seemed admirable. Enemies feared the aura of success that grew around Mossad.

Did they not rescue persecuted Jews trapped in hostile lands – in Iraq, Morocco and Ethiopia; bring to justice murderers and torturers like Adolf Eichmann; and rescue airline hostages in famous assaults when all seemed lost? The long-range rescue of hijacked passengers aboard an Air France flight taken to Entebbe remains a classic example of operational anti-terrorist daring and efficiency. The skill of Mossad agents became legendary as they fought against the forces of terrorism throughout the world, and supplied a fund of information enabling security forces in the West to ward off many perils.

Many of them did not live to tell the tale. Some were murdered in lonely alleys; some were blown to pieces by bombs; others were publicly hanged in the main squares of Damascus, Baghdad or Cairo. There were those who did not return from desperate missions, and their fate will never be known. It was to commemorate the lives and deaths of many such heroes that their families banded together to demand a public memorial to them. Bowing before such poignant pressure, a former head of Mossad took over as chairman of the organizing committee which raised $2 million to build a dignified shrine. Constructed of monumental angular blocks of sandstone, it stands at the Centre for Special Studies in Herzliyah, north of Tel Aviv. Suitably enough, the building was conceived as a kind of labyrinth with five alcoves, each representing a period in the history of Israel's intelligence operations. 'The idea of such a maze', explained a veteran of the service, 'was to create the impression of an interminable search of changing direction. Complexity and infinity are at the core of intelligence-gathering.' On the walls have been engraved with pride the names of 360 of the fallen who were members of all three branches of the intelligence community, Mossad, Aman and Shin Beth, the counter-espionage service.

The first agent to lose his life in the service of the new state was Jacob Bokai, a Syrian-born Jew executed in August 1949 after being arrested as he entered Jordan disguised as an Arab refugee. A painter named Shalom Dani died of natural causes in 1963; his name is inscribed on the roll of honour for his crucial skills as the man who

4

forged the documents for the Mossad team which snatched Eichmann in Latin America. One secret revealed by the memorial was the name of Yacov Bar Simantov, a diplomat murdered outside his home in Paris. The fact that he is remembered in the memorial confirmed posthumously, and for the first time, that he was a Mossad agent. Some of the names recorded, like that of Eli Cohen, a master-spy finally caught and executed in Damascus, are famous. For secret agents the price of fame is exposure and death, for only then are their exploits revealed. The deeds of many of those commemorated here must remain secret for ever, except to their colleagues, and sometimes to their relations. Former intelligence officers who act as curators say that the work of some of their dead colleagues remains so confidential that their names may not be recorded. Even in death their clandestinity is preserved. It is entirely in keeping with the brave and sentimental ways of Israelis and of Mossad that it should become possibly the only secret service in the world to have its own public memorial.

The CIA may have greater technical resources; the KGB is no doubt bigger and more methodical; but no intelligence service is more feared than Mossad. The popular view of its activities in the outside world is of an efficient, cunning and dreadnought secret service. I have been struck by the fact that, whenever it was mentioned that I was writing a book about Mossad, the question asked most frequently by those without knowledge of such things was, 'Isn't that a dangerous thing to do?'

It is true that on occasion Mossad does not shrink from borrowing terrorist methods from its Middle Eastern enemies, which in any case were familiar to some of its original agents who had carried out assassination and kidnap raids in the battles for Israeli independence. After the Munich massacre of 5 September 1972 they conducted a long hunt across the world for twelve suspects and killed them, one after the other. Operatives broke many laws, and their interrogations were fierce, prolonged and scientific. But other agents went out into hostile countries to rescue fellow Jews in danger of persecution simply because they were Jews. Nor should it be forgotten that, because of Israel's peculiar diplomatic problems, intelligence officers were forced to act in the role of clandestine diplomats in Africa and Asia. In Arab countries which, out of friendship for the Palestinians, refused to recognize the state of Israel, Mossad performed the complicated tasks of hidden diplomacy without benefit of immunity.

Mossad agents have helped to win wars; they have overthrown Arab regimes; and they have irritated European governments and the US administration by flouting the accepted rules of international behaviour. Using underhand tricks they procured uranium for Israel's

5

atomic bomb, and bombed and raided in Iraq and France to delay the moment they dreaded – when an enemy Arab state might acquire its own atomic bomb. Agents dramatically spirited away from Cherbourg the gunboats under construction for Israel in France when the French refused to deliver them as a mark of their disapproval of Israel's policy.

When it comes to assessing Mossad's most spectacular exploits, judgement must remain in the eye of the beholder. For some, it seemed an heroic and historic act of vengeance when the team seized Eichmann, the Nazi war criminal, and brought him to trial in Israel. To others, this was an act of kidnapping perpetrated against an ageing German in a foreign country, which set a bad example in international lawlessness and produced a show trial long after the crimes undoubtedly committed.

Isser Harel, one of Mossad's founders and the man responsible for that kidnapping, once said: 'They should stop spinning legends around Mossad. I think that we just work harder and collect more information than the others. No other country in the world has such urgent need for an efficient secret service. Israeli is surrounded by enemies. We have no diplomatic relations with these nations whose agents clobber us as terrorists. For us it is a question of survival.'

You cannot kill a legend with a breath of realistic modesty. For many years, the illusion was that Israeli intelligence men could do no wrong. To sympathizers, there was brave little Israel standing up to the wrath of the hostile Arab millions. In those days the high reputation of the Israeli service seemed almost too good to be true. That a small country could furnish an intelligence service with such a formidable record in a world dominated by the giants of the CIA and KGB, not to mention the British SIS and allied services in Europe, seemed little short of miraculous. So exhaustive was the quantity of information made available to their friends by Mossad and Shin Beth that the CIA came to rely upon it for analysis at critical times. In the heyday of James Angleton, the CIA master of counter-espionage, the Agency had a special department for liaison with Mossad, over which he presided. After all, it was Mossad alone of the free world's spy networks which managed to purloin a full copy of Khrushchev's now famous initial denunciation of Stalin at the 20th Party Congress. Israel set world standards for secrecy and professionalism, even when its aims were sometimes debatable and its methods so high-handed as would only be tolerated in a country continually at war. No wonder that Yehosophat Harkabi, one of the most notable of the early heads of military intelligence, could say to me in London in 1988: 'I am proud of the achievements of Israeli intelligence.' He had every right to be; and,

6

moreover, he could afford to take that high-minded, yet hard-headed Israeli approach by roundly declaring: 'We live in an imperfect world. It must be realized that intelligence is an amoral business and must be wisely used. Those involved must be strong internally. I am stating a fact. Many of the acts committed are immoral but constraints must be observed.'

Once upon a time it appeared that to work in Israeli intelligence was like being at the court of King Arthur – every day a new adventure. Every adventure seemed to be a sacred quest, as the wicked were punished and the innocent rescued. Then things started to go wrong and doubts clouded that image. This was not a sudden transformation, for, ever since Mossad came into being, despite the posture of high morality adopted by 'holier-than-thou' Israeli statesmen, cruelties and harsh methods were tolerated and even encouraged. And the efficiency of the intelligence operatives and their leaders was by no means all that it was cracked up to be. There were always disastrous failures side by side with the acclaimed and publicized successes. Like other people's secret services, the Israeli one fell victim to scandals, and on at least one occasion – the case of the traitor Israel Beer – the Russians managed to install their mole in high places.

The rot really set in through Israel's preoccupation with the Palestinians and terrorism. Containing the Palestine Liberation Organization's campaign of subversion was a job that had to be done, but the task was a corrupting one. As underground war became a way of life, some elements turned to counter-terrorism in combating enemies at home and abroad. Brutality raised its head. It is one thing to use intelligence information to pinpoint a terrorist lair and then attack it, but quite another to send out hit teams deliberately to terrorize the terrorists and to fall into the habit of using their unspeakable tactics.

Stern punishments handed out to terrorists, the hard-line attitude, the raids against the raiders – all were held up as an example to the 'soft' Americans and Europeans accused of being people who just talked and never did anything. Then Mossad became involved in an infernal round of counter-actions to wipe out the terrorist gangs. And what was the result of it all? Did terrorism go away? No, by 1989 Israel faced new and more formidable perils. When Yasser Arafat and the PLO abandoned international terrorism, rightly convinced that they achieved more success through diplomacy than by shoot-outs, the Israeli authorities were reluctant to face the new reality. Then began the *intifada*, the new problem, for which Israel was ill-equipped to cope after the years of battle. Within the borders and in the occupied territories there was a spontaneous uprising of the Arab population. At first it was not even directed by the PLO. Yet within two years

7

the demonstrations and the riots had created more sympathy for the Palestinians than had two decades of armed struggle. Mossad and Shin Beth were equally puzzled about how to deal with young demonstrators and stone throwers. They had been capable of dealing with their armed elder brothers, who were guerrillas, but were as bewildered as the Israeli government when confronted by violent civil disorders. Israelis were enthusiastic enough to be soldiers or spies, but Jewish folk memories of sufferings at the hands of Cossacks and the secret police of eastern Europe ensured that nobody wanted to serve in a police riot squad.

The great intelligence effort in the 1970s was directed at fighting terrorism and the battlefield was Lebanon, which had become the base for Palestinian forces once they were driven out of Jordan by King Hussein at the beginning of the decade. Israeli policy remained constant: it was always considered right to strike back hard at the guerrilla forces which constantly tormented the Jewish state. In order to do that Mossad was kept fully stretched in spying out the arms depots and bases, and in trying to discover the enemy's plans and targets in advance. The intelligence service was also required to probe the international contacts of the Palestinian movements and find out where their arms came from and who organized their training.

Mossad's best tactic was to insert into the Palestinian groups their own agents, sometimes Arabs paid or blackmailed into carrying out this dangerous task and sometimes patriotic Israelis with special knowledge of the Arab world and its language. But undercover agents have a dual purpose: to wage clandestine war behind the enemy lines, but also to achieve secret initiatives which would fail if they were attempted publicly. When such qualities were required Mossad dipped into a pool of talent in a population of immigrants, many of whom were Jews brought up in Arab countries. A good example of a Mossad agent operating in an Arab country in a quasi-diplomatic role was provided by Sylvia Raphael. In Jordan she posed as a French journalist in order to keep track on Palestinian goings-on there, but she was also in contact with Jordanian notables.

On each side of the northern border with Lebanon both Mossad agents and those of Shin Beth – which is, theoretically at least, an organization concerned with internal counter-espionage – were active in preparing the way for the eventual invasion of Lebanon, and then being used as the intelligence shield of the occupying army. Responsibility for the ill-fated adventure rests upon General Ariel Sharon, defence minister to Menachem Begin, when that leader of the right-wing Likud party finally succeeded in becoming prime minister. It can be argued that from then onwards the reputation of both intelligence services began to plunge. Old men with bitter memories of internecine fights among the various pre-independence factions made a comeback as advisers in special offices close to the prime minister. One of them was Rafael Eitan, the man ultimately blamed for exploiting Jonathan Pollard, an American Jew in US naval intelligence, to spy upon America, the oldest and firmest ally of Israel. That affair shocked the Americans and Jewish-American opinion too. According to Isser Harel, the man who made the reputation of Mossad, it was 'the worst-bungled affair in Israel's history'. Until then Israel had made a point of trying whenever possible not to make use of diaspora Jews in espionage operations which might prompt foreign governments to consider Jews a security risk and lead others into anti-semitism.

Troubled times and confused events and actions moulded Israeli intelligence into its present-day form. During the first forty years of Mossad's history admiration for its style changed to suspicion about its methods.

2. In the Beginning

In the beginning were the spies.

Until recent times every aspect of the work of the Israeli intelligence community was ultra-secret. Only when a slip of the tongue led Ben-Gurion to breathe the word in the Israeli parliament, the Knesset, did it became possible even to use the name Mossad in print; in a country where military censorship still prevails, any mention of it had previously been suppressed. As recently as 1980 a reporter who dared to reveal the name of the then head of the service was punished by being deprived of his press accreditation. In the memoirs and personal accounts of the early years of the modern state of Israel the name of Mossad, the organ of state respected for its mysterious zeal, was scarcely whispered. As Menachem Begin once said, 'In spying, as in war, the legend of success is in itself a success factor' – and legends depend upon secrecy. The deep discretion surrounding the intelligence service is easily explained by a backward glance at the time shortly after the end of the Second World War when the Zionists engaged in the final battles in order to place again upon the political world map a state called Israel.

It is not going too far to say that the Jewish clandestine private armies and secret services actually created the new state. Israel became a nation through underground warfare. Jewish refugees from many lands were smuggled into Palestine, despite the best efforts of the British forces during the Mandate years, and particularly in the late 1940s, to prevent them from swamping what was at the time essentially an Arab land. There were moles and agents within the British army, and secret agents were embedded in high places in the neighbouring

Arab countries which became increasingly hostile to the prospect of a Jewish Palestine. Zionists sought out arms supplies and arranged to smuggle them into Palestine to equip the armies and the underground militias being formed by the Jews as the vanguard of the new Israel. Spies kept watch over dissident Jewish minority movements.

Israel is a nation which thrived upon covert operations and espionage. Its first leaders had been forced by circumstance to enter this occult world, and it was by a natural process that the new state became a 'spyocracy'. Many prominent figures current in the Israeli political establishment are former members of the intelligence community. The president himself, Chaim Herzog, was in military intelligence; Yitzhak Shamir, the prime minister, served for years as a Mossad field man in Europe; David Kimche, who became the senior foreign ministry civil servant, is a former deputy director of Mossad. From the beginning the tradition was there, and it was only to be expected that secrecy would remain a normal pattern of conduct after independence.

The secrecy principle had other origins, too. Like many institutions in the new Israel, the secret services were influenced by British example. Many Jews served in the British forces and in military intelligence during the Second World War. By the time it ended, 130,000 Palestinian Jews had joined the British army to fight against the Nazis. Moshe Dayan, the victorious general and successful cabinet minister whose career blossomed in the Haganah intelligence unit, was a wartime pupil of the Secret Intelligence Service, SIS, and of the Special Operations Executive, SOE. Of the Jewish recruits to the British services, thirty-two had parachuted into Nazi territory. Isser Harel, who became head of the official secret service, received his early training in a British-run force, the Palestine Police.

It was the United Kingdom which first produced the ground rules of total secrecy. Whitehall had always been reluctant to admit that a secret service and a security service existed at all. Although spying and intelligence are as venerable as human conflict, it was not until 1909 that Britain began a new trend in this field by creating the first modern intelligence agency as a government department, financed and controlled by the administration. Its task in peace and in war was to obtain foreigners' secrets and to protect those of its own government. The great powers of old Europe seized upon the idea and set up similar bureaucracies of espionage: Germany in 1913, Russia four years later. The French service officially came into being only in 1935 and the United States hesitated until 1947 before creating the CIA, the Central Intelligence Agency, to take over from the wartime OSS, Office of Strategic Services, which had been disbanded after victory.

11

For Israel, worldwide intelligence operations began with the founding of the Jewish Agency at the Zionist Congress in Zurich in 1929. Haganah, the Zionist underground force, set up its own information service, named Shai, which from then until 1948 had as its objective the promotion of an independent state of Israel. To achieve this it concentrated upon infiltrating the British administration in Palestine, so as to inform Jewish leaders about British attitudes and to anticipate the actions of the Mandate authorities. Simultaneously it spied upon Arab opponents in the surrounding countries. Zionist agents also sought to monitor and control extremist groups of their co-religionists both in the Middle East and in Europe. Security men were responsible for collecting information in Nazi Germany to protect the Jewish underground and to establish escape channels, before and after the Second World War. Shai became expert at smuggling into Palestine weapons and illegal immigrants. It was particularly successful in getting its agents into positions of influence in the British-run customs, police and transport services; exploiting these positions, they were able to make sure that the authorities seized quantities of arms being smuggled in by the Arabs ready to fight against the new settlers in Palestine.

Rekhesh was an agency given responsibility for providing arms and ammunition to the Jewish underground forces establishing themselves in Palestine. To achieve this task, its agents became expert at setting up dummy corporations, adjusting export licences and providing themselves with false identities. The other direct ancestor of Mossad, and the pre-independence organization from which it took its name, was Mossad le Aliyah Bet, the Institute of Illegal Immigration. When the British attempted to settle the vexed problem of Palestine by limiting Jewish immigration to 75,000, the Jewish Agency decided to adopt a policy of smuggling in Zionists. The old, original Mossad, with just ten agents in Europe, had the job of establishing escape routes, providing ships and arranging safe houses and false passports to ensure the safe passage to Palestine of thousands of incoming refugees. Head of both Mossad and Rekhesh was Shaul Avigur, a Russian immigrant trained in a kibbutz and a natural conspirator with a passion for secrecy so ingrained that when he sent a packet of Hebrew newspapers to his daughter in London he marked it 'Private and Confidential'.

These organizations formed the nucleus of a kind of tough, learn-as-you-go university for spies and secret agents. Working within them in conditions of danger and stress, the men who would become the backbone of state intelligence acquired their skills the hard way. The Zionist services provided on-the-job training for the clandestine people who were ready and able to serve the state of Israel which finally flew its Star of David flag on 14 May 1948. The Zionist dream had became a reality, thanks in good measure to the work of these clandestine groups. Two weeks later, on 30 June, the Israeli intelligence community came into being officially as a secret, though fully recognized, branch of the government service. At that stage it was simply known as the secret service.

The birthplace of this newcomer in the field of state intelligence services was a simple room at 85 Ben Yehuda Street in central Tel Aviv, situated in a nondescript building boasting a café in the basement, a flower shop and a few apartments on the upper floors. On the door of one of them was a plaque proclaiming it to be the office of the 'Veterans' Counselling Service'. Until then, the place had served as the undercover headquarters of the old Shai, which was now disbanded.

The purpose of the meeting which took place in Ben Yehuda Street on 30 June was to lay the foundations of the Israeli intelligence community. It was attended by district heads and leaders of the many different bodies which had plotted and fought to build the nation. As a result of this modest conference the IDF, the Israeli Defence Forces, issued an official order setting up a sub-division of the operations branch of its general staff. In the beginning was military intelligence, which came to be known as Aman. To help it collect classified information internationally, the pioneers also set up the political department of the foreign ministry, under Boris Guriel. The third prong of the community was to be a general security service known as Shin Beth. This initial structure survived only until 1951, when Mossad proper in the form that it is known today emerged after a complete overhaul of the hastily created intelligence structure, which from the start was discredited by scandals and quarrels.

David Ben-Gurion, the first prime minister, chose Isser Be'eri as the man to head the new military intelligence service in 1948. A colonel in the newly constituted Israeli Defence Forces and head of a construction company, he had been a member of Haganah since 1938. He had come to prominence only when he took control of Shai during the desperate battle for Jerusalem a few months earlier. The choice of Isser Be'eri soon proved to be a disastrous one, for his brief period in charge of military intelligence served only to introduce into it the kind of knavish tactics which later brought Israel's secret services into disrepute.

Within a few months, the officer in charge of the newly established service was arraigned before a secret court-martial for actions committed in the violent period before independence. He was charged with murdering an Arab notable named Ali Kassem, who was suspected of betraying Zionist conspirators to the British security people and of running a protection racket. Be'eri simply defended himself by saying that the man was a traitor – 'so we killed him'. That was not the only act with which Be'eri was reproached. So anxious was he to expose a powerful Labour party politician called Abba Hushi for having collaborated with the British during the Mandate that he had one of Hashi's aides tortured in an attempt to obtain evidence. Not content with that, he arranged for documents to be forged in a further effort to prove the point. On the very day that he assumed his new command over military intelligence another shameful event took place. A drumhead court-martial, presided over by Be'eri himself, found Captain Meir Toubianski guilty of spying for the British, and he was summarily executed by firing squad on the orders of Be'eri. A subsequent enquiry ordered by Prime Minister Ben-Gurion found that the captain was innocent. His army rank was restored to him posthumously, and by way of compensation he was given a military funeral.

Isser Be'eri, held responsible for these disgraceful events, was dismissed after only twelve months in office, then arrested and charged with murder. The only defence put forward at the secret hearings was that his position as head of the secret service gave him the right to act outside the law and to use what methods he thought fit. It was an argument of *raison d'état*, unacceptable even in such troubled times as those facing the new nation. The founding fathers of the new Zion had always assumed a high moral stance, and for them to accept the idea that their security service, for all its zealous patriotism, had a right to brush aside all normal codes of decent behaviour was totally unacceptable. Isser Be'eri was found guilty and stripped of his rank and title. In recognition of his past services to the cause he received only a token sentence of one day's imprisonment, and even that was commuted by President Chaim Weizmann. The mildness of the sentence was to set a precedent when the state was later confronted with problems in dealing with security misdemeanours.

The life of Israel's brand-new secret service had started with brutality and a clash of wills between its leader, who favoured harsh methods, and the authority of the state represented by Ben-Gurion. Only the prime minister's strong conviction that the law must be upheld prevented continual recrimination over what had been done in the lawless times before independence. In some ways the situation was comparable to that in newly liberated France after the Second World War, when fresh crimes were perpetrated by the Resistance against those suspected of collaboration with the former German conquerors as the process of formalizing wartime units into regular state services proceeded in peacetime.

Ben-Gurion's original plan, which was largely adhered to later, had been to create three divisions responsible for intelligence. First came

14

the bureau of military intelligence, known by its abbreviated Hebrew title, Aman. Linked to that was the department of counter-espionage (Ran) and the political department of the foreign ministry, headed by Boris Guriel. The foreign ministry people were given the worldwide task of collecting all intelligence considered to be of importance to Israel. Isser Harel, later to become the most famous spymaster, made his first appearance when he was appointed head of the third division, the department of security – Shin Beth.

In the nature of things it was not always easy to draw boundaries between the activities of these different departments. When the state was starting from scratch all its institutions had to make their own rules as they went along. Things were made more complicated by the fact that the services were staffed by people from many diverse backgrounds – refugees from Hitler's persecution in Europe, Zionists from the Soviet Union, and Jews born and bred in what was then known as Palestine. Although united by their Jewishness, their faith and their customs they were separated by language, experience and acquired national characteristics.

The traditions merging in the foundation of the Israeli secret services were on the one hand those of the Zionist clandestine groups, accustomed to breaking the law in what they believed was a good cause, and on the other that of military intelligence, itself inspired by more classical methods and organization. The officers of the new service, recruited from the old pre-independence bodies, were a pretty wild crew accustomed to the rougher forms of clandestine warfare. They had had their field training in nasty operations to smuggle in arms purchased by trickery and, using similar dirty and violent methods, to prevent their Arab foes in Palestine from doing the same thing. To mould such desperadoes into a disciplined state intelligence force was not a simple task. Stewart Steven in his well-informed book *The Spymasters of Israel* pointed out that such men 'found it hard to take the trammels and restrictions placed upon them by what was necessarily a bureaucratic structure, however loose, answerable to the rule of law and the *diktat* of government and parliament'.

After the disgrace of Isser Be'eri in 1949, the armed forces' intelligence organization was headed by Chaim Herzog, later to become president of Israel. He convinced Ben-Gurion of the need for a properly funded and more formal military intelligence service with its own budget. The new chief was an experienced intelligence officer, with previous service in the British army, and this early training enabled him to transform Aman into an efficient and well-organized service. He soon created a tidy unit with a proper chain of command and its own efficient training establishment.

15

By the time that his deputy, Colonel Benjamin Gibli, succeeded him as head of the service in April 1950 Aman was a going concern.

At that point Chaim Herzog was sent to Washington as military attaché at the Israeli embassy, a posting which was to become more significant than the modest title indicated. The United States was a firm ally and supporter of the new state of Israel, and had agreed to exchange intelligence information with its secret services as soon as they were formed. The CIA and the FBI were ready to provide their new friends with state-of-the-art equipment for coding and decoding and to instruct Israeli officers in its use. Both Herzog and his talented diplomat colleague and former intelligence agent, Reuben Shiloach, were in the USA at a critical stage in the early days of the Cold War. It was a time when the Soviet Union, which at first had been a supporter of the new state, was turning its attention to improving relations with the Arab world and beginning to plot against Israel. This development helped to bring the Americans and the Israelis closer in face of a common opponent. Chaim Herzog forged the first links with the CIA, which over the years were to prove so important, both for Israel and for the American service itself. The connection was further strengthened through the efforts of James Angleton, the redoubtable CIA officer who eventually took under his wing the Agency's Israeli desk.

Aman military intelligence under Gibli had yet to win its reputation. It was a descendant of the Haganah underground movement, formed into a department of the army general staff operations branch. In the early days the controllers found some difficulty in sorting out areas of responsibility for their people, and a certain confusion prevailed. Individual field agents who were sometimes required to work for Mossad and sometimes under the control of Aman competed with each other all over the world, often in a less than professional manner. This state of affairs led to a good deal of manoeuvring by individual controllers, sometimes designed to increase their own authority, but also as genuine attempts were made to make operations more efficient. The final arbiter in all such disputes was Ben-Gurion, who set up a select committee to advise on restructuring the intelligence establishment. By a prime ministerial directive dated 1 September 1951, this committee announced the setting up in its definitive form of Mossad, the agency whose task was to gather intelligence from abroad and to run whatever special operations were considered necessary. Its director was Reuben Shiloach, who was directly responsible to the prime minister. The founding text might well have been taken from the Old Testament: 'And Moses sent them to spy out the Land of Canaan . . . and see the land, what it is; and

16

the people that dwelleth therein, whether they be strong or weak, few or many.'

The reorganization was prompted by Reuben Shiloach's enthusiasm for the American way of doing things, acquired during his time as minister at the Washington embassy. Impressed by what he had seen of new espionage techniques being pioneered by the CIA, this son of a rabbi strongly recommended that Israel should follow the American example and set up an independent agency responsible to the head of government. His suggestion was put forward at a time when the political department of the foreign ministry was the subject of carping criticism about the behaviour of its diplomats, who were accused of high living in foreign parts. Animosity against the personnel of the department was increased by the fact that Boris Guriel, its chief, had recruited mostly intellectuals with European Jewish backgrounds whose grand manners were resented by Palestine-born and -bred Jews. What had been in essence a diplomatic intelligence department was dissolved. The replacement, renamed the research department, was given the much more limited function of carrying out research and evaluation and lost its overseas intelligence role. This change was made specifically so that a rival organization would not interfere with the work of the new service, Mossad.

This was an arrangement which caused high indignation among the old political department's field men, many of whom returned home to protest and resign in a huff. Boris Guriel, head of the service, and a man who held strong beliefs in the need for careful evaluation of intelligence material, retired to private life. That was a great loss, for it turned out that the new services were, as he had predicted they would be, better at acquiring information than at assessing its value and significance.

So it came about that David Ben-Gurion formalized the status of the intelligence services, with Mossad, the Institute, looking after the collection of all foreign intelligence and with responsibility for mounting any special operations deemed necessary. The original directive complicated matters by laying down that in the field of special operations Aman was charged with nominating the targets and planning operations which had then to be approved by Mossad. Shin Beth became the home security service, aided in police work and surveillance by Reshud, which was the Israeli equivalent of the Special Branch of the British police.

Nobody was entirely satisfied by the compromise arrangements. Mossad at the beginning was a pretty small agency. Its field of action was circumscribed by lack of manpower as well as by rivalry with Aman. Aman itself, during the period up to the war of 1956, appears to have relied upon signals intercepts of Arab traffic, much of it furnished wittingly or unwittingly by France, for a substantial amount of its intelligence material. Raymond Cohen, lecturer on international relations at the Hebrew University of Jerusalem, having carefully examined declassified files in Israeli state archives, concluded in a paper published in *Intelligence and National Security* in 1988 that at least a dozen significant items originated from French sources, and at least one possibly from a British source. This demonstrated that by no means all Israeli intelligence coups were the work of daring field agents. In return for French help, Israel was able and willing to provide valuable information about the sources of finance and arms being supplied to the Algerian rebellion.

At first it seemed that Mossad's main role was simply to give its sponsorship to special operations, many of which were carried out by agents of military intelligence. On some occasions Aman asserted its right to veto operations demanded by Mossad. Changes took place after the prime minister set up a joint intelligence committee and made the head of Mossad its *ex officio* chairman. Isser Harel, who took over in 1952 and whose close relationship with David Ben-Gurion greatly strengthened his influence, became known as *Memuneh* – the patriarch – as did all subsequent chairmen. He was the one with direct and constant access to the prime minister. The rival military intelligence head reported to the chief of staff, and seemed obviously lower in the pecking order.

Initially the most flourishing branch of the industry was Shin Beth, the general security agency, which had been built up energetically by Isser Harel to combat communist infiltration of the political parties and of the new apparatus of state. He had recruited large numbers of agents, some of whom were eventually pressed into service by the infant Mossad. This was a state of affairs calculated to provoke quarrels between him and Reuben Shiloach, the coordinator and first head of the rival service. This soon led to the resignation of the Mossad man and his replacement by Isser Harel on 14 September 1952. Harel, now firmly established as overall boss, was in a position to gain control of both services and to set Mossad upon the road to success.

Organization had not been its strong point up to this time. The new chief found that his headquarters staff, working in a three-room office in Tel Aviv, consisted of only a dozen people. There was so little money available that the secretary had not been paid for months. David Ben-Gurion was persuaded to provide a suitable budget and new offices were found to accommodate recruits brought in from Shin Beth. The next step was to purge Mossad agents already in the field, so as to get rid of ineffectual ones, to retrain others and to reorganize the network.

Although he came to the task with only limited experience of international espionage operations, at the age of forty Isser Harel was quick to learn. One of those diminutive sandals-and open-necked-shirt veterans of the kibbutz, born in Russia, he had learned his trade as the security man of Haganah, the Israeli guerrilla army. His task was to spy out dangerous dissidents and extremists in rival movements, at a time when Jew clashed with Jew and simultaneously fought the Arabs and the British. He had been chosen in 1948 to crush Irgun Zvi Leumi, the extremist Jewish group in conflict with Haganah, which broke the truce in the Arab-Israeli war, signed in June that year, by trying to land on a Tel Aviv beach from the ship *Altalena* a load of weapons for its own sectarian forces. His next battle had been against the Stern Gang of ultras after they murdered Count Bernadotte of the United Nations in Jerusalem. He succeeded in both enterprises. In this fashion, and long before he took charge of Mossad, he had become keeper of the dossiers and a man to be reckoned with in underground warfare.

The nickname he enjoyed, which differentiated him from the previous officer of that name – Be'eri – was 'Little Isser'; it was an inappropriately innocent description, for Harel was a hard man with cold eyes and overweening ambition as well as Zionist fervour, and almost entirely lacking in humour. Through the next decade this right-wing political action man built Mossad in his own image. He had a passion for secrecy, and kept his own files secure in a special building. Despite the fact that he spoke out against murder he never hesitated to launch violent and questionable operations whenever he considered them necessary in the interests of the state. His staff liked and admired their boss, and he gradually gathered into his own hands supreme power over one of the most devoted intelligence communities in the world.

One of the first tasks after Harel's original appointment was to use the Shin Beth branch of his command to spy upon the United Workers party, an extreme left-wing group thought to be infiltrated by communists. Some of its members were in fact agents within Shin Beth and, doubting their loyalty, Isser Harel set up a special department to carry out surveillance of the party. One of his own former agents made the discovery that a bug had been planted in party headquarters and managed to trap and expose two special department agents, whom he then denounced to the police. Shin Beth had been caught red-handed in an internal political operation, and scandal followed.

3. The Way It Is Now

Twice a week at least, and more often in times of emergency, the bosses of Mossad and Aman meet for an orders and planning session. In what for Israelis is a rare use of understatement, they call it their 'coffee morning'. In attendance at these top-level talks are the director of Shin Beth; the inspector general of police; and the senior man from the foreign affairs ministry, together with his head of research and political planning. Also present are the special advisers to the prime minister on political, military and anti-terrorist affairs.

These meetings at the top of the pyramid of the Israeli intelligence services bring together the men of the central control body – the committee of heads of services. The function of Va'adat Rashei Hasherutim, known simply as Va'adat, is to coordinate all current activities in the field both at home and abroad. In the course of their gatherings, which are of course held in conditions of maximum security, each director presents a briefing on the headline activities of his people. 'Cooperation is the secret of our success,' was the judgement of Meir Amit, the only man who has served as head of both Mossad and Aman.

In theory at least, all those present at such sessions are of equal standing, but some are more equal than others. The Mossad man presides, and by the fact that he is addressed by the ritual title 'Patriarch' it is generally recognized that he and his service predominate. It has been claimed, however, in a CIA report on Israeli intelligence, that in recent times the director of Aman has often been able to outrank his Mossad colleague in power and importance.

The German *Stern* magazine, in a rather fanciful and excited

20

account of such meetings, claimed in the 1980s that they took place in an anonymous-looking office block in Tel Aviv inhabited otherwise by insurance men and lawyers. It was said that the place could only be entered by way of a special elevator starting from the underground car park. No doubt it is true that the leaders of such highly sensitive services do take many precautions, such as using armour-plated cars; but when I was received by Rafael Eitan, who was anti-terrorist affairs adviser to the prime minister, the meeting took place in a modest office within the defence ministry compound in Tel Aviv, and it seems likely that the intelligence bosses hold their regular meetings in such a place. Certainly great security precautions are needed. For one thing, there is the danger of conversations in Tel Aviv being picked up by the Soviet electronic spy ships which constantly hover in the Mediterranean off the coast of Israel. The intelligence people are always on the alert, knowing that the Russians can monitor their communications and may pass on their findings to the Arab powers.

There is nothing flashy and extravagant about Israeli intelligence. It is not housed in the modern splendour of the Langley headquarters of the CIA; its chiefs are not to be found chatting in the faded grandeur of the kind of gentlemen's club frequented by senior men from the British MI6. Nor do its officers favour smart clothes or a high lifestyle. Indeed, in the early days of Mossad special courses in social behaviour had to be arranged, so that agents recruited from the stern and puritan simplicity of the kibbutzes would not stand out as oddities in sophisticated Western capital cities.

The head of Mossad is chosen by the prime minister and his statutory term of office is five years, though some chiefs have stayed on longer – and some have left before their time. Mossad is not a generous employer; it demands a lot from those who volunteer for service with it, and pays them modestly. Its people are considered to be normal civil servants on a pay scale suitable to their grade. The usual pension amounts to 70 per cent of the final salary rate, and the average spy retires at fifty-two, although he may well be dug out of retirement to reinforce younger colleagues in time of crisis. One of the strengths of the organization is that a pool of old boy back-up agents is constantly available. Extra points, ensuring higher payment, are awarded for dangerous or delicate missions. Agents may retire early, if they so choose. 'We consider that it is always a mistake to keep people in the service when they have decided in their own minds that it is time to go,' was how one member of Mossad put it.

There is a completely different scale of payment for outsiders who provide Mossad with secret information. Jonathan Jay Pollard, an American Jew who spied for Israel in the USA, received a salary

21

of $2500 a month which was doubled while he was in prison. As is customary in the case of agents who are captured, the Israeli government raised the $200,000 to pay for his defence, although they pretended that the money was raised by public subscription.

The service prefers to recruit average-looking, inconspicuous, though talented people. Few of the Mossad operatives with whom journalists come into contact over the years are flamboyant personalities or the kind of people who would stand out in a crowd. Almost all are highly intelligent and have a wide range of interests. Mossad seems to favour tough, practical intellectuals who tend to place themselves back to the wall in all public places and are rarely willing to tell even a friend exactly where they are staying, or for how long. In preliminary vetting recruits are thoroughly checked for faults, and their background is probed to discover whether they have Arab friends. Talent spotters for the service recommend young people such as those who, for example, have shown promise during their military service. The children of the kibbutz are favoured as potential recruits; indeed, kibbutz education gives the same advantage to an aspiring agent that attendance at a good public school would impart to an English boy keen on joining MI6. Likely young men who have displayed special skills and aptitudes at school or university are often marked down as potential agents.

There are signs that the service is beginning to suffer from a shortage of Arabists; in the early years Jews brought up in Palestine spoke Arabic naturally. There is increasing concern that young people of a generation brought up in times of continual conflict with the Islamic world as nationalist Hebrew speakers are reluctant to learn the language. According to one intelligence officer, 'Our linguistic advantage is slowly disappearing. Young people just do not want to absorb what they think of as "enemy" culture.' Statistics show that of the thirty thousand children a year who start learning Arabic most now drop out.

Each candidate is made to pass a series of psychological aptitude tests. That process is followed by deep vetting. Despite great care in selection, mistakes are made; it would be absurd to suppose that every agent recruited by Mossad is a model of perfection. Case histories have been recorded of new officers who seemed promising enough under instruction but who turned out to have some inner weakness which made them useless for field work. One such agent, having been sent on a dangerous posting to Beirut, could not bring himself to leave his hotel room. He was simply paralysed by the difficulties of the task he had undertaken and had to be brought out of the country.

The average initial training course lasts for one year. To begin with a Mossad recruit is required to learn basic tradecraft – codes, use of handguns, self-defence, fieldcraft and surveillance work. Foreign languages are regarded as essential tools and Mossad men and women are required to speak them expertly and colloquially. They must also learn cosmopolitan social accomplishments so as to pass unnoticed in foreign countries. How to dress, what small talk to make on what subjects in which countries, how to tip – all such apparently trivial elements are considered important.

'The worst thing in training is the memory tests,' said one ex-Mossad man. 'They make you watch a video film, then suddenly stop a sequence and demand a list of all the objects seen for a split second just before the cut.' The selection is rigorous as the course proceeds, and from each intake between 30 and 45 per cent of the candidates either give up or fail. This is not surprising when the difficulties of some of the spy survival tests are considered. One recruit told how he was despatched on a dummy run to the north of England without money and equipped only with instructions to meet a contact. There was no contact and it was left to his initiative to find a way of getting back home. He used his wits to break into a supermarket and stole enough money to buy an airline ticket. Others have been 'kidnapped' and interrogated in foreign countries by their own people pretending to be Arabs, to see how they stand up to unexpected and alarming treatment.

On passing out, candidates receive different ratings which decide whether they are best qualified to become analysts capable of assessing the value of raw intelligence, or field men whose task is to go out and acquire information. High fliers may be posted to the special operations training school at Herzliyah, north of Tel Aviv.

Mossad takes pride in asserting that, in what is often a dirty game, its people are urged to place themselves on high moral ground. Under international law all covert activities and intelligence gathering are illegal. Yet every nation is involved in such activities. Therefore each state must set its own guidelines when launching such illegal operations. Israel takes the idealist view that any such act is just, provided that it is sanctioned, not only by the government and the political leaders, but also by the intelligence chiefs and the agents themselves. This is a rigorous standard, not always adhered to. But when the Wrath of God hit teams were sent out to assassinate those considered responsible for the Munich massacre, every member was provided with a detailed dossier deemed to provide proof of the guilt of their target. The aim was to provide each individual with evidence that the person he was under orders to kill was guilty beyond reasonable doubt.

Although killing is sometimes considered to be necessary in the higher interests of the state, those in the service maintain that their acts are as just as those of soldiers in war. For Jews, who are as

23

preoccupied by the sanctity of life as they are by intricacies of the law, the spectacle of Jews killing is deeply disturbing, especially when it is done unjustly. This is the curse of Saul. Even David, the greatest king, because he was a man of blood could not build the temple. Many energetic debates have been conducted about the morality of certain actions, and as much intellectual energy goes into such disputations as it does into the planning of operations. 'We do not recruit criminals,' said a former Mossad man. 'The service employs citizens who must be assured that their acts have a moral basis.'

A senior officer indignantly explained that Mossad would never blackmail someone into becoming one of its agents. This was a fact, he said, and the policy was based partly on morality, partly on the conviction that such an agent could never be completely trusted because the original act of blackmail would simply serve to alienate him. 'The whole essence of persuading someone to work for an intelligence agency is to make that person dependent upon the recruiter and to establish a feeling of trust so that he is under an obligation to do his will. That would be totally destroyed by an act of blackmail.' Such statements run absolutely against the tide of fiction written about Mossad. Certainly the outside public image is one of a service without scruples. It has been claimed that Arabs living in Israel and in the occupied territories who apply for papers to go and visit or to work in neighbouring Arab countries are required to provide information about those countries, and that they are threatened with imprisonment if they refuse. Pressure of this kind has undoubtedly been put upon Arabs in the occupied territories by Shin Beth.

Mossad claims that it does not prevent an agent from resigning once the desire to serve has gone. It is obvious that once a spy becomes disaffected he becomes careless, or even worse he may be susceptible to attempts at recruitment by the enemy as a double agent. Nor does the service like to employ cranks and emotionally unstable people. But examination of the records of those agents who have been exposed shows that, as might well be expected, the Institute does not always manage to live up to its own high standards. Jonathan Pollard, the American in naval intelligence who spied for Israel, was highly emotional, indiscreet and boastful. In the words of William Webster, then head of the FBI and now director of the CIA, 'I think a lot of people were surprised because it didn't fit the pattern of Israeli intelligence. The utilization of Pollard was unusual.'

A dilemma which confronts those responsible for recruiting Mossad agents is whether or not it is wise to involve diaspora Jews in espionage work. It is natural that some of these people are more than willing to serve in order to help Israel. If they do so, and are caught, it creates fears about persecution of Jews in some countries and about raising the old ghosts of anti-semitism everywhere. The problem caused anxiety right from the early days of Israeli intelligence work. In Iraq, back in 1951, the activities of Mossad agents were discovered, and this put at risk the emigration of threatened Jews from that hostile Arab country. As a result of that crisis, Shaul Avigur, one of the pioneers of the service, asked David Ben-Gurion, the prime minister, for an undertaking that never again should local Jews, or their organizations, be used in intelligence work. He argued with force that the state of Israel should be a symbol of hope for regional communities around the world, and not a cause of further suffering. He believed that, once it was discovered that local Jews took part in secret service work, the whole Jewish population of that country might suffer.

In general, Mossad has tried to apply the rule that it should, if possible, avoid the trap of recruiting overseas Jews, the more so as hostile counter-espionage officers smelling out spies would automatically think of combing out the places they frequented. In general the service regards the recruitment of diaspora Jews with the same suspicion with which the KGB looks on calling upon the services of card-bearing foreign members of the communist party. It is asking for trouble and making things easier for the opposition.

A contrary view was suggested in a CIA report on Mossad, discovered in the US embassy in Tehran by the revolutionaries who seized the building, which reported that Israel did use diaspora Jews to serve its interests both for recruiting agents and for getting general information:

> The aggressively ideological nature of Zionism, which emphasizes that all Jews belong to Israel and must return to Israel, has had its drawbacks in enlisting support for intelligence operations, however, since there is considerable opposition to Zionism among Jews throughout the world. Aware of this fact, Israeli intelligence representatives usually operate discreetly within Jewish communities and are under instructions to handle their missions with utmost tact to avoid embarrassment to Israel. They also attempt to penetrate anti-Zionist elements in order to neutralize the opposition. Despite such precautions, the Israelis frequently experience setbacks and there have been several cases where attempted recruitments of Americans of the Jewish faith have been rejected and reported to the US authorities.

The name Mossad sounds more sinister and romantic than its actual rendering into English, which comes out as more respectable and banal. The facts are that the Institute is responsible for what is called in the trade human intelligence, for covert action including disinformation, and for counter-terrorism. Its main task is to conduct operations against hostile Arab nations and organizations throughout the world, but particularly in western Europe and in the United States. There is a military side to the agency's work in that it reports on the state of Arab forces, especially with regard to their leadership, morale and armaments. It also takes a keen interest in their internal politics and diplomatic activity. Mossad agents are constantly on the look-out for news of the shifting relationships among Arab leaders. Middle Eastern commercial negotiation is a subject of continual investigation, the more so when it concerns the purchase and supply of armaments. Analysts constantly monitor and attempt to counteract Arab propaganda. A suspicious eye is always kept on the United Nations, generally considered to be hostile to Israeli interests. Such intelligence work is frequently put to practical use by Mossad covert action teams charged with arranging disturbances intended to create distrust among Arab states and their leaders.

Of the eight departments created in 1977, which in organization have changed little since then, the collection department is the biggest. It is responsible for foreign espionage operations and for processing the reports from them. Some of its people in the field work under diplomatic cover and are 'legals', while others have unofficial cover as traders or businessmen. The action and liaison department looks after relations with friendly foreign intelligence services and keeps in contact with nations with whom Israel has no diplomatic relations. Subordinate to it is the special operations division, the action people who run covert operations against Arab terrorists and also against wanted Nazis and neo-Nazi groups. They go in for sabotage, paramilitary activity and psychological warfare.

Although the head of Mossad is responsible to the prime minister, circumstances vary according to the personalities of the people involved. The service head does not always feel it necessary to keep the defence minister informed about operational details. The final decision on a major operation is reached by a cabinet committee consisting of the head of Mossad, the prime minister and any other ministers closely concerned. In Ben-Gurion's day, when the Eichmann affair was mooted, the initiative came from his intelligence chief, as Harel admitted later, saying, 'I warned him that we would have to do something unlawful in a friendly country. And he told me only in this case, because there was no way, no chance in the world to get Eichmann in a different, an official way.'

On another occasion Michael Bar Zohar, the biographer of Harel, recalled 'a very diabolic plan . . . very clever and very efficient' being put to General Moshe Dayan. To this Dayan answered, 'Now that you ask me, I'll have to say no. Why do you ask me? The moment you ask me, I have to say no.' This response certainly implies that it is not unusual for Mossad to act on occasion without authorization, which has the advantage for the political decision maker that, if challenged later, he can truthfully deny all knowledge of the operation. It was General Dayan who produced the phrase of convenience – 'plausible deniability'.

The Soviet bloc is another target of the intelligence service, as Mossad tries to discover how much Soviet support is going to Arab nations. In addition, the Israelis are ever-conscious of the need to see to the interests of the substantial Jewish minority in the Soviet Union and eastern Europe. The problem of the emigration of Soviet Jews requires the attention of the intelligence community.

A further task which devolved upon Mossad right from the beginning was to keep in touch with oppressed Jewish minorities anywhere in the world. It needed to build up contacts and have agents ready to go to the aid of such groups whenever the need arose. The Institute sent teams to Iraq, Iran, South Yemen and Algeria to arrange for the evacuation, either openly or covertly, of thousands of fellow Jews whose lives were in danger. In one of its most remarkable operations Mossad succeeded in making arrangements to rescue from Ethiopia sixty thousand Falashas, black Jews who are reputed to be the descendants of one of the lost tribes of Israel. This 'gathering in' was the more impressive because it involved an airlift from the neighbouring Arab state of Sudan, whose then ruler, President Numeiri, was persuaded by Israeli diplomats to turn a blind eye to what was going on. The officer who paid the price for this cooperation was General Omer Mohammed al-Tayeb, head of state security, who was later sentenced to life imprisonment for allowing the planes to land secretly in Sudan.

Because of the long and tormented history of the Jews, which led to the dispersal of their people throughout the world, Israel has inherited a kind of imperial responsibility. This obligation to watch over the interests of the diaspora as well as those of its own citizens forces the state to take on responsibilities in a wide international field. The intelligence services have also become a means to prevent the isolation of Israel through international disapproval. To this end its operatives become involved in trade and in arms dealing as well as in training programmes for third world intelligence services and armies. The collection department of Mossad and its political action department maintain stations in a great number of countries. They are established in the United States, in Central and South America, in the USSR and eastern Europe, in the EC countries, in Africa,

Asia and Oceania, as well as in the Mediterranean countries and, obviously, in the Middle East. For Israel the great disadvantage, which greatly stretches its resources, is that it is forced by circumstances to run a Rolls Royce intelligence agency on a mini-car economy.

4. Hi-tech and Brute Force

In the convoluted world of Israeli intelligence, the area most difficult to comprehend is the shifting relationship between Mossad and its military brother – Aman. Ever since the name Mossad first became publicly known, it has been in the eyes of the outside world the adventurous service, enjoying a reputation for dash and vigour. Aman, so far as its drab-sounding name is known at all except to professionals, is the one which took the blame for two outstanding intelligence disasters. First there was the covert operation in Egypt that went wrong in the 1950s; then came the failure to draw correct conclusions from incoming reports that Egypt and Syria were about to invade Israel in 1973.

To balance that record of failure there were undoubtedly brilliant successes. In the Six Day War the military intelligence people displayed their talents to great advantage. Agents were able to provide detailed information about the Egyptian air force which made possible Israel's pre-emptive air strikes: Egyptian warplanes were caught on the ground within minutes of war breaking out and destroyed on their own airfields. Aman field men went to great trouble to compile a databank with dossiers said to include information on every officer in the Arab armies of the surrounding nations. These were intended to be circulated not only to field commanders, but also to lower-ranking officers, the better to enable them to know their enemy and his tactics. The facts were compiled using the tried methods of military security, through interrogation of prisoners, and from poring over newspaper cuttings and military gazettes.

Aman certainly became the best research organization in the Middle East. Its soldier spies and analysts have always been good at collecting

29

facts, but on occasion they have shown much less confidence in the business of interpreting the material so painstakingly acquired.

For this state of affairs the perpetual clash of prerogatives between Aman and Mossad was partly to blame. Only insiders could fully understand the subtleties of the somewhat vague demarcation lines of responsibility, written and unwritten, between the two. For example, a secret military liaison unit would sometimes find itself involved in covert operations conducted jointly by Aman and Mossad. Before the operation started it was Mossad which made the decision to choose a soldier as the best qualified person available for this particular foreign job. No doubt the ability to combine resources helped to give flexibility, but it sometimes puzzled even those concerned, and led to personality clashes and disputes. On occasion each side of the intelligence service made use of personnel from the rival partner. Military intelligence had the right to choose special operations and to plan them, but in order to activate such operations it had to get authorization from Mossad. This arrangement made it inevitable that Mossad became the senior service.

Aman started life as the intelligence branch of the Israeli general staff, working from within its operations branch. But in 1953 the army reorganized its structure, abandoning the original British model in favour of the French set-up. It was then that military intelligence became a branch in its own right, and began using the title Agaf Hamodi'in and its acronym – Aman. At the head of it after the reorganization was Colonel Benjamin Gibli; his deputy was Lieutenant Colonel Yehosophat Harkabi.

Aman had already emerged as a distinctively military service with its own green and white flag, a fleur-de-lys badge and all the outward signs of an army hierarchy which distinguished it from the civilian cloak-and-dagger rig of Mossad. To complete the structure, it later became customary for the head of the service to be promoted on appointment to the rank of general.

The structure established in 1953 put Colonel Gibli (who did not become a general) in control of both the army's intelligence corps, consisting of six hundred officers and men scattered through the forces, and of the intelligence branch of the general staff which disposed of some two hundred men. The sharp edge of this branch was the collection department, aided by the research department. A number of 'desks' were set up within the research department, one for each Arab country; their job was to analyze incoming information, some of which was provided by Mossad, the service that retained responsibility for operations outside Israel. This structure, although adapted to changing needs, remains much the same today.

In the 1980s the Israeli Defence Force intelligence branch still has the job of collecting military, geographical and economic intelligence about all nations in the Middle East. For this purpose it is divided into departments – production, intelligence corps, foreign relations and a fourth department responsible for both field security and military censorship. All media reports affecting defence matters in Israel must be submitted to the censor, even in time of peace.

The most important task of the production department is to prepare annual 'Risk of War' estimates and the national intelligence estimates. One of the department's segments has the forbidding title 'enemy doctrine'; this section issues daily bulletins containing both raw and analyzed information. The most recent available figures suggest that in the 1980s Aman employed some seven thousand men and women, six hundred of whom, working to the regional desks, were occupied in intelligence production. They are recruited by recommendation from commanding officers, or are head-hunted in schools and universities for special training.

The intelligence corps is charged with the job of collecting information both by above board means and by secretive ones. The agents branch, as its name implies, runs military espionage – the collection of secret military material. But Aman operatives of this unit are not free-ranging like those of foreign military intelligence organizations; they are limited geographically to cross-border sorties into neighbouring Arab territory. To support them, the service also operates a long-distance observation unit which keeps watch upon all enemy movements just across the frontiers. Known as Unit 10, or Katam, it also has responsibility for running agents in nearby enemy territory. Some of them are Jewish 'arabizers' who go into long-term deep cover with Arab identities; others are simply Arab informers, always known in the service by the Hebrew word *shtinkerim*, which is a borrowing from the English word 'stinker'.

Aman has its own foreign relations department for, among other things, liaison with foreign military organizations. It also deploys Israeli defence attachés posted abroad, who are useful for garnering available intelligence, especially about the development of weapons and equipment. The service maintains contact with, and also keeps a watch over, the activities of foreign attachés accredited to Israel. British and American embassy military staff in Israel have from time to time been arrested for acts such as photographing military installations.

Military intelligence and Mossad in their peculiar way share the tasks of what might be called conventional espionage. What finally distinguished Aman from its 'civilian' partner was its dominance in

31

two specifically military spheres of activity. It brought as a dowry control over the army special troops, which had to be called in to provide heavy support for some operations; and it had control over radio signals work.

The ancestor of Israeli special forces was a pre-independence formation, the 'night squads' established in the 1930s with the benefit of military advice from Orde Wingate, an unconventional British soldier and Talmudic scholar who later in his career achieved fame and glory as commander of the Chindits fighting behind the lines against the Japanese in Burma. Their tactic was to make pre-emptive raids on Arab groups preparing to launch attacks upon Jewish villages and kibbutzes. As Arab raids multiplied in the troubled times after independence, the chief of staff, on the proposal of Brigadier Michael Shacham, created an army unit in August 1953 which modelled itself on the night squads. Designated Unit 101 (because it trained at Camp 101), it was commanded by Major Ariel Sharon, who later achieved fame in the Yom Kippur War. He recruited forty experienced Israeli guerrillas into what became a private army, trained to hit back at cross-frontier terrorist bases. The squads usually fought in plain clothes and in the style of a posse of Indian fighters in the American West.

The unit drew unwelcome attention to its brutal ways because of a fierce revenge attack upon Quibya in Jordan which killed sixty-six villagers. Even so, it was never entirely disbanded, and the tradition lived on when the unit was merged with a more respectable and conventional parachute battalion. Still under Sharon's command, it continued to fight out its own brand of dirty clandestine war against Arabs on the borders and in Gaza after that area fell under Israeli control at the end of the 1967 war.

This was the ancestry of Sayaret Matkal, the new unit which finally emerged to cope with special operations required by the intelligence services. Outside regular army control, it was based at a military airfield, with a strength of around two hundred men ready for instant action. Specialists could easily be called in, either from the secret services or from the armed forces and their reservists. Its soldiers undergo hard physical and weapon training, and learn the techniques of parachuting and underwater swimming. Training missions are sometimes carried out in hostile territory, just to make things tougher. The emphasis is on initiative and endurance; the pattern would be familiar to soldiers in similar foreign units, such as the British SAS or the American Delta commandos. Secrecy and speed are the watchwords.

Everything about this force is secret and the name itself, simply 'The Unit', maintains an aura of suitable anonymity. Within Israel, military censorship prevents the name being mentioned in print. The unit is answerable only to the chief of military intelligence, and although it carries out conventional military operations too, the real purpose is to serve as heavyweight back-up for Mossad operations when military might is needed. One of its early operations took special squads on a helicopter-borne raid deep into Egypt in 1968 to blow up Nile bridges and a power station. In the same year the unit made a reprisal raid on Beirut international airport where it destroyed nine planes operated by Middle East Airlines.

Sayaret Matkal developed into Mossad's heavy unit in the war against Palestinian terrorists, always ready to supply army muscle for revenge operations as well as for attacking hijacked aircraft in order to liberate passenger-hostages. In the course of Mossad operations against Palestinians in Europe a number of troopers from the unit were in fact seconded to Mossad. In a joint operation with Mossad, the unit took the war into enemy territory with a raid launched from the sea upon Arab guerrilla offices in Beirut. The unit's greatest triumph was the Entebbe raid, again a combined operation with intelligence. Its most recent operation was the seaborne raid in 1988 on the PLO headquarters at Hammam Beach in Tunisia, in which Khalil al-Wazir, a founder member of Fatah, was killed. As the man responsible for gaining control over the Arab uprising on the West Bank, he was an obvious target for Israeli covert action.

Commando operations were a significant part of the function of military intelligence. But in the long run it was the service's control over radio and signals, the so-called 'sigint' as opposed to human intelligence, which ensured the increased status of Aman. The one great advantage enjoyed by the military over their civilian rivals is that the intelligence corps looks after the signals activities of the whole Israeli intelligence community. So Mossad also depends on its technical abilities for all its intelligence traffic.

With the development of military technology, and as electronic warfare began to dominate battlefield tactics, it became ever more important for Aman to concentrate on the signals side of intelligence work. Although it cannot compete with the great powers in terms of spy-in-the-sky satellites, international listening stations and other expensive luxuries, it was able to develop a network of listening posts around the borders of Israel. For example, during the war of attrition, the long period of military stand-off in Sinai which lasted from 1970 until the Yom Kippur War of 1973, an installation twenty miles from the canal at Umhashida listened in to Egyptian military signals traffic. Near the northern border, on Mount Hermon, a similar station is still in operation within forty miles of Damascus, the Syrian capital. Unit

33

2, specially formed of army experts and technicians to collect signals and electronic intelligence, is of great importance militarily.

It was the realization that a small country like Israel, beset with economic difficulties, would never be able to provide the intelligence people with the expensive hi-tech equipment needed to keep long-range watch over enemy states which drove the Israelis into attempting to get the information in other ways. They came to rely upon crumbs from the table of the rich man, America, and then, when the USA drew the line at passing on all the fruits of its research, Israel sent spies to acquire that information by other means from its most loyal friend and ally.

Part II
Wider Yet and Wider

5. Security Mishap

For a public accustomed to legends about the brilliant infallibility of Mossad and Aman, with their impeccable skill at special operations, the story of the sabotage network set up in Egypt by the military service must come as a great shock. The time was 1954; David Ben-Gurion had left office and retired to a kibbutz, leaving in his place as prime minister Moshe Sharett. The new incumbent was a politician who seemed incapable of imposing his authority, especially over his defence minister, Pinhas Lavon, who as a union boss was more at home with the intricacies of industrial tactics than with military strategy. Two ambitious young men at the defence ministry, the chief of staff, Moshe Dayan, and the director, Shimon Peres, were waiting to make their mark, and seemed keener on going off to consult the former prime minister than on serving the new one.

The final period of Colonel Gibli's time as chief of military intelligence was a miserable one. Prime minister Sharett wrote in his diary that the Colonel was dogmatic, guilty of 'frightening ignorance about the Middle East' and capable of 'malignant one-sidedness'. Obsessed by fears of incursions into Israel by guerrillas from the Arab states, Aman was ever-ready to counter all such threats with military action to prove that the authorities of the new state of Israel were not prepared to take things passively.

In the period of tension caused by the attack upon the Jordanian frontier village of Quibya by Unit 101, military intelligence warned the prime minister about westward movements by the Jordanian Arab Legion, formed with British military aid to protect the Hachemite kingdom of Trans-Jordan. In fact there was no attack from Jordan, but

37

in the panicky atmosphere another alarm bell sounded when 'Ahmed', an Arab agent working for the Israelis, wrongly reported that an attack was imminent on an Israeli outpost near Jerusalem.

Then there was a coup in Damascus which caught military intelligence off balance, followed by misguided Aman reports that the Iraqis were actually invading Syria. Happily, calls from the military hotheads for warlike intervention there by the IDF were rejected. The political consequences of such moves were not properly considered, and in any case military intelligence had made the cardinal error of getting its facts wrong.

Despite that, Aman considered itself top dog in the intelligence community. It had the edge on the rival service, Mossad, in the sense that its chiefs continued to enjoy more influence over the government. Originally, it had been laid down that the head of Mossad had to be involved in the planning of all special operations on enemy territory and that his consent was required before such operations were carried out. As soon as Lavon became defence minister, he changed the rules and terminated this arrangement at precisely the moment when Aman was at its most aggressive. Its special operations crowd planted a bomb in Beirut; they had a pointless scheme to blow a bridge in Jordan.

Further evidence of Aman's incompetence was provided when an ill-prepared group of five Israeli commandos on an intelligence mission in Syria were captured while changing the batteries on a listening device to monitor Syrian army telephones on the Golan Heights. One of the soldiers killed himself, fearing that he might break down under torture and reveal classified information.

It was a worrying time, the more so as events had taken place in Egypt which, although welcomed at first, began to cause disquiet. King Farouk was overthrown. His departure brought few tears, but when Gamal Abdel Nasser, leader of the revolutionaries known as the 'Free Officers' who had carried out the coup, began to get into his stride as an anti-imperialist, Arab socialist dictator, storm cones were hoisted in the Middle East and Europe. It soon became plain that the new man in Cairo had ambitions to become leader of the Arab world, and that his first objective was to gain control of the Suez Canal, at that time run by an Anglo-French company. His further aim was to end the strong British military presence in the Canal Zone. If that were achieved, it would have important military consequences for Israel too: the removal of British buffer forces would leave the country vulnerable to an Egyptian attack up through Sinai, and it would also provide the means to tighten the Arab blockade against the new state of Israel.

What irked the Israelis was the tolerant attitude to the Egyptian revolution being adopted by the Western powers. The American secretary of state, John Foster Dulles, seemed convinced that Colonel Nasser might become an ally in helping to hold the line against Soviet communism in the Middle East. There were even indications that the CIA had helped and encouraged President Nasser, in the hope of seeing a strong and friendly government being installed in Cairo. The British government was disposed to reach an accommodation with the Cairo regime for the eventual total withdrawal of British forces from Egypt. In the summer of 1954, within two days of the event, details of an agreement reached by Winston Churchill, then prime minister, with President Eisenhower concerning a new British plan for the evacuation of the Suez bases were discovered by Aman.

'Something must be done' was the reaction of Israeli leaders when their intelligence revealed that the British government intended to start troop withdrawals from Egypt. The action they finally chose was a half-baked conspiracy inside Egypt, to be mounted with the intention of destabilizing the Nasser regime. Exactly who first thought up the scheme remains a mystery, but it was approved at high level and operational planning soon began. In outline what they schemed to do was to set up an Israeli terrorist network in Egypt pretending to be an Arab one. It was to be activated to organize a bombing campaign against British and American targets such as the British Council and the US Information Centre in Cairo, for which the Egyptians would be blamed. With any luck Colonel Nasser would turn on his old enemies the fundamentalist Moslem Brothers, and the Anglo-Saxons would begin to have second thoughts about the viability of his new regime. Only a convinced and over-eager, conspiratorial secret service could ever have imagined that such a plot might conceivably succeed; the whole concept on which it was based displayed a surprising degree of ignorance about Egypt and the Arab world. Yet nobody in authority vetoed the idea as preparations went ahead.

An amateurish network of Egyptian Jews, set up several years before by military intelligence for special operations behind the lines in case of a war between Israel and Egypt, was run operationally by Unit 131 (not to be confused with Unit 101). From headquarters in the old Arab town of Jaffa, near Tel Aviv, Lieutenant Colonel Mordechai Ben-Tsur organized the training and preparation of the network which was being readied for what was to be called Operation Suzanna. Both Mossad and Shin Beth were involved, along with their colleagues from military intelligence. Moshe Dayan later wrote of the affair: 'The Unit initiated an operation which thereafter was always referred to as "the security mishap".'

On the ground the network of 'sleepers' was controlled by Colonel Avraham Dar, using the cover name John Darling which fitted his pretence of being English and working for a British company. The first blunder was that he recruited a man who, wearing another hat, was also the local head of a Zionist organization responsible for arranging the emigration of Egyptian Jews. His name was Dr Victor Sa'adi and he enthusiastically agreed to help. Together the two men assembled local Jews to support the sabotage network. The danger of this procedure was that, when detected, this fact might put at risk the whole Jewish population of Egypt – which in any case was viewed with suspicion by the highly active Egyptian intelligence people. None the less, plans went ahead and Dr Moshe Marzouk from the Jewish hospital took charge of the Cairo cell, while Samuel Azar, a young schoolmaster, headed a similar one in Alexandria. Each was responsible for his own team.

The plotters were a young and enthusiastic bunch of friends. That was another drawback, for if any one of them fell into the hands of the Egyptian police it would be only too easy to discover the rest of the circle. In their unprofessional way, and ignorant of the trade tricks of cut-outs and cell organization, they innocently foregathered for planning sessions in a public place or in the home of one of them. Among the recruits was an attractive young woman, Victorine Ninio, and a dashing young engineer named Victor Levy. Before the operation began, Colonel Gibli decided that they should be brought secretly to Israel for espionage and sabotage training. This was properly arranged, although the training officer became alarmed at once when he saw the kind of people who had been recruited for the perilous task of operating in an enemy country. Although charming and cosmopolitan, they lacked toughness and experience. For the skilled trainers this material was singularly unpromising. A party of well-meaning civilians, with only the vaguest idea of how to operate the radios supplied to them, were required to improvise incendiary devices using condoms filled with acid and spectacle cases packed with combustible chemicals. None the less, trained as best they could be, they were spirited back to Egypt to await orders.

By the time that Operation Suzanna was ready in the summer of 1954 the original team organizer, Avraham Dar, had been replaced in the field by a new man, Paul Frank (real name Avraham Seidenwerg), who passed himself off in Cairo as a former Nazi SS officer. Frank was a real intelligence man recruited after his military career had been blighted by court-martial for theft. With its normal thoroughness in such details, the Israeli secret service arranged for him to spend several months establishing his so-called legend, a false life story. So equipped, he submerged himself in the German colony in Egypt and prepared for activation. He was astonished to find that when he went to make contact with the Alexandria cell he was warmly greeted as the 'Spy' whose arrival they had been awaiting.

In July 1954 Unit 131 received this bizarre order:

Begin immediate action to prevent or postpone the Anglo-Egyptian agreement. The targets are, one, cultural and informational institutions. Two, economic institutions. Three, cars, British representatives and other British citizens. Four, anything else that might complicate diplomatic relations.

Inform us of the possibility of action in the Canal Zone.

Listen in to us daily at seven o'clock on waveband G.

Despite many difficulties, the group did manage to plant small explosive charges in the letter boxes at the central post office in Alexandria. Some damage was caused, although nobody paid very much attention. The Israeli terrorists succeeded in making a bit more of a splash on 14 July when they contrived to place explosive devices in sunglasses cases at the libraries of the US Information Service in Alexandria and Cairo. Encouraged by this partial success, they got together enough explosives for similar small bombs to be planted at Cairo cinemas and in the main railway station to mark the anniversary of Colonel Nasser's revolution. None of them went off. That was bad enough, but worse was to happen in Alexandria. While Philip Nathanson, a nineteen-year-old recruit, waited in a cinema queue for his chance to place a bomb, the device in his pocket exploded prematurely. Prompt action by Captain Hassan el-Manadi of the Egyptian police special branch saved him from being badly burned; he quickly realized what had caused the accident. Within hours Egyptian police and intelligence men had rolled up the vulnerable Israeli network. Because its members all knew each other, the cells collapsed like a pack of cards.

A graver blow for Mossad was that Max Bennett, a truly professional agent operating independently in Egypt on more important business, himself became a victim. Because he had been having radio transmission trouble, he was forced to get in contact with the amateurs and therefore he was exposed when they were. The capture of Bennett was a serious setback for Israeli intelligence: after his arrest the service found itself without a single top-class operative left in Egypt when spies were most needed there. Partly as a result, the Israeli government was completely taken by surprise about the Czech arms deal by which President Nasser began receiving copious supplies of up-to-date Iron Curtain weapons and jet fighters.

41

Within four days Egyptian security triumphantly announced that it had arrested ten men and a woman – as the Cairo newspapers put it, 'a bloody Zionist gang'. For Gamal Abdel Nasser it was a propaganda victory, exploited to the full by a show trial. Dr Marzouk and Samuel Azar, the cell leaders, were both sentenced to death and were hanged in Cairo in January 1955. The victims of an ill-conceived and pointless operation, they became the first agents in the history of Israeli intelligence to be executed in Egypt. Max Bennett, like the well-trained secret serviceman that he was, killed himself in prison by opening his veins with a rusty nail. The other agents received long prison sentences. Victorine Ninio, who had not been involved directly in the bombings, got fifteen years and suffered terribly from torture and ill-treatment before she was eventually allowed to return home, a broken woman. Twice she had tried to kill herself after being arrested in Max Bennett's Cairo apartment, when he was caught in the act of transmitting to Tel Aviv by radio. It was not until 1968 that she was finally repatriated in a prisoner of war exchange. Once back home she was treated as a national heroine. Within three years she totally recovered from her harrowing experiences as a failed secret agent and in 1971 when she married a Colonel Eli Boger her rather grand wedding was attended by Golda Meir and a cluster of top intelligence officers.

For Israeli intelligence, Operation Suzanna had been a deeply embarrassing disaster. When news of the arrests first came out the government issued panicky denials, which could not, however, hold the line for long. The chase was soon on in Tel Aviv to discover who was responsible. Just after the executions in Cairo, Pinhas Lavon, the defence minister, resigned in an hysterical letter addressed to the prime minister which was kept secret at the time. His departure provoked a government crisis that only ended when David Ben-Gurion, still ostentatiously wearing the kibbutz clothes which he affected in exile at his Negev retreat, appeared in the Knesset and consented to serve the country once more as minister of defence.

The matter did not end there, for many people and several agencies were involved. The dispute centred upon who gave the order for the Cairo bombing campaign to start, and the political ramifications of this affair poisoned Israeli politics for many years. A committee of investigation began its secret hearings in a Tel Aviv apartment. Lieutenant General Yaacov Dori, a former chief of staff, and Judge Yitzhak Olshan, president of the supreme court, had the task of attempting to sort out the truth of different versions of the story put forward by the principals concerned. Colonel Gibli and his military intelligence officers claimed that the orders had come from the defence minister, Pinhas Lavon.

Lavon claimed that Aman itself had launched the bombing operations without prior ministerial authorization, an allegation heavy with consequence – if the minister was correct, that would mean that the military intelligence service had conspired to make a terrorist raid on another country without bothering to consult its own government.

What does seem clear is that the idea of unleashing Unit 131 was inspired by gloomy estimates about the consequences for Israel of British military withdrawal from the Suez Canal Zone. Colonel Gibli considered that this would be an 'unmitigated disaster', for it would remove 'a foreign barrier separating Egypt from direct physical contact with Israel'. Throughout the period, his service had displayed strong tendencies to overestimate both Egyptian military strength and President Nasser's desire to make war on Israel. For this reason, when Anglo-Egyptian talks on the Canal Zone were about to resume, his preoccupation was to prevent the agreement at all costs, even by resorting to sabotage operations in Cairo and Alexandria.

The question of responsibility for the plot was never satisfactorily resolved in public. The enquiry committee's verdict left it open by summing up: 'In the final analysis, we regret that we have been unable to answer the question put to us by the Prime Minister. We can only say that we were not convinced beyond any reasonable doubt that the senior officer did not receive orders from the minister of defence. We are equally uncertain that the minister of defence did, in fact, give the orders attributed to him.'

In leaving it at that, the government set a precedent which was to be followed later. Whenever embarrassing actions came to light, the reaction was to claim that because the security of the state was involved, and because security counted more than any other consideration, it would be best not to dig any further.

One further embarrassment in this disturbing affair was still to come. One of the survivors of the débâcle was Paul Frank, now in Europe. Using his cover as a former SS officer, for his part in the operation he had succeeded in becoming friendly with influential Egyptians. The suspicion in Israel now was that, by the time he became enmeshed in the Israeli bomb plot in Cairo and Alexandria, he had been 'turned' by the shrewd head of Egyptian counter-intelligence, Colonel Osman, and had been paid 40,000 Deutschmarks. In due course he was arrested by the Egyptians together with the other Israeli plotters. They held him in prison for long enough to establish an alibi which would convince Mossad of his loyalty, and then allowed him to escape to Vienna.

What raised Israeli suspicions was the fact that in Europe, where he continued to work in intelligence, he went on using the cover name Paul Frank under which he had been convicted and sentenced to death *in absentia* by the Egyptians. Also, there was evidence that he remained in contact with Egyptian secret service officers. Despite his dire threats that if he was forced to return to Israel he would blow the lid off what was by then known as the Lavon affair, Mossad was determined to get him back to face trial and made counter-threats. Evidence introduced at his trial in Jerusalem in 1959 did succeed in reopening the whole affair. The court found him not guilty of betraying Operation Suzanna, but guilty of photographing and being in possession of military intelligence documents and of making unauthorized approaches to Egyptian officers in Europe.

For these lesser offences he received a sentence of twelve years. The severity of this punishment was taken as a sign that although, as is often the case when spies are brought to court, it was impossible to prove that he had betrayed fellow agents, the court had little doubt about his misbehaviour. It was an episode which left a bitter taste at the end of an unfortunate affair. After serving his sentence Frank went to live in the United States.

6. From Gaza to Suez

The main preoccupation of the IDF in the early 1950s was border trouble, as Arab raiders sneaked across the old ceasefire lines to seek vengeance on the Israelis. These sorties were in fact spontaneous gestures by Palestinians living in harsh conditions in the refugee camps, many of them in sight of places where the inmates had once lived and which were now in the possession of strangers. But the army, convinced that the attacks were organized by the Egyptian authorities, struck back in counter-raids. Because these actions were based on a misapprehension, their principal result was to make things worse. In fact the surrounding Arab states were at first not responsible for the attacks, and indeed, fearing the military consequences upon themselves, Egypt, Syria, Lebanon and Jordan did their best to discourage the *fedayeen* from military activity. In Gaza the Egyptians were constantly arresting suspected fighters and blocking their entry routes into Israel. But as the result of an Israeli cross-border raid into Gaza, the Egyptians changed their policy and began setting up a *fedayeen* movement under their control. Israeli hawks thought that by attacking the Arabs they would protect their borders; instead they encouraged further attacks.

In the spring of 1955 began the process which transformed an ill-organized collection of Arab raiders into a professional Palestinian guerrilla force. President Nasser invited to Cairo the Arab leaders from Gaza and announced that he would provide them with military training, money and weapons to attack Israel. Egyptian officers and NCOs in Sinai began to take control over the scattered groups and warring factions, and formed a force which soon showed itself capable

45

of carrying out night attacks on buildings and vehicles. In August the Palestinians killed five soldiers and seventeen civilians, and so began the long-running subversive war. It was a conflict which was to absorb the activities of Aman and Mossad for many years to come.

Aman's first reaction was to turn to assassination as a means of pacification. Target number one was a talented Egyptian intelligence colonel based in the Gaza strip as organizer of the new Palestinian resistance. His name was Mustapha Hafez and he became the first victim of Israeli counter-terrorism, blown to pieces by a parcel bomb delivered to him by a mercenary Arab double agent working for the Israelis. Another Egyptian colonel who was military attaché in Jordan also died as a result of a mysterious explosion.

It was the job of military intelligence to discover the facts behind the activity of the infiltrators and so to prevent their raids. But Aman was also kept extremely busy, as the senior arm of state intelligence, trying to assess not only the wider diplomatic significance, but also the extent of warlike preparations being made for full-scale Egyptian assault. For, partly as a reaction to an IDF raid on Gaza, President Nasser had decided that he might have to go to war and he was negotiating with the Soviet Union to get new weapons with which to fight it.

Both Aman and Mossad were found lacking in this crucial period, for they failed to provide detailed information about relations between Egypt and the Soviet Union. They were both shocked and surprised when in September 1955 President Nasser announced his arms deal with Czechoslovakia. This was an arrangement by which Egypt was eventually to acquire two hundred Mig-15 fighters, fifty bombers, artillery and tanks in quantity. The Israelis were then forced to try to find out when the arms would be delivered and – even more important – how President Nasser intended to use his new arsenal.

The accepted view was that the Egyptian leader was planning to use the *fedayeen* to frighten Israeli settlers on the southern border in the Negev, and then under cover of such operations to launch an all-out attack upon Israel. While Aman turned its attention to probing the Egyptian order of battle, Israeli hawks like General Moshe Dayan spread the gospel that an attack was imminent. Dissenting voices went unheard. Mr Sharett, the foreign minister, complained about the 'blatantly tendentious' approach of Aman, which he said seemed determined to make use of whatever facts were available to prove its political case that war was inevitable.

When Yehosophat Harkabi took over as chief of Aman in May 1955, it was a service whose prestige and pride had been seriously harmed by the 'mishap'. Pinhas Lavon, the defence minister, was the first to lose office as a result of the Egyptian fiasco. Then Colonel

Gibli was dismissed; but in the ranks of intelligence many of Gibli's colleagues soldiered on. Colonel Harkabi decided none the less that to undertake a further enquiry into the conduct of the service would demoralize it even more. The scandal continued to haunt the service for many years; despite its shortcomings, however, Aman remained the predominant branch of Israeli intelligence as the new chief took on the task of rehabilitating it.

Israeli military intelligence owes a particular debt to Harkabi, an intellectual soldier who had joined it in 1950 fresh to the world of intelligence. When he took command he was only thirty-five years old. What he was able to offer was a lively mind, analytical ability and a deep knowledge of the philosophy and literature of the Arabs. He preached the doctrine that the best way to anticipate the plans and actions of the opponent was to 'get under his skin' and understand his thinking. Knowledge, according to this former philosophy student, was often more important than 'Intelligence' in its military sense. To his mind this process was more useful than simply counting the number of enemy tanks and guns. Harkabi prepared two book-length 'worst case' scenarios anticipating renewed war with the Arab states. In these, he analyzed the whole spectrum of factors, political and economic as well as military and geographical. His studies had a profound influence on the work of the department over the next three decades.

A more urgent task confronting the new boss was to satisfy constant demands from Moshe Dayan, the exigent chief of staff, for more information about Egyptian military preparations, which he was already convinced were well under way. It seems that the service now had few, if any, agents in Egypt itself and its analysts were mostly officers of European origin, unable to read Arabic and unfamiliar with the ways of the military in Cairo. To a large extent it had to rely upon signals intelligence, which managed to bring in useful practical material. In fact Aman at this period of its history performed well when it came to collecting facts, but, despite the best efforts of Harkabi, its record was less impressive in interpretation.

Once President Nasser had announced his decision to nationalize the Suez Canal in July 1965 the war party in Israel became active and, with the approval of Aman, began preparing a pre-emptive attack upon Egypt in cooperation with France, a country which had reasons of its own to settle the Algerian score with Nasser. Both Aman and Mossad were already closely tied in with French intelligence services, and all were united with the aim of toppling the Egyptian dictator. Britain too now became an ally, and as preparations went ahead Aman was able to show off and win friends by providing the European partners with valuable information about the enemy order of battle.

It also found time to indulge in a programme of disinformation and deception so as to confuse the Egyptians about the aim of Israeli military preparations. Through broadcasts which repeated that Israel had no intention of allowing itself to be used as a tool by the old imperialists, Britain and France, it managed to convince President Nasser's intelligence that Israeli did not intend to become involved in aggressive action. The myth was reinforced by news that mobilization in Israel was in fact directed against the danger of an attack from Jordan and Iraq.

The real triumph of Mossad and Aman was to keep secret all the covert contacts throughout the summer and autumn of 1956, as Israel began to collaborate with the governments of France and Britain in preparation for the attack upon Egypt. At a final clandestine meeting at Sèvres near Paris, senior British, French and Israeli ministers finalized their plot to destroy President Nasser. Israeli troops were to launch an attack into Egyptian-held Sinai, then the French and British agreed to issue an ultimatum ordering both belligerents to withdraw their forces from the Suez Canal zone. Egypt's refusal would provide a pretext for Anglo-French forces to land in Egypt in a 'police operation' and take over the Canal. The first stages of the plan were accomplished, but the threat of American and Soviet counter-measures forced Britain and France to agree to a ceasefire and the operation ended in failure.

So successful was Israeli intelligence in concealing the truth about meetings where the crucial decisions were taken that even Israeli ambassadors in London and Paris were not aware of what was going on. Apart from Golda Meir, the minister, nobody at the foreign ministry itself was let into the secret. But this intensive subterfuge, no doubt commendable from a professional point of view, had a malign effect. Because the Israeli ambassadors in Washington and Moscow (Israel was still represented there at the time) were kept in total ignorance, they were unable to report upon and appraise the likely reaction of the two superpowers. This was a sad omission, for it was the hostile response of both the USA and the Soviet Union which eventually ruined the Suez operation and the plot to overthrow Nasser.

7. Nazi Hunt

The failure of the Suez adventure and the ignominious withdrawal of the Anglo-French expeditionary force produced a mood of self-pity in an Israel convinced that it had been betrayed by the lack of political will of the European allies. The army felt resentment that its military successes had failed to destroy President Nasser, who was now seen as the ogre. It was this mood which encouraged the secret service to move into another field of endeavour. For years its agents had been in communication with Nazi-hunters like Simon Wiesenthal, keeping tracks on the persecutors of Jews who had escaped at the end of the war to find asylum in Latin America. The time had come to strike a blow against the surviving tormentors which would also help to reinforce national self-confidence at home, and to remind the world of the tragic sufferings which had led to the exodus of Jews into the new state of Israel.

Isser Harel, by this time firmly established as head of Mossad, received what he instinctively felt was sure information that Adolf Eichmann, the monster who had organized the gas ovens in which millions of Jews perished, was alive and living in Argentina. It was a piece of news which launched a complicated and devious two-year operation under the personal control of Harel to kidnap the Nazi and bring him to Jerusalem for trial. No matter that for months on end it absorbed most of the resources of Mossad; it was a good cause.

This deed, more than any other, established the worldwide reputation of Mossad as the boldest and most dynamic intelligence service in the world. And Isser Harel, a man whose name had never appeared in print, head of a service which had never been mentioned in public, enjoyed the moment of triumph when he sat in the Israeli Parliament to hear prime minister Ben-Gurion make the official announcement of the mission's success. In May 1960 David Ben-Gurion rose to declare:

> I have to announce to the Knesset that a short time ago, one of the greatest Nazi criminals was found by the Israeli Security Services, Adolf Eichmann, who was responsible together with the Nazi leaders for what they called the 'Final Solution of the Jewish Problem' – that is the extermination of six million Jews of Europe. Adolf Eichmann is already under arrest in Israel, and he will shortly be brought to trial in Israel under the Nazis and Nazi Collaborators (Punishment) Law of 1950.

In due course Eichmann was found guilty by an Israeli court, sentenced to death and hanged. These events raised many questions which were debated at length, both internationally and in Israel. Doubts were expressed about the morality of the kidnap and trial of an old man so many years after his crimes had been committed. Obviously the covert mission to seize him in Argentina, without the knowledge of the Argentinian government, was a breach of international law and custom. What was not in doubt was the impeccable style and manner of Mossad's behaviour in carrying out the operation. The secret service had resisted the temptation simply to kill the man they knew to be guilty of abominable crimes. Isser Harel gave strict orders that, if the team were detected after what they regarded as a kind of citizens' arrest had been made, Eichmann was not to be killed. In those circumstances, he was to be handcuffed to a Mossad man with instructions to ask at once to be taken to a senior Argentinian official so that he could explain who the prisoner was.

Harel's own book, *The House on Garibaldi Street*, published fifteen years later when he finally got cabinet permission, revealed the scope and complexity of the successful plan which employed a team of eleven men and one woman, backed up at home by a special unit. The role of the non-liberated lady agent involved, Dina Ron, was simply to give credibility to one of the half dozen safe houses taken over in Argentina by posing as the girlfriend of the man who had rented it. Two specialists, one named in the Harel book as Shalom Dani, a skilled forger and a specialist in make-up, were also employed. It was of crucial importance that the overseas unit should have a variety of identity papers and personality changes available. For the most difficult trick was not the actual detection and seizure of Eichmann, but to

50

make sure that the Argentinian authorities should not become aware that Mossad was operating in their country at all.

In unprecedented fashion, the head of the service himself took charge on the ground in Latin America. He took maximum precautions to avoid detection and ensured that his team of veterans drawn from all branches of the security service did the same. Harel also had the authority to make sure that the national airline, El Al, was ready to cooperate in the difficult business of flying the prisoner back to Tel Aviv. For this purpose he used a special Britannia airliner which had flown to Buenos Aires to take the foreign minister, Abba Eban, to attend independence day ceremonies in Argentina. Eichmann was finally smuggled past immigration officers, drugged and wearing the uniform of an El Al crew member. The final Mossad touch was that, had questions been asked at the last moment, they could have produced medical papers prepared in advance for a member of the team in whose false name the Nazi war criminal was in fact travelling. No clearer proof has ever emerged of Mossad's scrupulous attention to detail in its sensitive work.

Naturally, the publicized success of this mission had a great and beneficial effect upon morale within the service. There is a limit to the amount of time that even highly motivated secret service officers, often cut off for years at a time from their friends and controllers, can continue to work in an atmosphere of total clandestinity in which not even their achievements may be recorded and praised. For once Mossad was able to bask in the kind of public recognition normally only granted to soldiers after some great victory. The Eichmann affair even encouraged bright young men and women to volunteer to join the service.

Nothing could more simply illustrate the up-and-down nature of the life of a spymaster than the events which unfolded while the Israelis were still vaunting the success of the Eichmann affair. One evening in March 1961 Isser Harel was interrupted by a telephone call as he was about to leave home. The call came from his counterpart at the head of Shin Beth, the home security branch, who was passing on the report of a surveillance mission with a Soviet diplomat as its target. The watchers had seen him hand over a black briefcase to a man whom he had encountered in the street. That man was Israel Beer, a reservist colonel and a defence adviser to the prime minister, who on the grounds that he was writing an official history of the war of independence, even had his own office at the ministry of defence. What made things worse was that he was also a friend and confidant of David Ben-Gurion. It is difficult to imagine a trickier job for a head of intelligence than to have to inform a prime minister that his friend is a spy.

Mossad and Shin Beth had long had their suspicions about the activities of the curious Mr Beer, and Isser Harel positively disliked him. Already evidence had accumulated against him as a result of investigations initiated because of his high spending on a modest salary. But finally, Shin Beth got proof of his activities when the Soviet agent was caught red-handed. In the briefcase which the Russian was handing back to Beer at the time of the arrest were confidential documents including Ben-Gurion's official diary, which had been photocopied. Beer himself readily admitted that he had been spying for the Soviet Union ever since the Suez war.

When the news was transmitted to him the prime minister sadly ordered, 'Do your duty.' But he was angry for all that, because when suspicions about his friend had first been mentioned he forbade the security men to put him under surveillance, and he refused to believe that Beer had now been detected simply by chance.

At his trial Beer did not deny the facts, but justified his actions by arguing that he felt it was his duty to save Israel from falling into the hands of the Western imperialist powers when it ought to ally itself to the Soviet Union. In prison serving a ten-year sentence – raised to fifteen years on appeal by the prosecution – he wrote a book of self-justification. The account which the spy gave of his life was full of fantasy, and Mossad had no difficulty in proving that. But they never did manage to discover the whole truth about his origins, though it was proved that a real Austrian named Israel Beer had disappeared in 1938, the year that the man using that name emigrated to Palestine. This supported the belief that he had been placed in deep cover during the mass emigration from Europe, ready for exploitation by the Russians later when he had embedded himself in the Israeli establishment.

David Ben-Gurion was so put out and embarrassed by the revelations about his former friend that he never quite forgave Isser Harel, whose instincts in the Beer affair had been proved correct. It was an incident which continued to rankle and was responsible for the head of Mossad losing the strong support he had formerly received from the prime minister. In fact it marked the beginning of the end of Harel's period of glory as the master of Mossad. For this affair was still fresh in the memory of the prime minister when the two men quarrelled over the correct assessment of the importance of the aid being given to the Egyptians in modernizing their armoury by German scientists at work in Cairo.

8. Spymasters' Clash

Of the Mossad spies sent out into Egypt in the early years when that country seemed to be Israel's most threatening adversary, the most audacious and successful was Wolfgang Lotz. He created a dashing legend, reinforced by the publication later of his account of his own exploits under the catchy title *The Champagne Spy*.

Lotz's widowed mother, a Jewish actress who had married an Aryan German theatre director, fled from Germany in 1933 and settled in Israel. Eventually her son joined the British army in the Middle East and, as a senior NCO speaking impeccable German, was employed interrogating prisoners of war from the Afrika Korps. With this military background he later joined Haganah, the Israeli underground army, and after independence signed on as a major in the regular IDF. He caught the attention of the military intelligence people because of his Aryan features and German background at a time when Israel was particularly worried about the activities of former Nazi scientists working for President Gamal Abdel Nasser. The Egyptians had brought in the foreign missile and aircraft engineers with the ambitious aim of producing weapons for use in future wars against Israel. In addition to the obvious military danger, Israel concluded that the alliance against them of Egyptians and former Nazis must be evidence of continuing and dangerous anti-semitism in Germany. Many unemployed former Wehrmacht officers had gone to Egypt to find employment as instructors with the Egyptian army. They were followed by a number of German scientists; although most of the talented rocket engineers who had worked on the early wartime missiles were headhunted for recruitment by the Russians and the

53

Americans, some of the less distinguished ones made their way to Nasser's Egypt.

Wolfgang Lotz seemed an ideal choice to pose as an ex-Wehrmacht officer so as to infiltrate this group of German scientists. The advantage of using him as a spy in Cairo was that his wartime experience as an interrogator of officers in Rommel's 115th Division provided him with detailed knowledge of that unit; it was simple for him to pretend to have served in a division whose record was familiar to him. Against all the normal rules, he was ordered to use his own name – which, of course, could be backed up with a genuine birth certificate and identity documents, once the secret of his mother's Jewish birth was suppressed. To strengthen the cover story of his life still further, he married a lady who looked convincingly German, Waldraut Neumann, whom he met for the first time on the Orient Express.

Further operational support was provided after Isser Harel, the Mossad head who took over the Cairo operation from Aman, had done a deal with the West German espionage organization established by General Gehlen in the postwar years. The Germans agreed to help in the matter of the ex-Nazis in Cairo: Lotz received special training at one of their establishments in Bavaria and was furnished with letters of introduction to high-ranking German ex-officers.

Posing as an Arabic-speaking German of independent means, he arrived in Cairo and took a fine villa in Heliopolis. The next move was to set up as an opulent breeder of Arab horses at a stud farm in the smart Zamalek district. From there, and as a member of the Cavalry Club at Gezirah, he began cultivating the friendship of equestrian enthusiasts in the Egyptian hierarchy and within the international community. It was a role which satisfied his natural inclinations towards a lifestyle which he thoroughly enjoyed. It even gave him a wry satisfaction to pretend that he, a Jewish intelligence officer, had been a Nazi. He was received in the homes of prominent Germans, and in return gave lavish parties, spending freely from the funds provided by his intelligence bosses. The stud farm too cost a small fortune and Lotz, who was better at spying than at accounting, was in constant trouble with the parsimonious accounts department in Tel Aviv, which constantly demanded paperwork to back up his expenses. But the high cost of his champagne life in grand surroundings was justified by the amount of intelligence material he was required to provide.

One side of his task was to gain insight, through personal contacts at the riding school, into the personalities, thinking and behaviour of senior Egyptian officers such as Colonel Abdel Rahman of military intelligence. After six months, when he travelled to Europe to consult with his masters, he was able to report being on excellent terms with

General Youssef Ali Ghorab, the influential officer in charge of the Egyptian police. By cultivating the friendship of General Fouad Osman, head of security at the rocket sites, Lotz was able to get an invitation to visit SAM missile bases newly installed in Sinai, and claimed that he even persuaded him to pose for a photograph in front of one of the missiles. Mossad demanded details about the rocket programme and plans of secret establishments, as well as the names and records of foreign technicians. The spy's only weakness was that, although he could provide a mass of hearsay information picked up in the smart clubs, he was not gifted at assessing and interpreting that material.

Lotz was operational in the field at a critical time in the tense relationship between those two rivals, Mossad and Aman. Isser Harel, his immediate boss, was in conflict with Meir Amit, head of military intelligence, on the issue of the size of the threat to Israeli security of the work being done in Egypt by the German technologists. In July 1962 the Egyptians launched four demonstration missiles, two with a range of 175 miles and two others capable of flying 350 miles. President Nasser proudly announced that they could destroy any target 'south of Beirut'. This event caused great alarm in Israel, made worse by the fact that Mossad had nothing in its files about the missiles.

The sarcastic Meir Amit enquired: 'What are we spending our intelligence budget on if we get our information from a public speech of Gamal Nasser? All we need for that is a portable radio.' He had already clashed with his opposite number over his complaints that Mossad was too busy with flashy operations such as the capture of Eichmann to have time to discover the extent of the military threat from the Arab neighbour states.

The indignant Harel made a big effort and within a month provided prime minister Ben-Gurion with a full report on the Egyptian rocket programme, a good deal of which was provided by Lotz. Through him Mossad received blueprints of Project 333 for the design of missile control systems, and discovered the location of places where rockets were to be assembled. But the key piece of evidence it obtained was a letter from one of the German scientists, Professor Wolfgang Pilz. Written to Kamil Azzab, Egyptian director of the factory, it asked for more than three and a half million Swiss francs for the purchase of nine hundred rockets. The conclusion was that President Nasser was preparing to rain down missiles on Israel. It was left to the sceptical Meir Amit to point out that the danger was not immediate and that the enemy was still having great trouble with guidance systems for the missiles.

It was at this point that a mysterious Austrian scientist called Otto Frank Joklik conveniently walked into an Israeli embassy in Europe with information that the Egyptians were also working on a 'poor man's bomb', made of strontium and cobalt atomic waste, with which they were preparing to lay Israel waste. He said that he knew this information because his job was to procure the materials for two secret programmes, one codenamed Cleopatra to produce an atom bomb, and the other Ibis to create a strange radioactive weapon. This new development provided just the ammunition that Isser Harel needed to justify the extreme measures of covert action which he proposed to take against the German scientists. Mossad made ready to carry out Operation Damocles, which received final approval in September 1962. Israeli intelligence was going into the assassination and terrorism business.

Lotz's reports from Cairo, some of them based on odd bits of gossip, appeared to back up Joklik's remarkable story and he was promptly ordered to arrange the mailing in Cairo of threatening letters to fifty German scientists working for Egypt. More lethal action swiftly followed. In Munich Dr Heinz Krug left the office of a rocket-purchasing company with a stranger and was never seen again; an anonymous telephone call announced that he was dead. Two months later a parcel addressed to Factory 333, where missiles were assembled, exploded, badly injuring a secretary. Two other parcel bombs killed at least five people employed in firms connected with the rocket programme, and an attempt to shoot a German electronics expert narrowly failed.

Otto Joklik, the informer, was next called in for an attempt to persuade Professor Paul Goerke to cease working for the notorious missile factory. To accomplish this he arranged to meet Heidi, the professor's daughter, in Switzerland where they were joined by Joseph Ben-Gal, presumably from Mossad, who claimed to be an Israeli education official. They told the woman that her father was in no danger but that his colleague, Dr Pilz, was a Nazi who could expect no mercy. Heidi had taken the precaution of informing the Swiss police, who kept surveillance on the meeting and then arrested the two Mossad representatives not far from the Israeli consulate in Zurich. The West Germans promptly demanded their extradition on charges of attempted murder.

This was the event which launched the gravest of the series of crises which afflicted the state of Israel in its tangled relationship with the world of covert exercises launched by over-zealous spymasters. Capable though he was, Isser Harel was a bad-tempered man who allowed his emotions to over-ride his undoubted intelligence. He had detected what he felt convinced was a major German plot against Israel, a conspiracy being run by ex-Nazis. Historic memory clouded his judgement and he was willing to launch a campaign of terror against the guilty ones. And now, to increase his ill-will, the West Germans were demanding the extradition of Jews as a result of it.

Although the head of Mossad was not alone in seeing events in this light, and was receiving some support from members of the cabinet, including Golda Meir, a broader view was taken by David Ben-Gurion. The prime minister was intent on cultivating the friendship of both France and West Germany, believing that his country would need their support in the troubled times ahead. Ben-Gurion needed an alliance with West Germany, which he knew was becoming a great economic power and a force to be reckoned with in international affairs. For that reason, he strongly favoured diplomatic moves intended to obtain West German help in closing down the warlike activities of German citizens in Egypt.

This provoked a sharp quarrel between the prime minister, supported by Meir Amit, and Isser Harel. Harsh words were shouted, as Harel accused his opponents of sacrificing the security of the state in their efforts to cultivate German friendship. What stung most was the deeply cynical view taken by Meir Amit about Egypt's warlike preparations, and his heavy doubts over Wolfgang Lotz's reports that they were on the point of producing a missile force and an atom bomb on the cheap. He was particularly angry at Amit's sharp, sarcastic remark that, if all these reports were to be believed, 'Egypt was about to take over the world'.

Harel fought back with every means at his disposal. In the process he over-reached himself by playing politics, a tempting though dangerous game for a spymaster. Mossad launched a deliberate campaign of disinformation and news management by planting newspaper stories that Germans were preparing for the Egyptians all manner of sinister weapons – not just rockets, but chemical warfare substances and even death rays to wipe out Israel. Tel Aviv newspaper editors were given alarming briefings, and their investigative reporters were pointed by Mossad at various West German scientific establishments allegedly engaged in producing such fiendish devices. This had the desired effect of thoroughly alarming public opinion, the more so when such important politicians as Golda Meir took up the refrain in the Knesset.

The country was in a panic and the intelligence service seemed to be out of control. Ben-Gurion returned from holiday for an angry confrontation with Isser Harel who, although he admitted that he was the source of the press campaign, fought back in fury and finally offered his resignation – which was not accepted. It was an action intended to produce a political crisis which might result in the fall of the government, but the gesture failed. The prime minister promptly wrote a letter demanding that the Mossad chief should place on record his information about weapons production in Egypt and state precisely what was known about the Germans' part in it. Finally he required Harel to name the sources of his reports.

This was a bad blow to his pride, for the letter questioned his reliability and cast doubt upon his sources. Harel quit his office, handed over the keys and solemnly declared, 'I could not stay if I disagreed so profoundly with the prime minister.' It was the end of a long chapter in the history of the Israeli intelligence service.

In Cairo Wolfgang Lotz, the spy who had eagerly sought to provide his masters with the information they wanted, yet feared to receive, soldiered on. But after four years in the field he was being frantically overworked to produce more and more material to satisfy the requirements of controllers engaged in the political battle at home. Constant use of his radio transmitter finally drew the attention of detection equipment recently supplied to Egypt by the Russians, and they succeeded in locating the source of his broadcasts. He was arrested and in July 1965 a Cairo court convicted him. A sentence of life imprisonment was imposed, although Lotz was saved from the death penalty normally imposed on Israeli spies by maintaining throughout that he really was German. He served only two years before being released in an exchange of prisoners of war after the Six Day War and returned to Israel with his wife, who had also been imprisoned.

There the champagne life soon turned flat. His wife died, and the riding school he had established in Israel failed. He had no more success with a similar business venture in the United States. In 1978, with only $1000 left to his name of the compensation money paid him by Mossad, Lotz went to live in West Germany and took a job in a Munich department store. The disabused agent who had once lived in such style complained bitterly that all the state paid him for his dangerous service was $200 a month.

9. Damascus

Far away from the power disputes of intelligence chiefs and decision makers in Jerusalem and Tel Aviv, the field men and women of Mossad went about their dangerous task in the hostile neighbouring countries of the Arab world. Their lonely duty was to provide the raw material of intelligence upon which the security of the state would ultimately depend.

Superpower spying has become rather a cosy game. Many agents are covered by diplomatic privilege; they are licensed to spy, and when detected the worst that happens is that they are simply declared *persona non grata*. Although non-diplomats arrested in the field may be given long sentences, they are often exchanged after a while for someone caught by the other side. For spies engaged in the cruel wars of the Middle East, be they Israeli or Arab, the stakes are much higher – death is still the penalty for failure, and for those Jews taken by Arab states it is often preceded by torture. That was the fate of Eli Cohen, the most effective of all Mossad's undercover agents. In May 1965 he was hanged in full view of TV cameras and thousands of onlookers in Martyrs' Square, Damascus. After Cohen had said prayers with the Rabbi of Syria, the hangman threw a rough white shroud over him. They pinned upon the garment a sheet of paper recording his offences, and details of the sentence passed at the show trial to which he was subjected. What that paper failed to register was the fact that the high-grade military intelligence about Syrian military dispositions obtained by Cohen and relayed to Tel Aviv would become vital to the success of the Israeli assault upon the Golan Heights during the Six Day War.

Cohen, son of a Jewish family in the Egyptian port of Alexandria, spoke perfect Arabic and felt thoroughly at home in the culture of Arab countries. In his teens, as an enthusiastic Zionist, he worked undercover with Jewish organizations in Egypt. He had a narrow escape from becoming involved in the ill-fated Operation Suzanna before emigrating to Israel. Once there he married and settled down to a boring ministry job before being talent-spotted by Mossad. They considered that it would not be possible for him to return to work in Egypt, where his name figured in police records, and where, in any case, Mossad already had an agent in the shape of Wolfgang Lotz.

Instead, after careful preparation which involved perfecting the Syrian dialect – for Arabs are sensitive to nuances of speech patterns – he went into deep cover in Damascus. To prepare the ground for entry into Syria, one of the most difficult countries for the Israelis to penetrate because its people are both clannish and suspicious, he spent nine months in Buenos Aires as Kamil Amin Taabes, posing as a prosperous Syrian expatriate eager to return to his homeland. For this part of his mission Cohen spent some time learning Spanish in order to make his cover watertight. Mossad spares no effort in preparing its agents for the dangers and difficulties of espionage.

During his stay in Latin America the Israeli became acquainted with General Amin al-Hafez at the Syrian embassy. This same officer also returned home and in due course became President of Syria. This meant that Cohen-Taabes had excellent credentials. They were strengthened by contacts made with other prominent Syrians on the liner bringing him from Buenos Aires to Beirut, from where he travelled overland to Damascus, and gained for him an *entrée* into the highest Syrian circles. Supplied with smuggled and whitewashed Mossad money, he rented an elegant apartment near the headquarters of the army general staff, carefully chosen in an area where many of his neighbours were senior officers. One of his most useful friends turned out to be a Lieutenant Maazi Zahreddin, nephew of the chief of staff. In the company of this junior officer with influence, he was able to make a number of conducted tours of Syrian defence positions on the Golan Heights. In this military zone, where unauthorized intruders who penetrated were shot on sight, Zahreddin was able to show Cohen anything he wanted to see. On one trip he counted eighty 122mm mortars dug into the western slopes, and even took photographs looking towards the Jordan Valley. That kind of precise information gladdened the heart of Meir Amit, now the Mossad chief, for it enabled the IDF to pinpoint the mortars and their likely targets. Cohen also examined the deep bunkers where artillery pieces, newly received from the Soviet Union, were being positioned. Eventually, in 1964, Mossad's man in

Damascus was able to supply precise plans of the entire system of fortification around the strategic centre of Kuneitra, complete with details about the depth and strength of bunkers and scrapes for tanks and armoured vehicles.

A good deal of this precious intelligence material was transmitted to Tel Aviv by radio; but when it came to sending the plans he had acquired which revealed details of the Syrian army's concept of precisely how they planned to cut off the northern sector of Israel in a surprise attack, other means had to be found. Eli Cohen had set up an import-export business which involved the despatch abroad of pieces of Syrian pottery. He was able to pack top-secret documents and pictures into them and send them to Israel by way of third-party countries in Europe. On several occasions, he himself returned to Israel for clandestine holidays with his wife and family.

Among other intelligence coups to the credit of this brilliant spy were reports on the arrival of the first two hundred Russian T-54 tanks and pictures of the Mig-21 jet fighters from the Soviet Union. He did not neglect political moves, either. Mossad chiefs were brought up to date about manoeuvres and plots within the ruling Baathist party. They were also forewarned after one of Cohen's officer friends, Colonel Salim Hatoum, had shown him on a plan where Syrian saboteurs were planning to destroy the Israeli Jordan River water scheme for irrigating Galilee-Negev. In short, his work was invaluable for the defence of Israel, and without the military information provided the IDF would have found it much more difficult to storm the Golan Heights in the war of 1967.

Eli Cohen's downfall was due not to the vigilance of Syrian counter-intelligence, which claimed credit for unmasking him, but to a complaint made by the Indian embassy. The mission was located near to his apartment, and its radio operators complained of frequent interference with their transmissions. This was not surprising, for by that time the Israeli agent had so much material that he was exceeding safe time limits for such message sending and was sometimes on the air for up to an hour at a time. Even after the complaints, the Syrians were unable to trace the source of interference. But in 1965 there was a strong Soviet presence in Damascus and the KGB was only too willing to lend a hand in tracking down an Israeli spy; they had brought in state-of-the-art electronic equipment and were quickly able to pinpoint the apartment.

Eventually Syrian security men burst into Cohen's flat and caught him in the act of transmitting from a radio which had been concealed in a food mixer. He was forced to continue his transmission with a message dictated by them. It read, 'To the prime minister of Israel

61

and chief of the secret service in Tel Aviv. Kamil and his friends are our guests in Damascus. You will hear of their fate soon. Signed: the counter-espionage service of Syria.'

For a long time President al-Hafez hesitated on whether or not to execute the man he thought he knew so well; indeed it was said that his wife had once received an expensive present from Eli Cohen. Israel launched an international campaign to save its man from the scaffold, for Mossad always makes the most strenuous efforts to save its operatives in trouble. Despite that campaign for clemency the Syrian president, anxious because so many prominent Syrians had been involved with the Israeli, and fearing that mercy might compromise his political position, signed the death warrant.

Part III
World Gendarme

10. Electronic War

The quarrelsome departure of Isser Harel from Mossad left the service in a state of some disarray. His many loyal colleagues just could not believe that the man who for a decade had led them in so many successful operations was no longer in charge. What made matters worse was the fact that he had been replaced, at first on a provisional basis as acting head of Mossad, by his old antagonist, General Meir Amit. A crisp military intellectual with a good combat record as a brigade commander in the 1948 war, as well as of intelligence experience, Amit believed that the old Mossad had spent too much of its time and wasted its resources on such flamboyant operations as the kidnapping of Eichmann and in foreign adventures. So far as he was concerned, Nazi war criminals belonged to an era that was past. What mattered in 1963 was the intelligence war nearer home.

It was a time of recrimination and resignations as the old hands expressed their disapproval of the innovator. Not until September 1963 was Meir Amit's appointment as head of Mossad confirmed. Simultaneously his former deputy at military intelligence, Colonel Aharon Yariv, succeeded him as head of that service, with the rank of general. The two officers got along very well, and their friendly cooperation helped to form a useful new partnership in the intelligence game during the period leading up to the Six Day War of 1967. By this time David Ben-Gurion, the elder statesman, had again retired to his kibbutz, this time permanently. He was replaced by Levi Eshkol. As a compromise, and in the hope of healing the rift between rival branches of the service at the same time, Eshkol found a job for Isser Harel as prime ministerial adviser on intelligence and political information, an

65

arrangement which was not calculated to be very helpful in the end, for Harel had never cut much of a dash as a coordinator.

General Amit, the new man in charge, was intent on changing the entire style of the Institute, starting with the office furniture at headquarters. He established a proper chain of command, sweeping away the old lax arrangements by which Harel had had a hand in everything. One change which did win the approval of old hands from the previous regime was that he brought with him from Aman Unit 131, the special operations force of specially selected soldiers which was to provide useful back-up when its heavyweight skills and extra firepower were needed. Improved organization went hand in hand with the use of modern equipment.

Amit understood the importance of computerized data in intelligence work and quickly saw the important advantages of battlefield control by computer. During a visit to the USA in his previous command he had renewed acquaintance with Dick Helms, director of the CIA, and he had been impressed with the new technical material being used by the agency. Another strong influence on Amit, and therefore on the new model Mossad, was Professor Yuval Ne'eman, a scientist-soldier educated at Imperial College, London. It was he who urged the need for electronic listening devices to replace soldiers and human spies as guards along the borders of Israel. Amit was especially keen on developing the signals side of intelligence operations, and his men set up impressive equipment at vantage points to intercept enemy communications. Disguised though they are, the masts, antennae and radar discs can still be clearly seen on Mount Hermon above the Golan Heights. From there the powerful equipment remains on the alert, listening to telephone and signals traffic in Damascus, which is only forty-three miles away. The collecting department of military intelligence used computers to put together data about every individual officer in the armies of Egypt, Jordan, Iraq, Syria and Saudi Arabia, so that field commanders in war might have profile dossiers on their opponents. And General Amit made a special point of making sure that such information was provided right down to platoon and company level, so that unit commanders on the ground would know something about the officers facing them.

The technological revolution instituted in the early 1960s helped to make possible the military triumph of the Six Day War. Before and after it began, the IDF Signal Corps, which works with the signals branch of Aman, showed its mettle. Because of their ability to crack the codes of the allied Arab armies and their possession of powerful radio equipment in Sinai, Israeli intelligence was able to create military confusion by intercepting messages and transmitting false ones. To egg on Jordan to enter the war there were phoney signals about Egyptian successes in Sinai. Jordanian troops were asked to support an Egyptian counter-attack. In another piece of intelligence signals deception the Jordanians were told that Israeli jets about to raid their airfields were Egyptian aircraft. In one of the great coups of that conflict, the signals people managed to listen in to a radio conference between President Gamal Abdel Nasser and King Hussein of Jordan. It was in that conversation that the Egyptian president claimed that the United States and Britain had intervened on the battlefield to aid the Israelis. Despite the fact that the text of this conference was released as part of an Israeli disinformation campaign, it was still generally accepted in the Arab world that Western aircraft had attacked their armies, and this provided a useful excuse for the defeat of the allied Arab armies. The fact that the interception of high-level planning talks between the two enemy leaders was made public proved that in fact Israeli military intelligence used electronic deception for their own purposes as well. The suggestion is that they lured Jordan into the fighting at an appropriate moment when Israel was winning the war, in order to give themselves the opportunity to 'liberate' East Jerusalem which at that time was in Jordanian hands.

The Americans certainly believed this, and they had good reason to be well informed about the electronics battle being conducted by the Israelis. Offshore in the Eastern Mediterranean was the USS *Liberty*, a CIA spy ship capable of listening into and assessing all broadcast material in the war zone. Although the Israelis firmly maintained their own right to spy wherever the intelligence services thought fit, they expressed fierce indignation that the United States should pry into their war. Thoroughly alarmed at the thought that the Pentagon was able to read every operation order of the IDF and of the Israeli air force, General Dayan signalled the ship that it must leave the area. For whatever reason, that signal was never received by the *Liberty*. Without further warning Israeli Mirages and Mystères roared in to make a vicious strike which destroyed her electronic equipment. Not content with that, the Israelis, who seemed determined to destroy the spy ship, sent in three warships to torpedo the vessel. Finally, troop-carrying helicopters appeared to survey the damage.

Liberty was packed with Arabic and Hebrew speakers monitoring battle orders on both sides, and a number of casualties were sustained: the attacks killed thirty-four and wounded another seventy-five. Cynically, the Israeli government claimed to have mistaken the ship for an Egyptian vessel, despite the fact that (until it was shot away), she was flying the Stars and Stripes. It was unthinkable anyway that Israel's intelligence service should have failed to know the whereabouts and

67

nationality of the ship. The truth was that Israel was determined to put the listeners out of action. The aim was to prevent the US administration from knowing the full extent of their victory, in case Washington should impose a ceasefire before all their objectives had been achieved. Even though the US Sixth Fleet with the carrier USS *America* was only a few minutes' flying time away, it failed to intervene effectively. In response to a distress signal, the only response was a Phantom sortie which came too late. Eventually *Liberty* managed to limp away with her dead and wounded, and a half-hearted apology was wrung from the Israelis.

It may also be suspected that a further reason for the attack was that the Americans had stored away too much information for the Israelis' liking about how they had contrived a war for which they strove to put total blame on President Nasser. Israel, it can now be seen, bore a heavy burden of responsibility for the escalation which led to the war of 1967. Contrary to accepted belief, the Israeli intelligence estimate did not anticipate a full-scale conflict that summer. Their information about the Arab war machine led them to believe that the Egyptian and Syrian armies were not ready to make moves leading to war, and that not until preparations were complete in another year or two were they likely to attack. This assessment did serve to produce a contrary effect upon Israeli hawks who were tempted to strike a blow at the Arabs before they were ready to fight.

Two new factors took their effect on both sides. The Arab summit conference launched a scheme to divert the head waters of the Jordan and the Syrians started work on the project, to the great irritation of Israel. Then the PLO's Fatah force, which had made its first attack in January 1965, began the first round of the war of terror. The process of escalation began when Israel retaliated against the Syrians involved in the River Jordan scheme first with warnings to Damascus, and then by hitting terrorist bases across the lines. Arab intelligence, and very likely the Russians too, took these acts as an indication that Israel was moving towards a war which appeared imminent in the spring.

The scenario began to change in a way which had not been expected by any of the intelligence services concerned. As troops concentrated on both sides of the border, the Egyptians delivered an ultimatum demanding the removal of the UN buffer force in Sinai. Then, when it was withdrawn, President Nasser decided to occupy Sharm-el-Sheikh, and so threatened to blockade the sea route to the Israeli port of Eilat. And war became inevitable.

It was at this point that the mass of detailed information about the state of readiness and order of battle of the Arab armies gathered by the new model intelligence services of General Amit and General

Yariv became a vital factor in Israeli decision making. The government knew how vulnerable and unprepared the Arab armies and air forces were. President Nasser had wrong-footed himself in Sharm-el-Sheikh and Sinai, and here was an ideal moment to blame him and to mobilize, launch pre-emptive air strikes and win a quick and resounding victory. Despite the hesitations of Mr Eshkol, the prime minister, he finally decided it was a chance not to be missed and accepted the view pressed by General Yariv, on the strength of his intimate knowledge of the state of the Egyptian and Syrian war machines, that Israel could not lose.

11. Terror War

Total and spectacular victory in the Six Day War brought great rejoicing and hope that Israel's troubles were at an end, now that Jerusalem was a united city and a safe border had been established on the River Jordan. What was not realized at the time was that the resounding defeat of the Arab field armies would create a fresh menace as the dejected Palestinians started assembling their raggle-taggle guerrilla forces to begin a new kind of subversive warfare which Israel, even with the aid of its successful intelligence services, would be hard pressed to win.

Yet even before the war of 1967 the first ominous signs of future peril had been recorded. On a winter morning in 1965 a water engineer spotted a sack floating down the canal by the Nefuta Valley in northern Israel. He fished it out and found that it contained an explosive charge and a detonator. It did not seem like a big event in the history of Israel; but the symbolically floating bomb which failed to explode in the water system was the work of Fatah, the military arm of the Palestinian resistance. And this was the gesture which initiated a seemingly endless campaign of terror. Ever since, 3 January 1965 has been recognized as the day on which the Palestinian war of attrition against Israel broke out.

Cross-border raids from neighbouring Arab countries were already common enough; there had been incursions by armed refugees from the Palestinian camps straddling the old ceasefire lines. But this was the first small signal of a new phenomenon. Fatah originated in the Egyptian universities and was headed by Yasser Arafat. Its political manifestation, the Palestinian Liberation Organization or PLO, was

70

created in 1963 and at first enjoyed the patronage of President Nasser. Its ultimate aim was to destroy the state of Israel, referred to sarcastically as the 'Zionist entity', and to restore the land to the people of Palestine who had been forced out of it. Already in two wars the armies of Egypt and Syria had shown themselves unable to do this in battle. Young and fiercely nationalist Palestinians, spurred on by the success of the Algerians in winning independence from France through ceaseless guerrilla warfare and political pressure, decided that they would fight their own battle with covert armies.

At first, Arab defeat in the Six Day War produced a deeply gloomy effect upon Fatah and the PLO. Their champions in the Arab world had failed to shake the hated 'entity', so what could the Palestinians hope to achieve on their own? It was at this stage that the tougher elements in the leadership began propagating their theories of revolutionary warfare. The hope was that, when properly trained and armed, their men could make life such hell for the Israelis at home and abroad that eventually they would be forced to give in and leave. That was the thinking behind the terrorist campaigns launched by Yasser Arafat and in even cruder form by Dr George Habash, a Marxist Christian medical man with the soul of a left-wing revolutionary who eventually became boss of the PFLP, the Popular Front for the Liberation of Palestine. With him in the same group, though disapproving of his wilder excesses, was Wadi Haddad, a like-minded nationalist.

Within the Palestinian movement there were continual rifts and schisms, personality clashes and differences of opinion. Dissident groups hived off from the main body in pursuit of their own tactics. They fell under the influence of Syria, or Iraq, and later on of revolutionary Iran. In many cases the armed struggle degenerated into an armed squabble. For all that, the general aim of 'liberating' Palestine remained the goal, and as the birth rate among Palestinians boomed they saw an endless supply of young men ready and eager to fight as fiercely and as wantonly to create their supposed homeland as the Israelis had been to build theirs only a few years before. To paraphrase the words of the original verse of jingoism, they had the men, they had the guns – supplied in quantity by the Soviet Union – and they had the money too. Protection money came from the rich oil nations of Arabia whose leaders hoped to purchase immunity from revolution, and the Palestinians raised cash by taxes on their own people, by extortion, and by exploiting the Middle East drug production industry.

As the campaign developed over the 1960s and the following two decades, Mossad and Israeli military intelligence were forced to deploy practically their entire resources in combating Palestinian subversive warfare. Extra men were recruited and the service almost doubled in

71

strength. Diplomats in embassies around the world were called in to back up the effort with information, disinformation and propaganda. Councillors were always available to talk about 'the problem' in those familiar guttural Israeli tones. Every move was analyzed; each success recorded with detailed documentation. The word was always preached that the only way with terrorists was to strike back at them and never to give in to their blackmail.

The IDF, with the aid of the home security service, Shin Beth, proved itself as capable of coping with direct guerrilla attacks within Israel itself as it had with the external threat from the neighbouring Arab states. But when the Palestinians were thwarted in this way they developed new tactics by taking their war overseas and by internationalizing terrorism. Israel had influence throughout the Western world, they reasoned; therefore the friends and allies of Israel must realize that they too might become the targets of Palestinian wrath. It was this line of thought which persuaded Yasser Arafat, and the other leaders working both with and against him, to turn from targeting Israel to making raids on Western interests. It was the Palestinians who developed the craft of hijacking airliners – vulnerable, highly mobile vehicles – for a refined form of hostage taking. Such attacks were certain to achieve maximum publicity. The flying theatre stage, with its cargo of people from all nations as actors, could be moved from country to country in dramatic fashion. The first example, in 1968, was the taking of an El Al Boeing 707 heading out of Rome for Tel Aviv. It was forced to fly to Algiers, a destination chosen as a tribute to the example which Algerians set to fellow Arabs in fighting against foreign domination. Israeli passengers were imprisoned there for two months before being exchanged for Arabs held by their government. The series of acts of air piracy which followed succeeded in drawing the attention of the outside world to the Palestinian cause. They were also intended to discourage foreigners from visiting Israel, from patronizing the national airline, and from sympathizing with the gallant little state fighting bravely against huge Arab armies. When hijacking became more difficult for the hijackers, because of precautions taken, the PLO and its allies turned to the bombing of aircraft in flight and the seizing of ships on the high seas.

Shin Beth took charge of the business of improving airline security by vetting passengers and thoroughly searching them. Ben-Gurion airport at Tel Aviv became the pace setter because of its meticulous searches by men and women who mastered the art of fairly polite interrogation of passengers in search of the slightest indication of guilt or nervousness which might betray a potential hijacker or bomber. Armed guards trained by Shin Beth were placed in airliners, armed with Beretta .22

72

low-velocity handguns ready to engage in airborne fire-fights with any hijacker bold enough to try his luck.

Right from the beginning Mossad had been aware of the threats posed by terrorism. Enough of the old hands from pre-independence days remained in the service to know all about Arab raids on the kibbutzes. The counter-tactic then had been to get advance warning of enemy plans through spies and informers. The same methods were already being used by Shin Beth and its agents to keep watch over the sullen Arab population in the newly occupied areas. Although publicly the Israelis were forever buttonholing visitors with stories about how much more prosperous and contented the West Bank Arabs were under Israeli rule, they none the less took trouble to assess true feelings. Mossad began getting reports from its agents of activity in the training camps. It already had men in deep cover, posing as enthusiastic Palestinian fighters, and even in one case as a Syrian army officer who, when not spying, was actually engaged in instructing Palestinian guerrillas in the use of small arms and explosives.

Their watch also spread over the borders. By the time the PLO groups had established their war bands in Jordan, behaving with such arrogance that their armed presence threatened the monarchy, Mossad was well enough implanted within the Palestinian factions to be in a position to pass on detailed warnings about their activities to King Hussein; even his own excellent intelligence service could hardly match Mossad. Some agents were spies; others, although living in a country like Jordan which did not recognize Israel, were in fact acting in a covert diplomatic role. They were able to organize secret meetings between Israeli leaders and King Hussein. And when his regime was endangered by the overweening behaviour of the PLO with its bases in Jordan, he was strengthened in the knowledge that, should the Syrian allies of the PLO dare to assault the kingdom, then Israel would strike at the Syrian army.

Much attention has been concentrated upon the activities of Mossad hit teams, whose spectacular activities have been catalogued both in fact and in fiction. They were the hunters, trained to spy out enemy agents and sometimes to shoot them or blow them up. But for heavy operations they needed to call in special forces troops like Unit 131 to strike back across the borders at the bases whence guerrillas made their sorties. Two hundred of these troops were permanently on standby at the disposal of the intelligence services whenever their special capability was required. The air force was called in for what were called 'clinical' or 'surgical' strikes on PLO strongholds. The phrase was intended to convey the impression of a surgeon's knife cutting out the cancer, although it was conveniently forgotten that the knife of even

73

the most skilled surgeon sometimes slips. And sometimes he cuts off the wrong limb.

But the true work of the secret service was performed by anonymous field men and women who, at great risk to themselves, infiltrated the Palestinian groups to provide advance warning of their actions. The reports of most of these people remain forever secret, although there is no doubt that their penetration of the enemy's devious operational cells created a legend which alarmed the terrorist leaders. This led to constant and justified anxiety in the PLO about traitors in their inner councils.

During Isser Harel's term of office Mossad had been reluctant to employ women agents. The chief took rather an old-fashioned view of such activities: he once said he feared that sooner or later a woman agent would have to use her sexuality in order to get results, and that worried him. Yet much of the organization's success in the terror nests of Lebanon was due to the activities of women who managed to elude the attentions of vigilant Lebanese and Syrian counter-intelligence officers at a time when Beirut was the recognized espionage capital of the Middle East.

Even by the standards of the Israeli intelligence service, Shulamit Kishak-Cohen, a mother of seven living in the Lebanese capital, was a most unusual choice to run a spy ring. At her eventual trial before a Beirut court the prosecutor, with a taste for phrase making, described her as 'the Mata Hari of the Middle East'. Although she was undoubtedly an attractive, even an elegant woman, it might have been more appropriate to describe her as the Jewish mother of espionage.

It was through chance and circumstance that this lady, who was the child bride of a much older member of the surviving Jewish community in Beirut, drifted into espionage. Born in Jerusalem, she found herself living in what was then a peaceful Arab-Christian neighbouring country at a time in the late 1940s when Israel was becoming established as a new state. Her first act, carried out to the dismay of her merchant husband, was to help bring ashore illegally an important anonymous Jewish immigrant and to help smuggle him into Israel. An active, intelligent and patriotic woman, she then became involved in performing the same service for large numbers of Jewish refugees from the Arab countries.

Mrs Kishak-Cohen took up refugee smuggling rather as middle-class American ladies might engage in social work, while simultaneously she raised her large family with maternal devotion. She also found time to be forever busy preparing all those anniversary rituals and special ceremonies so beloved of Jewish families. From refugee work she slipped effortlessly into providing Israeli intelligence with state documents and political information from Lebanon and Syria. This she accomplished through her ever-widening social contacts with the high, and low, society of Beirut, where most commodities – including loyalty and secrets – may be bought, provided the price is right. Shula, as she was known, worked hard to extend her ring of informers and police protectors. A good deal of money, supplied by Mossad, was spent on purchasing favours and information. At one stage the spymasters in Tel Aviv agreed to pay up so as to launch the Star nightclub in Beirut, which served as a useful place of rendezvous.

Under her codename Pearl she made numerous visits to Israel where she was taught the elements of fieldcraft. After security was tightened on the Lebanese border, making it more difficult to cross, she journeyed by way of Istanbul, swapping passports on the way. Eventually the Pearl ring was itself penetrated by an ambitious young officer of the Deuxième Bureau, the Lebanese counter-intelligence service, and Shula was arrested. The court sentenced her to death by hanging on espionage charges, but later the sentence was commuted to seven years' imprisonment. After the war in 1967 Shula was exchanged for Lebanese captured during the fighting, and her family in Beirut were allowed to emigrate to Israel. Once back home she set up a flower shop near the King David Hotel in Jerusalem, thus providing a rare happy ending to a spy story.

In harsher times and places another woman agent of Mossad suffered much more severe consequences after being caught. A brief news item broadcast by the Voice of Palestine in 1980 was the first intimation to the outside world of another long espionage saga in Mossad's infiltration effort, featuring a woman agent in Lebanon when that country became the PLO's main base.

Two Palestine fighters, William Nassar and Mohammad Mahda Busayu, arrived in Beirut last night after their release from the Zionist prisons in exchange for the Zionist spy Dina al-Asan. The exchange took place in Larnaca. The two fighters were received at the airport by a representative of Abu Ammar [Yasser Arafat] and a number of cadres of the Palestinian Revolution.

Dina – a pseudonym of course – had indeed been an Israeli spy, an important and unusual one. Working under cover among Palestinians in Lebanon, she had helped to pinpoint PLO military installations and her information significantly aided a number of Mossad counter-terror operations. She made it possible for the Israeli air force to single out targets in the refugee camps in which they were often concealed. Most

Mossad operators in Arab territory are of Jewish origin, although brought up in Arab countries. Dina was in fact a Circassian Moslem born and bred in Jordan, a descendant of the people who fled from the Caucasus mountains in what is now part of the Soviet Union. Circassians were prominent in the forces of King Hussein when his army went into action in 1970 against Palestinian guerrillas in the Hashemite Kingdom; as a result Circassian officers were branded as enemies and harassed by the Palestinians.

Dina was born in Amman in January 1935 into a clan loyal to the King. After leaving school she began training as a doctor and practised without proper qualifications before marrying a Palestinian who turned out to be a wife-beater and from whom she later separated. Exactly how she was recruited by Mossad is not very clear, but Palestinian attacks upon Circassian communities may well have influenced her behaviour.

According to Mossad sources, she decided to work for the Institute while in Vienna, where she had gone in 1972 to continue medical training for a year after visiting her sister in Rome. On a second trip there she used the name Diana Schwartz. The story was that during the visit she had fallen in love with an Israeli pilot. Either he worked for the Institute and had became friendly with Dina as part of the plot to recruit her into the service, or he put her in touch with somebody who was an agent. Knowing that the woman had thwarted medical ambitions, the agency suggested that she might be given help to set up a clinic in Beirut as a cover for espionage. She agreed to do so, and before going to Lebanon early in 1973 Dina received training at a Mossad school in the use of clandestine radio transmitters, coding and photographic techniques.

Her clinic treated sick and wounded Lebanese, as well as Palestinians, and she was also able to travel south to the refugee camps in Sidon and Tyre where dysentery, hepatitis and malnutrition were rife. This gave her an opportunity to check on stores of the Red Crescent (the Islamic Red Cross) run by Yasser Arafat's brother. Rocket launchers and small arms were often hidden in crates labelled as medical supplies. In this way she was able to discover arms caches and HQ buildings which later became targets for air operations. The Palestinians frequently used medical centres for military purposes, and the wounded were employed as a kind of shield against enemy action. If the Israelis did attack such places, pictures of damage and innocent victims furnished a propaganda opportunity.

Dina was well placed to provide detailed information from within the camps, but she could not fail to be aware that when Israeli fighters raided they sometimes killed or wounded people who were her patients. At the time there were fifteen refugee camps with around two hundred thousand Palestinians living in them. Dina specialized in treating children, and also worked with gossiping Arab midwives. She lived in the clinic where she worked, which also became a community centre for Palestinians.

The place was, of course, secretly financed by funds from Israel; Dina's cover story was that she was using her own money from savings banked in Geneva. Mossad had invented for her the 'legend' that she had spent most of her life in Switzerland after her Arab family moved to Europe when she was still a child. Most of her relations and friends lived in Europe, but she had decided to return to the Middle East to support the Palestinian cause. The Israeli service with its customary attention to detail provided back-up to authenticate names, addresses and bank account details, so that if suspicions were aroused and Palestinian security men began checking they would find that everything was in order.

The odd feature of Dina's story is, that although she was prepared to inform against the guerrilla forces and to sabotage their warlike operations, she did in fact feel sympathy for the plight of the Palestinians. Indeed it is impossible even to enter the refugee camps, let alone to live there, without understanding the horrors of refugee life. Dina also understood Palestinian determination to secure a homeland. This, no doubt, served to build trust with the people among whom she was living and made it easier for her to spy there. She also managed to avoid the trap of appearing to be too fervently anti-Zionist, and on occasion went so far as to mention the rights of Israelis to have their land too. This helped to allay suspicion, for it seemed likely that an Israeli undercover agent would make every effort to seem more anti-Zionist-than-thou.

In the summer of 1973 Dina signalled her masters with detailed information that George Habash, leader of the PFLP, the would be one of the seventy-four passengers on board Middle East Airlines Caravelle Flight 006 from Beirut to Baghdad. Habash was high on Mossad's wanted list as the man who had specialized in hijacking aircraft since the 1960s and as the leader of the most active of the Palestinian fringe groups. His men had been responsible for seizing the El Al flight forced to fly to Algiers. The following year the PFLP had succeeded again, taking an El Al flight on the ground in Athens. In 1970 the same group launched the spectacular operation in which five international airliners were seized and four of them forced to land at Dawson's Field, a desert landing strip in Jordan, where they were blown up. Israel had many old scores to settle with George Habash and the information provided by Dina offered them a fine chance to get the enemy. Golda Meir, the Israeli prime minister, authorized her defence minister, Moshe Dayan, to take a chance and order the snatching of this active terrorist leader by forcing his airliner to fly to Israel.

A few minutes after take-off from Beirut Captain Mata, a senior pilot of MEA, reported unmarked hostile Mirage fighters approaching his aircraft. By radio, the Israeli squadron commander threatened to open fire, then ordered the Caravelle to follow southwards. The airliner was shepherded towards Israel and forced to land at Ben-Gurion airport, Tel Aviv. The passengers thought they had arrived at Baghdad and were amazed when, as the doors opened, Israeli soldiers leaped in and ordered them in Arabic to raise their hands. Male passengers were taken away for identity checks. It soon became apparent that George Habash was not among them and the airliner was allowed to fly back to Beirut. MEA later reported that it received a bill from the Israeli authorities for fuel and airport services.

The PFLP leader had indeed intended to be on that flight, which was an extension of the MEA service from Vienna. Its arrival from Europe was delayed, and after his long wait at Beirut airport, Habash, who suffered from heart trouble, felt unwell. Not relishing the idea of a 150-minute flight on to Baghdad, he changed his plans. This explanation emerged later, but at the time Mossad feared that their agent in Beirut had been rumbled. The suspicion was that the Palestinians had deliberately and deviously set a false trail in order to trap her. The Israelis were further provoked by George Habash's exploitation of the failed kidnap attempt. The great terrorist leader actually had the cheek to declare, 'This is the height of terrorism. It is time world public opinion knew who the terrorists really are.'

Shortly after this incident Christopher Dobson, the well-informed British journalist, wrote in his book *Black September*: 'From the intelligence point of view, the hijacking showed intimate knowledge of the movements of one of the most closely guarded and sensitive of Palestinian leaders. Such knowledge could only have come from someone very close to Habash. . . . The Palestinian organizations have in fact been penetrated through and through by the Israelis and the Jordanians.'

It was not the fault of Dina that the plot had failed. Indeed her ability to penetrate the highest levels of the PLO leadership was remarkable. She even succeeded in becoming friendly with the family of Salah Khalaf, known as Abu Iyad, who was at that time the PLO's chief military planner of the raid upon the Israeli Olympic athletics team. He was a leader of Black September, the Fatah covert squad which carried out the operation known as the Munich massacre, although he constantly denied responsibility for it. Abu Iyad was also chief of Fatah security, and in this capacity he recruited as special investigator

78

to ferret out traitors and Israeli agents within the organization a man named Ali Hassan Salameh, organizer of the Munich operation.

By chance Dina became a baby sitter in Salameh's family. It was not until she mentioned his name in a report to headquarters in Tel Aviv that she became aware of his close links with Abu Iyad, and Mossad realized in what exalted circles of the PLO leadership she was moving. She used the opportunities provided by child minding to work through the dossiers that Salameh kept at home, carefully photographing the ones she thought important for despatch to Tel Aviv. Among the details she provided were membership lists, false identity papers and even plans for forthcoming operations. Supplied with this high-quality material, Mossad was able to keep a look-out for terrorists and to pass on tips to Western intelligence and police, enabling them to keep watch for the arrival in their countries of terrorists bearing false passports.

After a Fatah seaborne attack on the Israeli coastal town of Nahariya in 1974 the IDF at once planned a retaliatory strike, and it was the woman spy who provided the information which helped them pick their targets for naval raids. Mossad signalled their agent in the camps with a request for pictures of PLO boats and fishing vessels in the southern Lebanese ports of Tyre, Sidon and Ras al-Shak, so that the raiders could seek them out. Dina had made special trips to the coast to treat Palestinian children, and also to take clandestine pictures of PLO boats – fishing vessels modified for terrorist needs with special equipment. The photographs had to be despatched through a 'dead drop', being left at a Beirut hotel and collected by another operator. The normal way in which she communicated with headquarters was through a radio transmitter concealed in her bathroom scales. Using her information, thirty PLO boats were demolished by the commandos.

Dina's most signal political service was to report back to Tel Aviv on the story she picked up from Palestinian sources about an Arab plot to assassinate President Anwar Sadat. It was a revelation which helped to pave the way for the first historic meeting between the Egyptian leader and Menachem Begin, the Israeli prime minister. For the government chose to pass on to the Egyptian leader information about the plotters, whom he was able to arrest. Naturally, he became better disposed towards Israel after this piece of cooperation, which probably saved his life.

Like many secret agents before her, Dina eventually began to feel invulnerable and to take unnecessary risks. She must have confided in her Lebanese lover, who denounced her as a spy, and she was arrested by the Beirut authorities before being handed over to the PLO at the beginning of the Lebanese civil war. Palestinian security interrogated her under torture and then, fearing an attempt at a rescue operation, moved her to a cave near Sidon. Chained to the wall, she spent five years in captivity before Mossad was able, through clandestine bargaining, to get her back in exchange for two Palestinians serving life sentences in Israeli prisons. In February 1980, under Red Cross supervision, the exchange took place in Cyprus. After her release, Dina went to work as a doctor in northern Israel.

It is a remarkable feature of Israeli spy operations that Mossad frequently succeeds in getting its people back alive. The controllers assume, of course, that once in enemy hands an agent will in the end confess. No one is expected to hold out against long periods of interrogation and torture. This realist attitude is also reflected in the willingness of the service to do deals with the Palestinians. Although it remains the official line that the authorities refuse to bargain over prisoners and hostages, this is a rule which has been broken on many occasions. The justification is that to recover an agent is always a boost to morale in the service and an encouragement to men and women engaged in perilous duties.

One thing has never varied since the terrorist war of attrition first began. That was the determination of whatever coalition government held office to mount quick strikes of retaliation against known terrorist leaders and Palestinian bases. Punishment had to fit the crime, and so Mossad became embroiled in a continuous process of strike and counter-strike.

12. Vengeance

From 1970 onwards Mossad set up not quite as the world's policeman, but at least as its counter-terrorist agency. Its full strength was directed towards mastering the Palestinian threat at home and abroad. The place of arms was Lebanon, which had become the base for PLO forces, but the secret service agents fought out deadly encounters too on the far-flung battle lines in Europe and Africa. The policy was always doggedly the same, to strike back hard at the guerrilla groups and terrorist bands which constantly tormented Israel. Moshe Dayan's estimate was that between the end of the 1967 war and the Black September civil war in Jordan no fewer than 5840 terrorist attacks were launched from Jordanian bases. They killed 141 Israelis and wounded 800.

The PLO and its many offshoots became an obsession. The Institute needed to know every possible detail about their internal policy debates and clashes, as well as to probe their relations and agreements with foreign governments. The service was given the job of penetrating the terror cells to discover more about their training methods and the plans for terrorist raids. These investigations were carried out, not only in neighbouring countries such as Lebanon, but also within the Soviet bloc, western Europe and the United States. The Institute was driven to spend more time getting cooperation from European intelligence services and those of the United States. The intelligence service also wanted to know about the international contacts of these movements, where their arms came from and who organized their training. Both Mossad and Shin Beth set up liaison links with the so-styled Kilowatt group formed by the western European nations, including even neutral Switzerland, and also with Canadian participation, to coordinate the fight against terrorists.

Mossad soon identified Wadi Haddad as its most dangerous and formidable opponent; he was the operations man in the PFLP faction of the PLO run by himself and George Habash. Although the two bosses frequently quarrelled on doctrinal points, that never prevented Haddad from developing his campaigns planned to eliminate the 'Zionist entity'. He even organized a plot to kill David Ben-Gurion after the old statesman's retirement, while the former prime minister was on a visit to Denmark.

Haddad himself became the hand-picked target of a Mossad hit team. In July 1970 six Soviet-made Katyusha anti-tank rockets triggered by a timing device crashed into the bedroom of the apartment in Beirut where he was staying. Haddad was in another room, where he was plotting with Leila Khaled, the woman hijacker. Neither of them was injured, but Haddad's eight-year-old son Hani, asleep in the bedroom with his mother, was badly burned and disfigured.

This was two months before the mass hijacking by the PFLP of international airliners to a landing strip in Jordan named Dawson's Field, and renamed for the purpose 'Revolution Field'. That was the incident which provoked King Hussein's Black September war against the PLO implanted in his kingdom. And as a result of that, the first Palestinian dispersal began. Driven by Bedouin soldiers from the refugee camps which had been turned into military bases, Fatah and the other allied groups were forced to leave the country. Yasser Arafat's mainstream PLO took up residence in Beirut. Other factions set up shop, according to ideological taste, in Baghdad, Damascus or North Africa. The PFLP went to Aden in South Yemen, to continue training for action. Mossad was then forced to spread its hunt further afield. No longer was it possible to keep watch on the Palestinians in Jordan and Lebanon alone.

The Institute had managed to cope with the first phase of terrorism's war in the air, and when he retired as head of the service in 1969 Meir Amit could at least reflect that the defences he had set up had stopped the hijacking of El Al flights. The air pirates were turning to other people's airlines in an attempt to win publicity for their sufferings.

Worse was to come, for new and more deadly plots were being hatched as the Palestinians spread their networks into Europe and began building cooperation with the continental terrorist groups then active in West Germany and Italy. The young European anarchist revolutionaries, prompted at first by their feelings of identification with the sufferings of the third world, had selected the Shah of Persia as their number one individual enemy. Israel became their least favourite nation as an oppressor of the Palestinians. Andreas Baader and Ulrike Meinhof, together with numerous followers, took themselves off to be taught the arts of guerrilla warfare in the Arab training camps.

Wadi Haddad was the great proponent of international terrorism. He preached this doctrine effectively at a conference held in 1972 in the Baddawi refugee camp attended by members of the Baader-Meinhof gang, the Japanese Red Army (JRA), Turks and Iranians, as well as by PFLP, Fatah and Black September. It was in September that the PLO had tasted the bitterness of defeat in Jordan, and the network established to take revenge was named Black September after those events. The various national groups agreed after the Baddawi meeting to help each other by providing weapons and intelligence data, and by offering safe houses and escape routes. The calculation was that security men on the lookout for Arab terrorists would be less likely to spot Europeans carrying out similar missions. Similarly, Western security on the watch for Europeans might not take notice of Arabs. Wadi Haddad had already recruited foreign nationals – people like Carlos, the notorious Venezuelan, and Patrick Arguelo, a Sandinista – to help with his operations.

The first result of the Baddawi conference was the massacre of disembarked airline passengers at Lod airport. It was carried out by Japanese from the JRA, in collaboration with PFLP. In a machine gun and grenade assault on the airport lounge twenty-seven people died. 'Our purpose was to kill as many people as possible', was the view of the PFLP spokesman.

Black September was already busy planning its own international coup. It had been organized as Fatah's covert strike force (although the PLO always denied the connection), by Abu Iyad (real name Salah Khalef), the chief military planner of Fatah. He was also boss of the Fatah security unit, Jihaz el Razd, whose main job was to sniff out traitors who had been recruited by Mossad. In this capacity he had executed twenty spies. The first act of the new terror group was to shoot and kill, at the Sheraton Hotel in Cairo, Wasfi Tal, the prime minister of Jordan; this was a pure act of revenge for their expulsion from Jordan. Even at that stage, in 1971, Mossad was already remarkably well informed about Black September, yet it had been unable to prevent the Lod attack, and Zwicka Zamir, who had become head of Mossad after the retirement of Meir Amit, came in for heavy criticism at home.

His main worry in the summer of 1972 was the forthcoming Olympic Games to be held in Munich. The Institute was already aware that this international occasion was a tempting target for terrorists. Their agents in place knew that some kind of demonstration was being prepared. At that time there was a West German of Jewish descent who was actually inside the West German terrorist movement, but even he was unable to get precise information about plans being coordinated with the Arabs. Two Mossad officers had gone to Munich to collaborate with the West German authorities on security. Their difficulty was that the Federal Republic, anxious to exploit the Games as final proof of a return to normality in the Federal Republic of Germany and symbol of its new power and respectability, did not want to spoil the occasion with heavy and obvious security precautions.

It was a bitter blow for Israel and a deep humiliation for Mossad when the Black September hit squad succeeded in taking hostage the nine members of their Olympic team. Back in Jerusalem there was fury and high indignation. Moshe Dayan angrily proposed despatching a special forces unit to battle it out with the terrorists on the spot, an act which would obviously be unacceptable to the Germans. Zwicka Zamir, the *Memuneh* himself, flew to Munich on hearing the terrible news and was present at the airport as a helpless witness of the final gun battle recorded by international television crews, in which the nine were murdered. He had never believed that the Palestinians would dare to attack and had left the athletes unarmed and undefended. The two Mossad advisers, reasonably satisfied that the Germans were taking sensible precautions, had returned home before the Games started.

There could be no doubt that the Israelis as well as the Federal Republic bore responsibility for failing to prevent the massacre. The embassy in Bonn took part of the blame and three of its staff, including one Mossad man, were found negligent by a commission of enquiry. There was strong criticism of Zwicka Zamir, and Mossad too found itself under fire from politicians horrified at the scale of the disaster. As a further reproach prime minister Golda Meir appointed a special assistant for terrorist affairs, which naturally reflected upon the leadership of Mossad. The man chosen was General Aharon Yariv, an officer just about to relinquish his appointment as head of military intelligence. This strengthened the impression that Aman was being called in to redress the balance of Mossad's incompetence.

It was an obvious turning point in the history of the service. The government and the public, alarmed at the upsurge of Palestinian terrorism, was demanding action. Golda Meir's orders were clear. The intelligence services were to go on the offensive in the subversive war. There was to be a change of policy, and the first step was to increase – almost to double – Mossad's budget, so that the means might become available to carry the war into the enemy camp. Mossad in fact was not only given a licence to kill (it had done that in the past), but a licence systematically to hunt down those deemed responsible for the Munich massacre. Golda Meir announced that from then on she would call upon 'all the spirit and determination and ingenuity our people possess to track down Palestinian terrorists wherever we can find them'.

Without waiting for instructions, the service had already struck in retaliation for the Lod massacre by the Japanese. First they assassinated Ghassan Kanafani, a Palestinian poet and novelist, a sophisticated and agreeable man known to many foreigners in Beirut. They booby-trapped his car, and when he started the engine both he and his seventeen-year-old niece were blown to pieces. Israel, embarrassed by her death, claimed at once that they had sure information that Kanafani, ostensibly the organization's information officer, had been a member of the inner council of the PFLP and had helped to plan terrorist acts. Outsiders suspected that his real offence was that he had publicly justified the massacre at Lod. Within weeks his successor as PLO spokesman, Bassam Abu Sharif, was blinded in one eye and scarred for life by an Israeli parcel bomb delivered to his home.

The man whom Mossad was really after was Ali Hassan Salameh, operations chief of Black September, specially chosen for the job by Abu Iyad. Their information led them to the conviction that he personally had supervised the Munich assault. The son of a Palestinian sheikh who fought against the Jews, he was a talented man with long experience in Fatah. It was obvious to the assassination planners that this man, who never moved without bodyguards, who had a variety of passports and safe houses at his disposal, would be the most difficult one to kill.

As the newly mobilized avenger squads practised their small arms skills and bombing techniques, Mossad's analysts combed through their bulging dossiers on Black September leaders and sympathizers. A special unit worked on the files at headquarters, while field men cultivated the German anti-terrorist specialists at BKA, the Federal police centre in Wiesbaden. Also helpful in the task of going through evidence about the Munich affair and the people involved in it was the West German intelligence service, the BfV, Bundesamt für Verfassungsschutz. Mossad was quick to make use of such friends, and constantly pointed up the connections between West German terrorists and the Middle East ones. The Israeli service was lavish in handing over any tit-bits which its operatives picked up about the so-called Red Army Faction, which took over where Baader-Meinhof had left off. In return, although it was strictly unconstitutional in Germany, Israeli agents gained a 'nod and wink' authorization to interrogate Arab suspects held in German prisons, such as Stadelheim in Munich.

Nor did Mossad neglect the disinformation side of its business. Information officers, who were moving around Europe at the time like travelling salesman to tempt journalists and politicians with juicy stories usually based on checkable fact, put it about in the Federal Republic that its generous laws allowing refugees to settle in Germany were being exploited by the Palestinians to strengthen their terror networks. Soon after Munich the magazine *Quick* ran a report from an Israeli source about Fatah and Black September, together with a picture of the man said to have organized the massacre. As a result of the publication of this article, the Federal authorities rounded up and expelled a thousand young Palestinians thought to have terrorist connections. Diplomats were also quick to remind the Bonn government how easy it was for Arabs to fly from the Middle East to East Berlin and then move to the West.

The first victim of the Mossad counter-terror offensive in Europe was Wadal Zwaiter, Black September's man in Rome who worked as a translator at the Libyan embassy. He was shot dead outside his apartment with twelve bullets from the Institute's favourite weapon for close-range assassination, the Beretta .22. Turning to more refined methods, the hit men next blew up Mahmud Hamshari in Paris. Explosives were planted in his flat by a 'plumber', and then detonated by an electronic signal on a telephone call. An added advantage of this method was that the victim first confirmed his identity by answering the telephone call. And so the bloody work of destroying the key men of Black September in Europe continued for month after month. 'It was not revenge,' said an Israeli member of the Institute. 'We were fighting a war, and the only way to win it was to destroy the network.' No doubt he was correct in believing that most of those killed were in fact plotters and organizers. Certainly the population of Israel shed no tears for those who died, but in the outside world these operations recalled biblical memories of 'an eye for an eye', and this period saw the creation of the Mossad image which still persists, that of an avenging force of great determination. And it should not be forgotten that one of the teams did call itself the 'Wrath of God', thus arrogating to itself justification from on high.

In fact the most devastating blow struck at Black September and Fatah was not strictly a Mossad operation. For the raid upon the terrorists' lair in Beirut in April 1973 the services of a special operations unit of the IDF were called upon. The Sayaret Matkal, spoken about in awed tones by compatriots and known simply as 'The Unit', already had a formidable reputation for daring actions. It was a compact, specially trained force, not unlike the British SAS; its men were held permanently on the alert at the disposal of the head of the intelligence service. Although secret servicemen had carefully spied out the targets and had prepared the infrastructure for the Beirut affair, the killing was done by Sayaret Matkal. By the time that their action started the Mossad scout team of six had either left or gone to ground, so as not to blow their cover locally. They arrived, of course, on false passports claiming to be British or European businessmen.

Thirty commandos in civilian clothes landed from Zodiac rubber boats on quiet beaches near the capital, guided in by an advance party of one man and one woman. From there they made their way to the first rendezvous where cars rented in advance by undercover agents awaited their arrival, and then drove to the suburban living quarters of selected Palestinian leaders. One block belonged to PFLP, the other to the PLO and Fatah. After a sharp fire-fight with Palestinian guards and a confused intervention by the Lebanese gendarmerie, the troops found and killed under the eyes of his wife and children Abu Youssef, deputy to Yasser Arafat and a Black September boss. Kemal Adwin, his assistant, and Kamal Nasser, the spokesman, were also killed. Two Lebanese lost their lives in the fighting and the raiding force suffered two fatalities and one badly wounded before they re-embarked. The care taken in preparation for the attack was illustrated by the fact that ambulance helicopters flew in the area, ready to take off casualties, the Lebanese authorities having been tricked into believing that they belonged to the Lebanese army.

Arab-speaking Mossad men with the expedition made a hasty search of the Palestinian headquarters building and grabbed quantities of papers and documentation before the buildings were blown up with demolition charges. Acquisition of this documentary evidence of terrorist activity was one of the secondary objectives of the raid, and back in Tel Aviv intelligence analysts got to work at once examining the hoard of material now in their hands. According to those involved, it provided precious clues about operational plans, international connections and infrastructure, knowledge of which helped with the next stages of the war against terrorism in Israel and Europe. Fresh information also helped to save at least one Israeli agent who was under suspicion in Lebanon by Palestinian security.

Despite the success of the mission, Zwicka Zamir's best-laid plans had failed to get the man at the top of Mossad's assassination list – Ali Hassan Salameh. And it was in the service's frantic attempts to track him down that it made its most notorious and public error of judgement. One of the teams roving in Europe wrongly identified as Salameh a harmless Moroccan waiter who was married to a Scandinavian girl. In July 1973 they shot him dead at Lillehammer in Norway. But their 'hard' information that Salameh was in Scandinavia planning a terrorist

87

enterprise proved to be based on hearsay; this was the mission which finally discredited all those confident boasts about 'surgical' operations conducted by Mossad.

The assassination hunt-and-kill team of fifteen people had been hastily assembled in Scandinavia as a polyglot unit, its leader concealing his identity under the name of Edouard Laskier and bearing a French passport. It was not easy for people looking like Israelis to pass unnoticed in a small Norwegian town, so at short notice he attempted to assemble the most Nordic-looking agents available, some of them part-time operatives. Others who were not practised in Mossad's dirty-trick operations were enrolled on the grounds that they would only be needed for the comparatively simple task of keeping observation. These were the excuses put forward after the event. They did not answer the question of how the intelligence service had either been fooled, or had failed to take careful precautions to make sure that the man in Lillehammer was in fact Salameh. The most likely explanation was that Mossad was overstretched in its campaign of counter-terror, and that in its eagerness to strike one more name off the list its normal rules of cautious analysis were brushed aside. What also worried the leaders in Tel Aviv was that bad planning for the agents' getaway when things did go wrong meant that a number of them were brought to public trial and Mossad suffered humiliation.

Among those caught in the bag was Sylvia Raphael. After years of quiet and efficient work disguised as a French woman journalist on operations in Jordan and elsewhere in the Middle East, she finally found herself the centre of much unwanted publicity. Sylvia was only part of the back-up, but the Norwegians none the less charged her and she was sentenced to six years and three months in prison. At that time she was working with a colleague named Abraham Gehmer, formerly an Israeli diplomat in the Paris embassy; they used false Canadian passports which identified them as Mr and Mrs Roxburgh. Because they had, in unprofessional style, noted down the telephone number of the Mossad 'legal' at the Israeli embassy in Oslo, their arrest led to the exposure of the semi-official Mossad agent for Scandinavia.

While in prison Ms Raphael kept a diary, extracts from which were later published by newspapers. She also achieved further publicity by sending the Norwegian prosecutor a facetious get-well card signed, '005 and a half The Spy Who Came in from the Cold'. A Norwegian who interviewed her wrote ecstatically, 'She was chic, attractive, with a terrific personality and eyes that looked at you and made shooting stars flare across your own eyes. A sweater and pants, a locket on a chain and a passion for surrounding herself with beautiful things – that was Sylvia.' Hardly the ordinary kind of person to pass unnoticed in a crowd, the sort normally favoured as a Mossad recruit. On her return home they put out the flags in her kibbutz and offered flowers, a curiously public homecoming for a secret agent whose operation had in any case failed. The gesture revealed something of the sentimental pride with which Israeli public opinion regards its intelligence service.

Sylvia Raphael was already known from the time she had spent in Jordan. In the period leading up to the civil war there in 1970 Mossad operatives working in the refugee camps gathered evidence on attacks planned against Israel, but in the process they also came into possession of information about Palestinian plotting with King Hussein as the target. Senior Israeli ministers had held secret meetings on numerous occasions with the King, usually in London where their embassies are almost next door neighbours in Kensington, and in general were well disposed towards him on the ancient principle that my enemy's enemy is my friend. Mossad therefore was content enough to pass on warnings about Palestinian machinations to the Royal Palace in Amman.

Sylvia Raphael, posing as a Parisian journalist, had already established an espionage network in Jordan, according to the well-informed British journalist John Bulloch, Middle East editor of the London newspaper *The Independent*. 'Through her charm, hard work, and through contacts already in place, she soon gained entry to the ruling groups in Amman', he reported. 'On one occasion she was invited to a party at which King Hussein was the guest of honour.'

There can be little doubt that, urged on by Yigal Allon, the Israeli chief of staff who favoured support for the King at a crucial time when he was in conflict with Palestinian forces established in his kingdom, Sylvia Raphael passed on to the monarch some of the fruits of the research in Palestinian camps. Hussein used her list of names and the subversive plans uncovered by Mossad when he finally felt confident enough to round up Palestinian dissidents.

Sylvia appears to have been a very laid back secret agent. She once showed journalists, including John Bulloch, her engagement book. He reported that 'it was crammed with dates for lunches, drinks and dinner parties with the élite of Amman'. On the one hand, it could be claimed that she was a spy ferreting out secrets; on the other that her role was closer to that of a diplomat under instructions to nourish a relationship with a country which in the nature of things could not agree to formal diplomacy. Although she had been highly visible on at least two occasions, it is generally assumed that the woman agent, who sometimes claimed to be a South African Jewess and at other times gave the impression that she was Canadian, continued to work less conspicuously for Mossad. However, her name was mentioned again. When PLO gunmen murdered two Israeli men and a woman on board

89

a yacht in the Cypriot harbour of Larnaca, there were stories that Ms Raphael was engaged in undercover operations work on the island. Indeed, Norwegian press reports claimed that the murdered woman was none other than Sylvia Raphael herself. It seems probable that this was a disinformation story put out by the PLO in an attempt to justify its crime. To clinch the matter, Ms Raphael wrote to Steve Posner, author of *Israel Undercover*, in 1986 saying that she was still alive.

The fact that Mossad was willing to use Sylvia Raphael in the Lillehammer affair when there were strong chances that she might have been recognized by Palestinians from her work in Jordan a few years earlier demonstrates that by that stage in the campaign against Black September Mossad was running short of personnel. In the prolonged period of worldwide operations, Mossad as well as Black September had taken casualties. Its most notable loss earlier in 1973 was that of Baruch Cohen. An experienced old hand in the service, he had left his base to fly to Madrid for a meeting in a café with an informant. While he waited there for his contact, Arab gunmen shot and killed him. His death made it necessary for the service to rethink its European operations and replace some experienced operatives; for it looked as though Palestinian security was beginning to penetrate the Mossad network, or at least to recognize some of its hard-working agents. Already suspicion had been aroused by the murder of two paid Arab informers in Paris, So hard pressed by headquarters to get results were operatives in the field that they began to place too much reliance upon such sources, which perhaps explains the disastrous failure to identify the correct target at Lillehammer. Some produced genuine information; others were simply after money; but there was a strong possibility that still others simply posed as informers in order to identify Israeli intelligence people.

After Lillehammer, which had drawn too much world attention to the sometimes brutal methods it employed, Mossad was put under strict orders to halt its deliberate campaign of assassinating Palestinian leaders. But in the end they did get their man. Salameh was blown to pieces by a radio-triggered plastic charge placed in a Volkswagen parked near his apartment in Beirut early in 1979. The way had been prepared by an agent using the name Penelope Chambers, who claimed to be British. She moved into Rue Verdun in Beirut a few weeks earlier, and, as a middle-aged woman painter fond of cats, found it easy to become friendly with Salameh's wife, Georgina. She spied out the movements of the Palestinian leader and prepared the way for the arrival of her two colleagues, who were explosives experts posing, respectively, as a British and a Canadian businessman. The bomb also killed four bodyguards and six people in the street, including a British woman secretary.

By that time Salameh had achieved a kind of diplomatic respectability as Yasser Arafat's right-hand man who appeared publicly with the leader at the United Nations when he made his famous 'gun and olive branch' speech. During the Lebanese civil war he helped to make arrangements for the evacuation from Beirut of a thousand American citizens. At that period he was in touch with American diplomats, and the Israelis suspected that he was hoping to use the occasion to promote the idea of US recognition of the PLO. Indeed, after his death Palestinian supporters gave the impression that Salameh had been negotiating with the CIA and that his murder was ordered by the Israelis to prevent further progress towards recognition.

So far as Mossad was concerned, his death marked the end of a long effort, and they were able to report that finally the Munich massacre had been avenged. Golda Meir told the Knesset: 'We killed the murderers who were planning to kill again.'

13. Atonement

So busy was Mossad prosecuting its obsessive war against international terrorism and the PLO that even its directors had little time to devote their attention to the graver threat hanging over Israel as the Soviet Union poured military resources into the Arab states. They had withdrawn agents from the so-called confrontation states, so as to concentrate on what was considered the more immediate threat of terrorism. While that battle filled the horizon, Mossad allowed its role as a strategic intelligence service to be almost entirely monopolized by Aman.

Significant events in the neighbouring countries had been taking place. Syria, under the firm control and harsh rule of President Hafez al-Assad, re-equipped its forces with the best and latest weapons produced in the Soviet Union. The Egyptians were armed to the teeth by the same power, and President Sadat felt confident that his army, now retrained and exercised after the long war of attrition which had been conducted against the Israeli army in Sinai across the Suez Canal, was ready to accomplish what his predecessor, Gamal Abdel Nasser, had failed to achieve in 1967. The two presidents of the biggest Arab regional powers began colluding to prepare a coordinated joint attack upon the old enemy.

The day they chose to launch the assault was Yom Kippur, Saturday, 6 October 1973, the Jewish Day of Atonement and a public holiday on which they calculated that the armed forces would be in their lowest state of readiness. On that afternoon the Egyptian divisions swarmed across the difficult obstacle of the Suez Canal and

92

quickly overwhelmed the Bar-Lev defence line, manned at the time by a brigade of reservists from Jerusalem. Soon they were advancing into Sinai with tank hunter teams by the hundred taking their toll of the armour.

There was bad news too for the Israeli general staff as the massed armoured regiments of the Syrian army roared forward track-to-track on to the Golan Heights and down through the defences towards the Sea of Galilee. Both Arab armies advanced under a rolling screen of anti-aircraft fire provided by SA missiles which prevented the Israeli air force from accomplishing its customary miracle by destroying their armour. The IDF's tank forces took heavy losses, and for several critical days it seemed certain that Israel might be defeated in battle.

The unthinkable was happening. Israel had been taken by surprise. Doomsday seemed nigh, for it had always been assumed that the first war to be lost by Israel would also be the last one. Everything was planned on the basis that intelligence would be able to provide forty-eight hours' warning. But so completely unexpected was the two-pronged invasion of that October that mobilization did not take place until after the attack. This was particularly grave, because the country had always depended on the fast assembly of the trained reserves, vital in a country whose small population and limited budget never enabled it to keep a large professional army on standby. In the tank depots around Beersheba armoured vehicles were not even ready serviced to be driven off to the front, and hours were wasted just getting them on the road while civilians rushed to join their regiments.

The war was hard fought and a close-run thing, almost a victory for the Arabs. The IDF took time to recover before it finally managed to hold the enemy on both fronts. It was only when General Sharon's divisions in Southern Command managed to split the Egyptian armies and get behind them by crossing the Suez Canal that the threat was finally contained. In the north General Yitzhak Hofi, who later took control of Mossad, drove the Syrians back to, and beyond, their start line on the plain of Damascus above the Golan Heights. It was a bitter victory at the end of Israel's longest war, which shook the nation to the core and shattered the mood of boastful over-confidence which had been generated by the rapid successes of the earlier Six Day War. Naturally, the intelligence services were the first to be blamed for falling victim to the elaborate and highly successful deception plans of the Syrian and Egyptian allies. The first in the critics' sights was Aman, whose responsibility it was to analyze the risk of war; but Mossad also came in for blame.

93

In a bold attempt to raise national morale, Mrs Golda Meir, the prime minister, spoke on television on the fateful Saturday evening as the battles began. 'For a number of days our intelligence services have known that the armies of Egypt and Syria were deployed for a coordinated attack on Israel,' she declared. 'Our forces were deployed, according to plan, to meet the impending danger.' She was telling the truth, but by no means the whole truth and nothing but the truth. Belatedly the regular army had been ordered to a state of high alert the day before, but it was too late because thousands of its officers and soldiers were already dispersing on leave to spend Yom Kippur with their families. Information about warlike preparations had been available before the attack, but the intelligence services were guilty of the grave mistake, which on occasion afflicts such organizations, of failing to interpret the reports correctly.

Three weeks earlier, Israeli intelligence did receive reports that Syria was massing its forces, and even more significantly was building up a dense mass of anti-aircraft missiles near the northern border. Despite their expert use of camouflage, Egyptian armoured divisions, lavishly equipped with SAM-6s, were observed advancing towards the Canal. Bulldozers were deployed on the Canal banks ready to cut gaps in the great sand wall on the western bank. It had hardly been possible not to notice that in Egypt warlike civil defence measures were being taken, with practice blackouts and appeals for blood donors. Perhaps the most decisive indication of what was afoot came two days before war started, when Soviet military advisers, ordered not to become embroiled in the fighting, left Syria. It has been claimed that on the same day a Mossad agent arrived at headquarters with detailed information about the Arab war plans. According to Stewart Steven, in his book *The Spymasters of Israel*, the final and conclusive piece of intelligence came from an Egyptian agent actually in the Canal Zone who radioed in that orders had been given to launch the Egyptian assault at 1800 hours – slightly inaccurate as it turned out, for the first artillery shells were fired at 1405 hours, while a group of Israeli part-time soldiers in the Bar-Lev line were playing football in the sand.

Whatever the truth of such stories, the information came far too late to alter the course of the first phase of the war. The failure of Aman and Mossad was that, although the final decision to invade Israel had been jointly taken by President Sadat and President Assad months before, Israel remained totally unaware of that decision. This shortcoming, although it could be interpreted as a tribute to Egyptian and Syrian security, was compounded by the fact

94

that Israeli intelligence then made a false interpretation of the signals of war preparations which did emerge. Despite there being at least uncertainty about what was going on, the intelligence chief presented to the ministers and the general staff a mistakenly over-confident and excessively reassuring assessment. This made it difficult for the Israeli leaders to take the decisive defence measures called for. If military intelligence had explained more carefully how difficult it was to tell the difference between preparations for war and preparations for strategic manoeuvres, then the decision makers would have found it easier to order precautionary moves. The truth was that the government had swallowed whole the myth of the infallibility of its own military intelligence service.

The assessment was affected by the personality of Eli Zeira, director of Aman, a gallant and successful soldier with a reputation for being totally fearless in action. He was, of course, the officer held principally responsible for the failure of intelligence and was dismissed from his post as a result of the findings of the Agranat Commission which subsequently investigated what had gone wrong. Zeira had persuaded himself that war was not going to happen in the autumn of 1973; he felt convinced that the Arab states were just not ready for war, a belief positively encouraged by the disinformation campaign executed by Cairo. The second part of this thesis was that they dared not launch a limited war because, if they did, Israel would at once turn it into a full-scale conflict in which the Arab powers were certain to be defeated.

This was known as the 'concept' and it was an article of faith subscribed to, not only by the staff of Aman and the general staff, but also by Moshe Dayan, the defence minister, and through him by the cabinet. Their belief was reinforced by the fact that twice within twelve months there had been false alarms about Egypt's intention to attack. A report was received in May 1972 of an impending assault and another in December 1973. Nothing happened at either time. What the Israelis did not know then was that President Sadat had indeed intended to launch his offensive in June, but postponed it because of the Soviet-American summit, and also because he was expecting further deliveries of Soviet weapons. As is well known, nothing is certain in war or in preparations for war.

It was the concept, 'that wretched term . . . which proved the undoing of intelligence just before the outbreak of the Yom Kippur War', wrote Shlomo Gazit, who himself became head of Aman after the war. In a thoughtful article on the subject of intelligence estimates and decision making published in *Intelligence and National Security* in

95

1988 he pointed out the perils facing those who estimate the risks of war.

An estimate that is nothing but an inventory of existing possibilities will contribute little to the formulation of a reasoned decision. Another danger, no less severe, lies at the other extreme. There is always some risk that intelligence men will lose their objectivity. Indeed, their participation in political deliberations and close contact with decision-makers may lead to an identification with policy to such an extent that they may ignore facts and dangers that contradict that policy.

That is what happened in the relationship between Zwicka Zamir and Mrs Meir's cabinet, in particular the minister of defence, Moshe Dayan. They all felt it in their bones that war was not imminent. Such a process has been analyzed by Norman Dixon, an expert in experimental psychology who examined the behaviour of military commanders in his fascinating study *On the Psychology of Military Incompetence*. He talked about a state called 'cognitive dissonance', which happens when a person comes into possession of knowledge at odds with a decision he has already made in his own mind. There is a strong tendency in such cases for the uncomfortable officer, whether he be a general or an intelligence chief, to search out extra justification of the original decision, rather than to risk loss of face by modifying it in the light of new information. Military history is littered with examples of the failure of commanders to change their mind because of new information. One notable case in the Second World War was when Field Marshal Montgomery refused to call off the airborne attempt to capture the bridge at Arnhem when new intelligence came to light that much stronger forces were defending it than had been reported when the plan was first drawn up. Israeli intelligence in 1973 was in numerous, though not good, military company.

Although it had always been taken for granted by the Israeli intelligence community that their country would be successful in any war against the Arab armies, there is little evidence that the directors had devoted much attention to attempting to assess what might be the consequences of victory. In 1967 neither Aman nor Mossad, swept along by general enthusiasm about the scale of the military success, foresaw that as a result of it Israel would need to face up to the burdens of being an occupying power governing a substantial Palestinian Arab population. They certainly did not anticipate the growth of the PLO, nor the development of its guerrilla and then its terrorist groups. Neither before, nor after, the Yom Kippur War was there much sign that they were aware of the dangers caused by other Arab powers rallying to the call for an oil embargo. It had been tried sixteen years before and had failed; therefore the assumption was that it would fail again. Yet the success of this wielding of what was called the 'oil weapon' finally had a much greater impact on the world at large than did the war itself. It was a retaliatory measure of great significance whose consequences had been underestimated.

Indeed, President Sadat's most brilliant coup was the use he made of this powerful economic weapon through the OPEC embargo on selling oil to the allies of Israel. The Egyptian leader scored two notable successes which left their mark on the Middle East – the oil embargo, and his near-victory in battle against the Israeli army in Sinai which so shook the self-confidence of that nation. Chaim Herzog, later to become president, admitted in his book *The Arab-Israeli Wars*:

> The first outstanding Arab military success – indeed the most important – was the strategic and tactical surprise they achieved. While this success was aided in no small degree by mistakes made by Israeli Intelligence and the political and military leadership in Israel, the bulk of the credit must go to the sophisticated deception plan mounted by the Egyptians and the Syrians . . . one of the outstanding plans of deception mounted in the course of modern history.

Although the combined Arab armies were in the end overpowered, there can be little doubt that their display of bravery and military efficiency in the handling of modern weapons and tactics destroyed the myth of Arab incompetence which had been fostered for so long by both Israel and its Western friends. The new spirit of pride and self-confidence in the Arab world at once inspired the PLO to further efforts, and finally made it possible for President Sadat to negotiate an honourable peace settlement with Israel.

It took the Israeli intelligence community several years to recover its poise, so badly shaken was it by shortcomings which put the very existence of the nation at risk. The Agranat Commission directly blamed Eli Zeira and three of his principal assistants for their failure to interpret correctly the information received about Syrian and Egyptian war preparations. They were all four relieved of their duties. The verdict on Zeira was that 'in view of his grave failure, he could not continue in his post as chief of military intelligence'. No similar measures were taken against the leadership of Mossad, whose men had faithfully fed in their bits of information which were not considered significant enough to alter the big picture. Mossad was quicker to recover its former status, especially when it undertook daring deeds which caught the public imagination.

The rescue operation in 1976 which came to be known as the Entebbe raid provided such an opportunity. An Air France flight with a passenger list including 103 Israeli and other Jews had been seized by the PFLP and forced to fly to Entebbe, capital of Uganda in the heart of Africa. The old spectre of vicious anti-semitism appeared when it became known that among the hijackers were Baader-Meinhof German terrorists. They were deliberately separating non-Jews from the other passengers, ready to slaughter diaspora Jews as well as Israelis if their demands were not agreed to. This was the factor which decided the government that, regardless of the dangers and the distance from base, action must be taken.

The success of the difficult and daring operation to fly in a special forces unit in three air force Hercules planes in order to free the passengers depended on fast preliminary intelligence work, which only Mossad was capable of providing. The Institute was already well connected in East Africa, especially in Kenya where only a short time earlier it had helped President Jomo Kenyatta's police to foil a Palestinian plot to use missiles to shoot down an airliner at Nairobi airport. The missile team of three on that occasion was arrested secretly by Kenyan security, which later seized two Germans, Brigitta Schultz and Thomas Reuter. These two had been flown to Kenya to search for the missing first three terrorists. All five were then handed over to Mossad and taken back to Israel under arrest. It was claimed at the trial that they had been drugged and removed from East Africa in clandestine fashion.

Because of this incident Mossad had friends on the spot ready to help as soon as it rushed half a dozen agents to Nairobi while negotiations with the hijackers continued. The Kenyan government agreed to allow an Israeli hospital plane to land, but was unwilling to become publicly involved in military action by allowing air force planes to refuel there on the way in. So four Mossad men with Kenyan helpers made their way in a fast launch across Lake Victoria on a reconnaissance mission to Entebbe airport. Others hired light aircraft and set off with make-shift equipment to photograph the airfield from high altitude, which at least provided evidence about how many Ugandan Mig fighters were deployed there. Not until the agents were able to radio back details about the number of troops on the ground and the strength of opposition likely to be encountered could the commander of the IDF special forces, busy rehearsing raid tactics in the desert, give the start order.

98

All but one of the terrorists perished. The IDF's only casualty was the raid commander, Lieutenant Colonel Jonathan Netanyahu, shot dead by a stray round. What had been achieved was the first great defeat of the international terrorists. The hard image of success was restored to the nation and Mossad was included in the vote of thanks when Yitzhak Rabin, the prime minister, said: 'This tribute is the least we can do for the anonymous soldiers of the intelligence community, the stouthearted paratroopers, the brave infantrymen of the Golani Brigade, the air force pilots and all the others who made the impossible come true.' Once again the Israelis basked in the warmth of worldwide approval and admiration.

Part IV
Violence of Lebanon

14. Massacre

'For the violence of Lebanon shall cover thee.'

Habakkuk 2:17

In the long struggle, Mossad and Shin Beth managed to contain the worst excesses of Palestinian terrorism. But the more they achieved in that respect, the greater were the fresh problems which arose to confront Israel. For all the dashing successes and cunning stratagems, the fundamental situation remained the same. Millions of Palestinians backed by the Arab world remained determined to achieve a homeland state on the same small piece of territory bordered by the Mediterranean and the River Jordan which was also the homeland of 4 million Israelis and holy ground for all three of the great religions. The endless armed struggle continued.

Yasser Arafat established a secure base in Lebanon from where he cunningly directed the onslaughts of his well-financed and lavishly armed PLO. Sometimes he stepped up the armed struggle; from time to time diplomatic offensives were launched. For a Palestinian leader can only make tentative steps towards peace if he demonstrates his martial enthusiasm and appetite for victory in war. Israeli leaders share the same predicament. Sensitive to the threat on their northern border in what came to be known as Fatah-land, the Israeli army was drawn into expeditions against the perpetual aggravator across the line. When air strikes against the camps failed to prevent raids, the IDF was called upon to send expeditions across the border into Lebanon, a country already riven by the civil war which began in 1975 with clashes between Maronite Christians and the Moslem majority. The strife became increasingly complex as one faction after another sent its private armies into action in a confusion of shifting alliances.

It was in Lebanon that Mossad fell into great error. Its field men cultivated allies among the Lebanese factions, the better to undermine the position of the PLO. First they made secret contacts with the Christians and helped to provide them with weapons and to train their forces. There were overtures also towards the Druze, a powerful clan united by their mysterious religion which is an offshoot of Islam. In such enterprises Mossad was in competition with Syrian intelligence, which was busy playing the same game with the same pieces. Next Israel sought an arrangement through its undercover agents with the Shi'ites, members of that dissident branch of Islam which had thousands of adherents in Lebanon. Many of them lived in the south and resented the high-handed and bullying behaviour of the Palestinian military who had built up their forces in the region. Israeli intelligence met with considerable success in its dealings with Amal, the 'respectable' political and military organization of the Shi'ites.

However, that happy arrangement became less profitable after the Islamic Revolution in Iran which overthrew the Shah and installed Ayatollah Khomeini and his fellow whole-hoggers in power there. Lebanon was marked down by them as the first foreign country into which the worldwide Islamic revolution might surge. Ayatollah Khomeini was the spiritual leader of the Shi'ites and soon the sect in Lebanon, or at least the most zealous members of it, rallied to his banner and established their militia and cells on behalf of the Party of God, Hizbollah. Before long Israel discovered that it had a new and dangerous enemy on the doorstep. Although Mossad had succeeded over the years in infiltrating the Palestinian organizations, its first attempts to penetrate the zealots of Shi'ism in their tight religious cells and family groups proved a much more daunting task.

But first the Israelis had to contend with a more immediate threat from the PLO. The mistake of senior Mossad officers was that in this tangled situation they began to place too much faith in their new-found friends the Christian Phalangists. Close relations developed between the leaders of the Phalange and the intelligence men, who came to believe that it might be possible so to strengthen the Christians in their heartlands in East Beirut and the coastal strip above it, that under Phalangist leadership and a Phalangist president, Bachir Gemayel, Lebanon might master the Palestinians. The dream was that covert plotting might induce the Christians to do in Lebanon what King Hussein had done earlier in Jordan – turn out the PLO and thus secure the northern border of Israel.

After a series of frontier clashes between Palestinian militias and the IDF, a sort of truce was arranged with American help in the summer of 1981 under which the Palestinians agreed to stop terrorist action against Israel. But military intelligence reported that under the cover of this arrangement the PLA, the Palestine Liberation Army – by this time equipped with artillery and tanks as well as lavish quantities of small arms and machine guns – was engaged in a hefty military build-up in southern Lebanon. If it were allowed to continue, the prediction was that terrorist activity would resume. Arafat's army was in a position to shell and rocket settlements in northern Israel. Raiding guerrillas who managed to get through the wire mesh and minefield defence line along the Israeli–Lebanon border known to the IDF as 'good fence' defences would also have a safe base where they could return to shelter under the guns of the PLA. From this time onwards, a preventive move by the IDF against the build-up became inevitable.

Under the disarming codename Operation Peace for Galilee, a full-scale invasion of Lebanon began on 6 June 1982. It followed closely upon the attempted murder in London, by one of Abu Nidal's terrorist gangs, of the Israeli ambassador Shlomo Argov, who was gravely wounded. This affair provided precisely the excuse needed by Menachem Begin, the hard-line prime minister, and his tough-talking friend and defence minister, General Ariel Sharon. Both were convinced that the time had come to use real military clout to rid Lebanon once and for all of the Palestinians. In strictly military terms the aim was to destroy the Arafat build-up in southern Lebanon. But as always in successful large-scale assaults the temptation was to go further, and the IDF, in a mood of gung-ho rather like that of Prince Rupert's cavalry in the seventeenth-century English civil war, went dashing ever forward in search of more and better enemies.

When the Syrian air force intervened, its Mig fighters were shot out of the sky and it lost most of its first-line strike force. On the ground the army reached the gates of Beirut, through which they were careful not to pass because the city still served as the stronghold of Palestinian and Moslem militias. It was a streetfighters' nightmare and there were already enough Mossad and Shin Beth agents in the city to provide warning reports about the perils of engaging in action there. But the invading forces did make contact with Israel's old allies the Christian forces, who had their own base in East Beirut.

It was at this stage that the bargaining began. After tough negotiations, agreement was reached for the evacuation from West Beirut by land, sea and air of Yasser Arafat and fifteen thousand Palestinians. They dispersed as a new military diaspora to destinations throughout the Arab world. As they made their way by the truckload

105

to embarkation points, Mossad's men with field glasses and cameras were hyperactive in cataloguing the 'fighters' for future reference. Aided by Shin Beth and military intelligence they removed from PLO bunkers whole cases of documents which provided more than enough raw material to keep terrorist hunters busy over the following decade. Never had so much data been freely available for the analysts to mull over. What they were unable to prevent was the handing over by the PLO, as it surrendered its weapons, of huge stocks of small arms and ammunition to Amal's Shi'ite militia. This provided an arsenal of which they were to make devastating use later.

For a while it seemed that a famous victory had been won, thanks to the old-style dash and vigour of the Israeli Defence Forces. It looked as though Mossad had been right to pin its faith upon the Phalange. Arafat and his men were leaving, the US Marines had arrived for thirty days on duty to supervise the evacuation, and Bachir Gemayel was about to become president of Lebanon.

Then there occurred a dramatic and unscheduled event so terrible that it threw the whole situation into confusion and turned Israel's victory into defeat. In the afternoon of 14 September 1982 Bachir Gemayel, the newly elected Christian president of Lebanon and close ally of Israel, was assassinated by a giant 45lb bomb which destroyed Phalangist headquarters in Achrafiyeh, East Beirut.

The instinctive reaction of the Israelis was to order the army to enter Moslem parts of the city to prevent a total breakdown of public order and to forestall Christian fanatics from taking the law into their own hands. Their advance was a cautious one which met with little resistance in the city streets, although the IDF did take some casualties.

The instant and dangerous decision to make this move was taken by prime minister Menachem Begin, his defence minister and the chief of staff. Although they could easily have done so, they did not consult the foreign minister or the heads of military intelligence and Mossad. Certainly the advice of the head of military intelligence on the possible strategic and military consequences of the move would have been valuable. And the head of Mossad, who was in charge of liaison with the Lebanese leaders, was better placed than any other officer to estimate Christian reaction to the murder of their chief. He would certainly have been able to advise upon what they were likely to do, and ought to have been aware of any plans for revenge.

Things were done with such unseemly haste that the operation order did not even specify what should be done about refugee camps in West Beirut, the city they were about to occupy. These camps were defenceless now that their menfolk and 'fighters' had been evacuated. Thirty-six hours later a further order made good this omission by forbidding Israeli troops to enter the camps. The fatal step proved to be a decision to leave any mopping up in the camps to Lebanese forces – either the Lebanese army, which was not in a position to do anything, or the Christian militias, which were eager for the task. Senior intelligence officers have since claimed that if only they had been consulted they would have expressed strong reservations and would have warned that disaster was inevitable.

Two days later units of Phalangist militia stormed into the two main Palestinian refugee centres, Sabra and Chatila, undeterred by Israeli troops ringing the area and meeting only sporadic resistance from the inmates. Under the eyes of the Israeli army the Lebanese Christian militia went berserk, fell upon the their old enemies the Palestinians and slaughtered 1300 of them – men, women and children. Even by Lebanese standards this was the most appalling atrocity. The horrific event brought worldwide condemnation and raised angry reactions in Israel, which forced a reluctant government to launch a judicial enquiry into how such a terrible thing had been permitted to happen and into the extent of Israel's involvement and responsibility.

Chief Justice Yitzbah Kahan, presiding over the enquiry, went to the heart of the matter and revealed a great deal about the intelligence activity which had preceded the Lebanese disaster. The charge against the director of the military intelligence over the massacres was that of negligence. He was blamed for failure to pay enough attention to the dangers of sending the Phalangists into Sabra and Chatila while they were still enraged by the assassination of President Gemayel. It seemed unlikely to the commission that the Aman chief was unaware of the role given to the Phalange by the army command in connection with the entry of Israeli troops into Beirut. The Phalange were to act in support of the IDF, provide local knowledge and enter areas forbidden to Israeli soldiers. The commission also identified for the first time the Phalangist officer who ordered his men into the camps and was the originator of the massacre as Elie Hobeika, commander of a 150-strong Lebanese intelligence and special forces unit. And he was a man who had been in close touch with Mossad during their long flirtation with the Christian forces. Before the invasion he had visited Israel, where he was given intelligence training; indeed, it has been claimed that he was a Mossad agent. Certainly Hobeika had the reputation of being a killer and an exceptionally nasty piece of work, and was also accused of being an agent of Syrian intelligence. This ultra-Phalangist was a born plotter, ready and willing to do deals with anyone in sight so long as it served his purpose; in short, a dangerous and unsatisfactory ally.

107

The report disclosed that military intelligence had repeatedly warned Mossad about the dangers of their rapprochement with the Phalange. Evidence from Major General Amir Drori, commander of Israeli forces in Lebanon, showed that at the time of the massacres a liaison officer from Mossad was present at Phalangist headquarters. Ariel Sharon, the defence minister, also stated that when he went to a meeting with the Phalangists the day after Bachir Gemayel's death the heads of Aman and Shin Beth were also present, together with a senior representative of Mossad. The secret services were there in strength at this critical moment shortly before the slaughter, although no use seems to have been made of their expert advice on how to handle the situation.

Justice Kahan commented, 'The Mossad, to a not inconsiderable extent under the influence of constant and close contact with the Phalangist élite, felt positively about strengthening relationships with that organization, though not ignoring its faults and weaknesses.' None the less, the prevailing view in the service was that the Christians were trustworthy and could be relied upon. In their evaluations Aman, the military intelligence people, emphasized the dangers of links with the Phalange primarily because of its lack of reliability. Despite the fact that military intelligence had proved correct in its assessment, the commission recommended the dismissal of Major General Yehoshua Saguy, head of the service. It exonerated the head of Mossad whom it did not name (he must have been Nahum Adnonni) on the grounds that he could not be held responsible for its earlier attitude because he had only assumed the post four days before the affair of the camps.

By implication therefore Yitzhak Hofi, director of Mossad at the crucial time, might have been thought to blame. But he, an experienced general and field commander before taking his new job, was not a suitable candidate for reproach. He did not accept the opinions of his own people without question, nor did he totally rely upon their reports. The confusion developed from lack of coordination. The Mossad officers who originally arranged political talks with the Lebanese leaders of the Maronite groups were acting neither as intelligence officers, nor as analysts, but as clandestine diplomats called upon to perform that function in the absence of diplomatic relations. As contact-making emissaries they fell into the error of becoming biased in favour of the unrealistic picture painted by their interlocutors. It was a trap which even experienced diplomats have found it difficult to avoid.

Before the decision to invade Lebanon was taken General Sharon, the defence minister, and an enthusiast for action in Lebanon, had visited the USA. Influential Israeli decisions makers formed the impression that Alexander Haig, the secretary of state, had agreed that America would support a big military operation. Nothing was done to correct faulty information upon which the government decision was based. Israeli military intelligence received no complete report which might have caused them to challenge the ministers' view. While the war continued the cabinet did not get full intelligence and analysis reports, because the intelligence services were rarely represented at important meetings. This was a strange omission, for it has since emerged that the head of military intelligence made a detailed evaluation of the military move into Lebanon nearly a month before it began.

Shlomo Gazit, Saguy's predecessor at military intelligence, pointed out in a shrewd analysis of Operation Peace for Galilee published much later that in 1982 the prime minister did his best to exclude General Saguy from cabinet meetings and did not give him a chance to present his appreciation of the situation. For lack of clear direction based on sound intelligence the Lebanon operation, which began with the aim of destroying the PLO military build-up in southern Lebanon, developed into a much more ambitious adventure. Instead of sticking to the original purpose, which was achieved, the IDF was ordered into a war to remove all Palestinian and Syrian forces from the country, then to link up with the Christians and impose a new order upon Lebanon under their hegemony.

Israel had over-reached herself and Mr Begin's government lived to regret the day that it had involved the country in the morass of Lebanon. Mossad too, because of its over-enthusiasm for the Phalangist cause, had failed to make proper use of its intelligence assets to prevent the political disaster. Shlomo Gazit placed the blame, not upon intelligence gathering, nor upon intelligence analysis and evaluation in the Lebanese crisis. The trouble, according to his view, lay in the poor relationship between the cabinet and the heads of intelligence. This made it impossible for the government to have balanced discussions before taking decisions. And although the Kahan commission recommended organizational changes to remedy this state of affairs, they were not introduced.

15. Iranian Adventure

Whatever the disasters, confusions and cruelties of Israel's Lebanese expedition, it did at least succeed in breaking the military power of the PLO in that country, at any rate for a while. It coincided, though, with the emergence of a new Shi'ite power in Lebanon, powerfully backed by Ayatollah Khomeini's Iranian revolutionaries. At first, the Israeli invaders had been positively welcomed by the Shi'ite population of southern Lebanon as liberators lifting the burden of the Palestinian occupation from their backs. Mossad agents cultivated the leadership of Amal at the same time that they were establishing a relationship with the Christians. Amal, under the middling leadership of Nabi Berri, a European-educated lawyer and by no means a firebrand, was for a time content to enjoy the benefits of Israeli patronage. The intelligence men took a cautious view, aware of the growing potential of the Shi'ite majority, which had already been stirred by the teachings of a Lebanese holy man named Imam Moussa al-Sadr, the founder of Amal. Southern Lebanon had indeed been the seat of the religious fervour which later swept Iran. Mossad warned of such dangers, but the government did not heed them.

All that changed as the mullahs, inspired by Islamic zeal from Tehran, built their private armies and terror teams to become the masters of the Beirut slums and of the Bekaa Valley, where they were reinforced by twelve hundred Revolutionary Guards from Iran. As things went from bad to worse within Lebanon, despite the presence of US forces aided by the French, the Italians and a small British contingent, the terrorists of Hizbollah, the Party of God, became ever more aggressive. A new terror force under the blanket description Islamic

110

Jihad (Islamic Holy War) had appeared on the scene and was ready to deploy its powerful new weapon, the suicide bomb. This had been given a trial run against the Iraqi embassy in 1981. Then two years later the suicide bombers struck at their foreign enemies. The target was the US embassy on the Beirut seafront. A truck loaded with explosive drove into it and killed forty-five people, including sixteen Americans. It was an event which created an enormous impact both in the Middle East and in America. More suicide bombs were exploded in the autumn at the headquarters of the US Marines and of the French contingent near Beirut, causing heavy casualties.

Taking over where the Palestinians had left off, Islamic Jihad succeeded in driving the international peacekeeping force out of Lebanon. Ultimately it forced the Israeli army to withdraw across its own border, leaving only token forces and Lebanese auxiliaries in the south.

On the ground the first task was to discover more about the new terrorist cells and their commanders. In this process Mossad agents in the Lebanese capital worked in conjunction with an FBI team and officers from French intelligence; Beirut at the time was full of unlikely stories about the old man selling nuts in Hamra who suddenly turned out to be a Mossad spy. The task was not easy, for the Islamic Jihad and its patron, Hizbollah, were tightly knit in religious belief and in clan organization. Israeli intelligence had to start at the beginning in attempting to find its way into these unfamiliar new structures. Among the bizarre pieces of information which Mossad picked up was that the Shi'ites had invented what was called a suicide vest. It was a sleeveless jacket with 10lb of plastic explosive sewn into it. The idea was that the wearer would walk up to his target and pull a toggle which detonated the plastic and simultaneously blew up the wearer and his victim. There is no record of this device ever having been used, possibly because of a shortage of volunteers to try it.

After the suicide bomb, the second new tactic of holy terrorism employed by Islamic Jihad was hostage-taking. Of course, the actual process of seizing people and demanding a ransom is as old as human conflict. But with the help of their Iranian allies the Shi'ites of Lebanon reduced the process to a modern fine art, and practised it with all the guile of a bazaar carpet seller. Beirut was still a cosmopolitan city with a sizeable European and American population which provided rich human pickings for the terror bands. The example had been set by the Iranian students who humiliated the United States and broke President Carter by seizing the US embassy in Tehran and holding prisoner its fifty-two diplomatic inmates. If that process could inflict such alarm on the satanic enemies of Allah's revolution, why

111

should not the process continue as successfully with the taking of individuals?

Over the following years more and more foreigners were seized. In 1989 thirty-five hostages of British, American and European nationality were believed to be still held in Lebanon. Mrs Thatcher steadfastly refused to bargain for the release of British prisoners, but this did not stop Terry Waite, the emissary of the Archbishop of Canterbury, from becoming involved with trading arrangements set up by other people. For his rather amateurish activities in an area where there was no room for innocent men of goodwill, he eventually paid the price by being taken hostage himself.

Despite bold words about not giving in to the terrorists, President Reagan sanctioned attempts to obtain the release of American hostages, and it was that process which led to the Irangate scandal. The President, who was given to seeing world problems in emotional terms, was sensitive to the pleas of the families of hostages and therefore anxious that everything possible should be done to rescue the prisoners. Behind the original plan to save the hostages was the vague feeling that, with Iran heavily engaged in the war with Iraq, it should be possible to convince the Ayatollah's men of the advantages of restoring relations with the United States. As a start was made in the process of contacting people in Iran believed to be 'moderate' and well disposed to the idea of taking the country back into the international community, Israel and Israeli intelligence were drawn in.

Israel's own relations with Iran were peculiar and complicated. They were based upon the belief that, as Iran was the only other non-Arab power in the region and an oil supplier at that, there was a community of interest which could be exploited. Israel had had reasonably good relations with the Shah. Israeli intelligence, thanks to its close connections in Iran, was quick to detect signs of trouble. As early as the spring of 1978 Mossad felt it was its duty to alert the Americans to the gravity of the threat to Shah Pahlavi's regime. It was a warning which went unheeded. Both the CIA and British intelligence took a much more relaxed view of the situation, which later they were to regret, for if it had been possible to convince the Shah that his power was beginning to crumble there would still have been time to take steps to avoid, or at least postpone, the catastrophe.

After the revolutionary mullahs seized power and began asserting that their war with Iraq was simply a stage on the way to Jerusalem, things began to look distinctly unpleasant for the Israelis. There was anxiety in Jerusalem about the fate of the eighty thousand Jews living in Iran. Ways had to be found to make sure that those who wanted to would be allowed to make their way to Israel. Those were the factors

112

which prompted Israel to start courting the Ayatollah's regime and making accommodations with it. In its attempts to renew contacts with the revolutionary regime through Mossad diplomacy, Israel had drawn attention to the fact that it was the Israeli air force which had taken out the Iraqi nuclear reactor, thereby saving Tehran from the threat of an atom bomb raid. When that strong card failed to persuade Tehran to cease proclaiming that after the USA Israel was the number two enemy state, other ideas were put forward. The obvious bargaining counter was the military supplies sorely needed by Iran for prosecuting the Gulf War. As a result of the Lebanese campaign, Israel had a surplus of equipment captured from the PLO which it was happy to dispose of. For in the immortal words once uttered to an Israeli commander by the late Brigadier Thompson, *The Daily Telegraph*'s military correspondent, 'I congratulate you, General. You keep a very tidy battlefield.' To sell weapons and spare parts had two advantages: it would give a lever for Israel to get something in return, and the munitions would be used in the commendable cause of weakening the military strength of another Arab enemy state, Iraq. In 1981 Ariel Sharon had explained to Alexander Haig, the US secretary of state, the advantage of the clandestine sale of quantities of Israeli-made tyres for Iranian Phantom jets. It helped to forge links with the new regime, he said, and to build a bridge with the new men who would one day succeed Khomeini.

The capture by Islamic Jihad in 1984 of William Buckley, the CIA station chief in Beirut, brought greater urgency to America's determination to do something about the hostages. William Casey, head of the CIA, felt under a special obligation to help his friend, whose fate had naturally produced a bad effect on morale in the service and had damaged its prestige in the Middle East.

The first suggestion that Israel, with its experience in the market, might be able to help with moves aimed at exchanging military equipment for prisoners came from David Kimche, the most senior civil servant in the Israeli foreign ministry. Kimche was no stranger to covert operations. Before moving into official diplomacy he had served with Mossad, and indeed became its deputy head. That was how he was in a position to call upon the services of Yaacov Nimrodi, a sixty-year-old millionaire contractor, an Iranian Jew born in Hamadan near Tehran who had emigrated to Israel in 1946. He was happy enough to come out of retirement to help with the Israeli-American operation to seek out Iranian moderates. His old friend Shimon Peres, then prime minister, outlined to Nimrodi the mission, for which he was exceptionally well qualified.

Although a fiercely patriotic Israeli, Nimrodi had never ceased to think of Iran too as his homeland. As Mossad's man in Tehran from

1956 to 1970, officially described as a military attaché, he had built up a spectacularly successful network which penetrated the secrets of Iran's Arab neighbours. He developed strong links with Savak, the Shah's secret police, some of whose senior officers had been trained by the Israeli secret service. Mossad was at that time part of a trilateral group comprising Israel, Turkey and Iran, established under the codename Trident, for the exchange of intelligence. Heads of service met regularly twice a year to talk about problems of mutual interest. Despite the revolution, Nimrodi still had many useful high-powered contacts and was able to get in touch with a number of senior Savak men, for although the Shah's police had been purged and denigrated not a few of them had made use of their specialized knowledge to find positions in the secret police of the new regime. Nimrodi, a fluent Farsi speaker, had gained his experience of arms dealing through his friendship with the Shah. Whatever reservations he had about selling arms to the mullahs, he was happy to be recalled to the service in the cause of freeing the hostages. Simultaneously he hoped to bring himself up to date on present-day Tehran. Later on, he was accused of making $10 million from his dealings in the process, but this he denied.

Nimrodi's first task was to talk to Iranians in Europe who had connections with the Khomeini regime and who might act as middlemen. First he saw Adnan Khashoggi, the flamboyant Saudi arms dealer and a man with a finger in many pies who was doing well out of the Gulf War. Second on his list came Manucher Ghorbanifar, known as Gorba, whom he had first met ten years before when he was a Savak officer. Gorba was a wheeler-dealer with interests in a shipping company, and a man constantly seeking to make contact with Mossad or the CIA to tell them about the high-level contacts in Tehran he hoped to exploit. A strange Mossad-inspired team finally met in London. David Kimche, accompanied by Amiram Nir, a former television journalist who had become the Israeli prime minister's adviser on terrorism, gathered with Nimrodi and his co-opted Israeli friend Al Schwimmer, well known as the founder of Israel's light aircraft industry and also a friend of the prime minister. Gorba was present and managed to convince the shrewd Kimche that he was the man capable of putting the Americans in touch with 'moderate' interlocutors in Tehran in return for a delivery to Iran of a consignment of TOW anti-tank missiles. Gorba gave the impression that he was dealing with the Iranian prime minister, and it was hinted that William Buckley might well be released from captivity as part of the deal he proposed.

There were difficulties, because to send the missiles would involve breaking the international embargo on selling weapons to Iran. Kimche's main contact on the American side was Robert McFarlane, the national security adviser, who thought this difficulty might be overcome provided that the quantity was not sufficient to alter the military balance in the Gulf War. A way round it was suggested by offering to despatch Israeli supplies which could then quietly be replaced by the Americans. This offered the further advantage that Israel would be getting new-for-old stocks. In August 1985 one hundred TOW missiles were flown from Tel Aviv to Tabriz in Iran aboard a DC-8 aircraft chartered by Al Schwimmer which was piloted by a Colombian.

No hostages were forthcoming, because the Iranian authorities were not expecting to take delivery of the cargo of missiles. That was because Mr Ghorbanifar's contact in Tehran was not in fact the powerful figure he had been made out to be, but a man of lesser importance and a grand title. With the help of the Israelis a second cargo of missiles was flown to Tabriz in two transport aircraft. This time Ghorbanifar went with them, bearing an Argentinian passport. This did not prevent his arrest on arrival, for he had been sentenced to death in his absence for plotting in an anti-Khomeini coup. He was released and soon reported the success of his mission, or at any rate partial success. Only one hostage was released instead of the four expected – the Rev. Benjamin Weir, a Presbyterian minister who had been held in Lebanon for a year. Of William Buckley there was no sign, for in fact he had been tortured to death some time earlier.

From this point onwards it was the Americans who took over the leading role, with Lieutenant Colonel Oliver North as the coordinator of Operation Recovery, and to all intents and purposes and for the time being he was in charge of American policy towards Iran. But most of the weapons subsequently passed to Iran continued to be transited by way of Israel. David Kimche was replaced by Amiram Nir, the anti-terrorist adviser from the prime minister's office who maintained the Israeli presence. Nimrodi and Schwimmer also continued to be involved, as did the extravagant Mr Ghorbanifar.

The fashion in which the US administration handled the hostage affair from then on drew a barbed comment from Amir Taheri, the well-informed Iranian expatriate journalist, in his book *Nest of Spies*: 'Surprisingly enough, they refused to look beyond information provided by exiles, arms merchants, foreign intelligence agencies, each promoting its own slant, and worst of all, profiteers whose bad faith had been recognized even by people close to the administration.'

It had not been a glorious chapter in the history of Israeli covert operations either, and when, after the failed mission to Tehran by Robert McFarlane and Colonel North, the Iranians deliberately released the story, Israel too came in for a good deal of unwelcome criticism for its shoddy part in the Irangate scandal. The only excuse was that Shimon Peres, the prime minister, had been anxious to help the American allies – especially at a time when the Jonathan Pollard spy case in the USA was arousing such resentment across the Atlantic.

The Israelis had insisted that Amiram Nir should accompany the North mission, probably to keep a watching brief, and he joined them as they flew from Tel Aviv to Tehran on the final ill-fated mission in May 1986. After a year of frantic activity and the official sale to Iran of 1500 TOW missiles and spare parts for 240 Hawks at exorbitant prices, little had been achieved. But after the initial arms deliveries to the mullahs the Americans no longer needed assistance.

Suggestions emerged in 1988 that Colonel North also planned other efforts by irregular forces to free the hostages in Lebanon. The source of this information was Amiram Nir. After his death in a light aircraft crash while on a mysterious journey in Mexico, the *Washington Post* disclosed details of a confidential interview it had had with him in London some months before. Nir had told the newspaper about a secret Israeli-American agreement which authorized counter-terrorist operations supervised by himself and Colonel North in 1985–6. It had been signed by prime minister Peres and by President Reagan. Such an arrangement had never been disclosed, and the White House was reluctant to discuss the matter. But Mr Nir had insisted that a series of covert actions were in fact organized. The starting point was a plan to recruit a force of forty Druze fighters in Lebanon to be trained for hostage rescue operations. There was also a plan to kidnap known terrorists or their relations to be swapped for American hostages, but this was rejected by the American authorities as an illegal covert operation. In Israel Nir was not taken very seriously, although he had managed to irritate Mossad by his amateur participation in the Tehran adventure and by becoming too closely involved with the Americans. His most notable contribution to the bargaining was to insist on higher payments for the weapons delivered. He had already left government service before going abroad on his fatal journey to Mexico.

16. The Twilight Zone

The third arm of Israeli intelligence, and the one with the least savoury reputation, is Shin Beth – sometimes known as Shabak – the general security service. Its methods are tough, usually disciplined, frequently brutal. It relies heavily upon informers, people who are sometimes paid and sometimes bullied to act as narks. The members of its interrogation unit are trained in the art of getting information from suspects on the subject of HTA, as they like to call it – Hostile Terrorist Activity. When he first became prime minister Menachem Begin, by no means thought of as a soft liberal, issued an order to Shin Beth recommending it to use its brains rather than its brawn in the quest for information.

By the nature of their watchdog job Shin Beth officers regard all foreigners, and many of their compatriots, with suspicion. They tap telephones, make use of electronic eavesdropping and surveillance, open letters and break and enter premises. The service is there to sniff out spies, stifle subversion from whatever quarter, and eliminate terrorism and sabotage. The polite designation of these duties is counter-espionage and internal security.

As if that were not enough, Shin Beth also has the job of providing security at airports and for the national airline, El Al; something it does with great efficiency. It also guards government buildings and embassies. The main counter-espionage targets are the Arab states and the Soviet and eastern bloc intelligence services. In the Arab affairs department it keeps a counter-intelligence index and a watchful eye on goings-on among Palestinians living in Israel and in the occupied territories.

117

As Palestinian resistance increased, Shin Beth expanded and became heavily involved in covert action against agitators and their cells inside Israel. It was a task they went to with a will. But there was less enthusiasm and more circumspection in the service for the other side of the internal security role – operations directed against Israeli terrorists attacking the Arab population. Despite the reluctance of some officers, action was finally taken after extremists booby-trapped the cars of three Arab mayors and conspired in an attempt to blow up the Dome of the Rock in Jerusalem, one of the most sacred shrines of Islam. Twenty-seven people were arrested and charged with belonging to a 'Jewish terrorist underground'.

In the curiously named Non-Arab Department, whose title itself seems to give an indication of the order of priorities, security officers are instructed to probe both communist and non-communist subversion. Its counter-intelligence activities concentrate on penetration of both hostile and friendly intelligence services. Shin Beth also has responsibility for the interrogation and vetting of immigrants from the Soviet Union as eastern Europe, for it is obvious that Israel must be on the alert for Jews who have been recruited and trained by the KGB before starting their new life in Israel.

With plenty of recruits available who had gained their experience in the tough struggles among clashing Jewish groups before independence, Shin Beth scored a number of successes in the early years after independence by uncovering Soviet spy networks. The most notable coup, with some help from the British MI5, was to catch red-handed a highly placed official at the defence ministry named Israel Beer as he was in the act of handing over material to a Soviet agent. They also arrested another spy, Professor Kirt Sitte, a nuclear physicist, who had been recruited by Czech intelligence before taking up his post at the Haifa Institute.

As mentioned above, Shin Beth's activities are by no means confined to actual or potential enemy countries. On numerous occasions its operatives were detected spying upon American embassy people. In one notable instance, they tried to recruit a man working at the consulate general in Jerusalem. He was having an affair with an Israeli girl and the service set up a fake abortion in an unsuccessful attempt to blackmail him. They also tried to persuade the girl to worm out secrets from her lover.

A good deal of information about this branch of the security services came from a secret CIA report on the Israeli intelligence services. The report catalogued a number of 'crude attempts' to turn US Marines guards at the embassy in Tel Aviv by means of financial reward. In 1964 a hidden microphone planted by the Israelis was discovered in the ambassador's office. They also found telephone taps on equipment at the defence attaché's residence. According to the report, 'The Israelis have shown themselves to be most adept at surveillance and surreptitious entry operations. Men and women are frequently used together on surveillance teams in order to allay suspicion. Shin Beth personnel are experts at entering private quarters where they go through visitors' luggage and personal papers.' Radio transmitters had been found concealed in record players, in coffee cans with false bottoms and in cooking stoves.

Much of Shin Beth's information about diplomats, journalists and other expatriates comes from informers likely to be in touch with foreigners such as taxi drivers, barmen, waiters and hotel staff, who earn a few shekels on the side by passing on bits of hearsay which may one day prove useful. Tip-offs also help in Shin Beth's work in unmasking spies and terrorists.

In 1979 Shin Beth, alerted by informers, began to keep surveillance on Rhona Ritchie, a Scotswoman recently appointed press officer at the British Embassy in Tel Aviv. They discovered that she was having an affair with Rifaat al-Ansari, a handsome Egyptian diplomat known to be an intelligence officer. A full intelligence report prepared by the Israelis showed that she had handed over confidential papers to her lover. Miss Ritchie was recalled to London, admitted her guilt and was given a suspended sentence.

Campaigning against Arab espionage in the 1960s the service managed to break Egyptian and Syrian rings, not to mention their discovery of a German engineer sentenced for conducting espionage on behalf of Lebanon, and a British engineer performing the same service for the Jordanians. They even discovered a former Israeli paratrooper named Dan Vered, an 'ideological' traitor spying for the Syrians and attempting to recruit Jews to be sent abroad for training in sabotage. Among them was another former paratrooper, Ehud Adiv, who actually went to Syria for explosives and instruction on using codes. Both of them received long prison sentences. Shin Beth has frequently had to match its wits against Syrian intelligence, the most active of the Arab spy services, which at one point in the 1970s was discovered to have set up a spy ring in Galilee. One hundred and fifty people, both Jews and Arabs, were involved in this network, thirty of whom were arrested.

As the Palestinian resistance in Gaza and in the occupied West Bank became first more vocal and then more brutal in its activities, Shin Beth faced a task of growing complexity. In its dealings with Arabs living both inside Israel and in the occupied territories, its officers relied more heavily than ever upon informers within the Arab community. Its officers also received useful briefings from friendly Arabs, some

119

of whom were appointed mayors by the Israelis. The spread of the uprising after 1987 closed many sources. The Palestinian activists began intimidating, and on some occasions murdering, such 'collaborators', and it became ever more difficult to obtain accurate reports about what was happening inside the Arab communities clashing openly with IDF patrols and settlers.

Increasingly frustrated in their task, Shin Beth officers themselves behaved on some occasions with great ferocity. The service was gravely compromised in a great scandal which began in 1984. Near Ashkelon, four Palestinian terrorists hijacked Bus 300 from Tel Aviv and forced it to drive towards Gaza with its thirty-five passengers still aboard. The hijackers were demanding, in return for the lives of the passengers, the release of five hundred Palestinian prisoners. Special troops accompanied by Shin Beth agents rushed to the spot and stormed the vehicle in traditional style. It was announced that in the shooting one hostage and all four terrorists had been killed. Two of the terrorists, it was then officially stated, had died on their way to hospital, which falsely gave the impression that they had been wounded in the assault.

But Alex Levac, an Israeli newspaper photographer, was present and took some pictures which, when eventually published, clearly showed two of the hijackers being led away after the attack still alive. The *New York Times* broke the censorship ban by describing the picture and drawing attention to the disturbing questions it raised about what had really happened by that lonely roadside. The picture eventually appeared in the Israeli paper *Hadashot*. In the photograph two hard-faced men in civilian combat-style jackets, jeans and trainers are firmly holding a dazed-looking young Palestinian named Majdi Abu Jumaa. One of them is pointing threateningly at the camera. This photograph provided clear pictorial evidence that Majdi was still alive after the shoot-out, as was his cousin, Subhi, both of them eighteen-year-olds. The implication was obvious.

Slowly the gruesome truth emerged. Security men had led the two young Arabs to a field where they were first interrogated and then bludgeoned to death in cold blood long after the fire-fight finished. Moshe Arens, the defence minister, condemned the murders as a 'clear contradiction to the basic rules and norms incumbent on all, and especially on the security forces'. He promised action against those responsible. Because the hijack siege attracted national attention while it continued, the minister and a number of senior officers had rushed to the spot when the assault was about to take place. But Mr Arens stated that neither he, nor the chief of staff, General Moshe Levy, was at the site at the critical moment.

As a result of the subsequent outcry and pressure from Knesset members the government commissioned Meir Zorea, a reserve army general, to investigate. He concluded that, although there was no evidence to show that formal orders had been given to kill the Arabs, there were signs of undue brutality which should be further examined in a criminal investigation. Shin Beth leaders were heavily implicated, for evidence from soldiers who were present at the time made it clear that the prisoners were interrogated and then murdered by Shin Beth officers. One witness described how the interrogators smashed the head of one terrorist against a rock and threw the other man to the ground from his stretcher. In their defence, the officers blamed claimed that they were acting on the orders of Avraham Shalom, head of Shin Beth.

To make matters worse, as the enquiry proceeded allegations were put forward that the service had been playing around with the evidence, forging some papers and destroying others, in order to justify their assertion that they had not been involved in the killings. Shin Beth witnesses called before the enquiry commission carefully coordinated their evidence to support the innocence of colleagues. Evidence was tampered with, so as to make it look as though the blame rested upon General Yitzhak Mordechai, the paratroop officer in command of the bus assault unit. The general admitted having pistol-whipped the two Arabs to get urgent information about a suspected booby trap on the bus, but he claimed that he had then handed them over to the security men. As well as Avraham Shalom himself, a number of high-ranking Shin Beth people were named in all this, and the affair took on a new dimension when he claimed that he had enjoyed the approval of his political masters, including Yitzhak Shamir. Later a ministry of justice investigation ruled that in fact this was untrue and he had not received high level instructions to kill the two hijackers. At the time, it was Mr Shamir who was taking Buggins' turn at being prime minister under the agreement made by the Likud and the Labour parties to alternate in power, so as to create a government of national unity. Neither he, nor his predecessor Shimon Peres, emerged unscathed from the scandal, for it appeared that Peres also had backed Shalom during his period of office.

The natural reaction of the politicians, as always seems to be the case in Israel when they are confronted by a dangerous scandal centring on national security and the intelligence services, was that things had gone quite far enough and any further probing would be damaging to the national interest. Morale in the service was at a low ebb in face of the unseemly behaviour of its officers, who were seen to be quarrelling and denouncing each other in public. Three top men decided that it was their duty to suggest that Mr Shalom, the head of the service, had been responsible for the order to kill. They were forced to resign.

In June 1986, two years after the events in question, Shimon Peres, the then prime minister, advised the attorney general, Yitzhak Zamir, that he should end his investigations into state security on the grounds that if they continued they could have a bad effect on the struggle against terrorism. He refused to do so and resigned. In the same month, President Chaim Herzog was persuaded to use his power of clemency to pardon Avraham Shalom and three of his deputies, even though they had not been found guilty in any court. He gave as a reason that the time had come to end 'the witch hunt surrounding this affair and to avert additional serious harm to the general security service'. The president went on to pay tribute to the sterling work of Shin Beth, which, he said, had cracked 320 terrorist groups responsible for hundreds of attacks throughout the land. 'The Israeli public has no idea what a debt we owe to all those unknown fighters . . . and how many lives have been saved thanks to them.' Part of the price paid was the dismissal of Avraham Shalom, who had become head of the service in 1980 after an active career as a secret agent. He was a member of the Mossad team which captured Eichmann in South America.

Thankful for being let off the hook by presidential decree, the cabinet turned down any idea of launching any further investigation of its own. The pardon was upheld by the high court and then extended to seven other Shin Beth officers, an act which effectively undermined attempts being made by the new attorney general to take a deeper look into responsibility for the bus killings. Public opinion was less satisfied than the government, and a number of newspapers expressed alarm at the success of what amounted to a great cover-up – 'the plot to silence', as it was called. It is one of the reassuring features of public life in Israel that, in true democratic style, the press is constantly alert to the dangers of official conspiracies to hide ugly facts. President Herzog's gesture in granting the pardon was severely criticized. The newspaper *Ha'aretz* felt that it implied that new norms had been established, permitting Shin Beth to murder terrorists and to give false testimony.

The security service emerged from the affair with a badly compromised reputation, but it continued to work in the old ways, constantly praised by hard-line senior politicians like General Ariel Sharon, who went very much further than the president in justifying Shin Beth in taking whatever action it considered to be right. Moshe Katzav, who served as minister of labour, admitted that the service had violated basic laws, but it was his view that the practice should be recognized and legitimized because 'Israel is in a state of war against terrorism . . . the normal laws don't apply.'

122

Further evidence of misbehaviour by Shin Beth became available in 1987 when the Supreme Court overturned a court-martial decision made several years earlier and predating the Bus 300 affair. Izat Nafsu, an IDF lieutenant of Circassian origin, was serving an eighteen-year prison sentence on charges of spying for the Syrians while serving in southern Lebanon. On appeal the Supreme Court overturned the conviction on the grounds that his confession, which was subsequently retracted, had been forced out of him during a two-week interrogation by Shin Beth. It found that the officers had used 'unethical interrogation methods' and that they had lied during Nafsu's original military trial. There was evidence that he had been beaten, kicked, humiliated and forced to stand for hours under interrogation in the freezing cold. To force a confession, the interrogators threatened to strip his wife and mother naked in public. The offence which Nafsu had in fact committed was that while serving in Lebanon he had failed to report meetings with an official of the PLO; for this misdemeanour he was reduced to the rank of sergeant major.

The combined effect of the Bus 300 and Nafsu affairs persuaded the government to set up a judicial committee of enquiry to look into the comportment of Shin Beth in general. Chaired by Justice Moshe Landau, formerly president of the Supreme Court, its other members were Judge Yahov Maltz and Major General Yitzhak Hofi, a former head of Mossad. Its conclusions utterly rejected the proposition 'that because of crucial interests of state security the activity of the security services in their war against terrorism occurs in a "twilight zone" which is outside the realm of the law, and therefore these services must be freed from the bonds of the law and must be permitted deviations therefrom'.

Having laid down that principle, the commission found that officers of the internal security service had indeed lied consistently and systematically in court over a sixteen-year period. They had done this to secure the admissibility of confessions obtained from prisoners under interrogation. Blame for this state of affairs was placed squarely upon three successive heads of the service and their legal advisers who permitted it to become the established code. The habit of perjury had grown from the desire of officers in the interrogation unit to avoid revealing their methods because, if they had done so, it seemed certain that the courts would have ruled confessions so obtained to be inadmissible. 'They simply took the easy way out', was the opinion of the Landau commission. There had never been a deliberate decision to lay down a policy of lying in court. The practice just took root and recruits to the service accepted it as an established and tolerated method.

In its conclusions the commission supported the principle that the law must lay down a suitable framework for the investigation and prevention of terrorist action. To this end it compiled a document of guidelines for interrogators, published in a section of the report which remained secret. In so doing it claimed to be codifying earlier guidelines which had evolved piecemeal from the time when investigations into terrorism expanded in the new situation created following the Six Day War of 1967, after Israel took over administration of Arab territory.

Enough hints appeared in the published section to give an indication of what Justice Landau had in mind. For example, in the cautious words of the commission, 'the exertion of a moderate amount of physical pressure is *not* [my italics] to be avoided' in order to get information when all else failed. But first, the interrogators were recommended to try psychological pressure, trickery, deception and non-violent, but prolonged and vigorous, questioning.

In short, it was recognized that Shin Beth had a difficult and important task to perform, and was therefore entitled to use harsh, though not brutal, methods in order to establish the truth about terrorist acts. Its role was different from that of the police, who were required to obtain evidence so as to get convictions in court; the security service needed intelligence information to thwart acts of terrorism, and for this reason the need to keep evidence secret might prevent an incriminated person from ever being brought to court. An insight into the philosophy of the security service was provided by an anonymous quotation included in the report from one of its ranking officials:

The network that deals with all this is mainly a collecting system. In the end, we thought, and we still think today, that the tool of interrogation is a system for collecting intelligence information. This also explains . . . why we were less interested in, or why we cared less about placing them on trial, because after catching the person [responsible] and solving the crime, I go on to the next stage – I go after the next suspect.

The commission hoped that Shin Beth could 'turn a new and immaculate leaf' within the framework of the existing law. It certainly needed to do so. The report itself spoke of the 'dismal and regrettable' picture which had emerged of a service which, whatever its achievements, had permitted itself to violate the law over many years and had gone so far as positively to encourage its officers to give false testimony in court.

124

Part V
Allies

17. Saving Sadat

The train of events which led to the first historic meeting between the leaders of Israel and Egypt developed from the exploitation of a Mossad surveillance operation early in 1973. One of their agents in Beirut signalled that two members of Wadi Haddad's PFLP were heading for London and Paris on a mission. The task of the watchers there was to discover what the target might be. After many weeks, it emerged that the PFLP was training a specially selected group of twenty men for a top secret operation. By raiding apartments, seizing papers and putting pressure on arms suppliers, the field men discovered that with Libyan help and encouragement the Palestinian group was planning to assassinate President Sadat of Egypt.

The plot arose in the first place from the justified anger of Colonel Muammar Gaddafi when a Libyan Boeing 727 with 108 passengers on board was shot down by the Israeli air force after it strayed over occupied Sinai. The air force tried to justify its act by claiming that, when the captain failed to respond to warnings, headquarters decided that the airliner might be on a kamikaze mission with orders to crash on to the centre of an Israeli city.

In revenge for this act the Libyan leader wanted to launch a raid on Haifa, but was dissuaded from attempting any such action by the Egyptian leader. Instead, Gaddafi conceived another plan. He would use an Egyptian submarine on loan to his navy to torpedo the British liner *Queen Elizabeth II*, then at sea cruising to Ashdod with mainly Jewish passengers intent on commemorating the twenty-fifth anniversary of the foundation of Israel. The Egyptian captain sailed on this mission, but wisely transmitted a coded message to Alexandria naval headquarters asking whether his orders were confirmed. According to the Egyptian journalist and author Mohammed Hassenein Heikal, President Sadat was woken at 1 a.m. to be informed about the signal. Promptly and firmly, he countermanded Gaddafi's order. But there was a nail-biting two-hour delay before the submarine next surfaced and was able to acknowledge his command.

This incident served only to increase Colonel Gaddafi's frustrated indignation. He felt further snubbed by the failure of his recent visit to Cairo, during which the Egyptian urbanites treated him as a young and boastful peasant come to town, rather than as the hero and rightful successor to Colonel Gamal Abdel Nasser that he considered himself to be. An additional factor which influenced his thinking was that signs were appearing of a real prospect of reconciliation between Egypt and Israel. Gaddafi decided that President Sadat was a traitor who must be eliminated. The man he chose to accomplish this deed was Wadi Haddad, the fiery leader of the PFLP, the breakaway group of the PLO, who had already made his reputation as the organizer of hijacks and other terrorist enterprises. Precisely for that reason, Mossad devoted a good deal of attention to keeping watch on his networks. Starting from the results of their surveillance work in Paris and London, the special team was able to ferret out details of the murder plot.

Menachem Begin had just become prime minister as a result of the success of his Likud party at the polls after nineteen years in the political wilderness. Both he and the former prime minister, Yitzak Rabin, were given details of the plot by the head of Mossad. To the amazement of the intelligence men, his reaction was to declare that Sadat must be warned that his life was in danger. It was a move which Mossad bosses at first opposed. But Mr Begin shrewdly saw that here was a chance to use a gesture of goodwill to isolate Egypt from the rest of the Arab world as a collaborator with Israel, and also to increase the chances of a peace settlement. The cabinet agreed that President Sadat should be briefed on Mossad's findings; the question was how this should be done.

There were precedents for Israel passing on such information to Arab leaders. King Hussein of Jordan had received timely warnings about threats to his kingdom which resulted from Mossad spying. When the intelligence service uncovered a plot to kill King Hassan of Morocco, that monarch had been told about it through the good offices of the CIA in the role of middleman. Mr Begin seemed amazed when Mossad told him about these earlier even ts, of which he knew nothing. But this time he was determined to do things his own way and ruled that President Sadat should be told directly by Israel. Some time later he made public, though veiled, reference to this matter, saying: 'We learned from a very serious source of a plot to kill and we didn't leave it a secret, so far as the proper authorities were concerned.'

The decision posed problems, for it was natural that the Egyptian leader might be suspicious about reports from such a normally hostile source. It was hardly possible to despatch the head of Mossad to a hostile Arab country to tell him about a murder plot. Eventually, King Hassan was selected as a suitable intermediary. Secret diplomatic links had already been established with the monarch, who for some time had cultivated a relationship with the Israelis, much though such encounters were condemned by the Arab world. Indeed, Colonel Gaddafi had even planned to kill the King as a punishment for such treachery. King Hassan's bodyguards were Mossad-trained, and frequent intelligence exchanges took place. In October 1976, Yitzhak Rabin himself, while still prime minister, had visited Morocco incognito for discreet talks as part of an attempt to arrange contact with President Sadat. He asked his host, King Hassan, to set up an Egyptian meeting with him. The Moroccan King put out feelers, but Sadat did not yet feel ready for such a bold stroke. Henry Kissinger advised him not to go, perhaps because the American adviser was worried that if Israel and Egypt came to be on speaking terms that might weaken US influence in the region.

The task of handing over his file on the Libyan terrorist operation to General Kemal Hasan Ali, head of Moukhabarat, the Egyptian intelligence service, fell to General Yitzhak Hofi, boss of Mossad. Even so, it was considered prudent to do this in the presence of Moroccan witnesses, because it was possible that Egyptians as well as Libyans were mixed up in the plot. Another reason why witnesses were considered essential was that the Egyptian intelligence chief might otherwise suppress the report rather than admit that he had been outsmarted by the Israelis.

The report revealed that Mossad had discovered two alternative plans to kill Anwar Sadat, either at a military parade or after a seaborne landing near his Alexandria home. It furnished details about the seven-man hit team specially trained at a camp in Libya, and of the location of the caches of weapons which had been taken into Egypt through the Libyan diplomatic bag.

Not all Egyptians were convinced by the data provided. Hassanein Heikal, by no means a great admirer of Mr Sadat, considered it an implausible story. The embarrassing question asked was, how had it come about that Moukhabarat intelligence men had failed to detect a plot to murder their own head of state when Mossad, from enemy Israel, had managed to expose it? In any case, President Sadat took no chances. His police arrested all those named in the dossier, and their

129

interrogation seemed to confirm the correctness of the Israeli report. In Cairo the affair was kept secret, the only item to surface being a newspaper report that several men had been executed for conspiring against the state. A week later, in July 1977 President Sadat massed Egyptian troops on the border and launched punitive raids into Libyan territory as a warning to Colonel Gaddafi that his plot to overthrow the Egyptian regime had been detected and thwarted. The offensive, which included air strikes as far west as El Adem, south of Tobruk, lasted six days.

Meanwhile, diplomatic moves to prepare the way for an Israeli-Egyptian reconciliation helped along by the Mossad revelations were proceeding under the auspices of King Hassan. The Moroccan ruler reported that President Sadat had said that he was ready for a secret meeting with Mr Begin. The first concrete result of Mossad's timely warning to President Sadat was his secret encounter with Menachem Begin, arranged in August 1977 in Bucharest during a visit there of a Cairo parliamentary delegation to meet the Romanian president, Ceausescu.

Mossad had also been called upon to help deceive the USA about clandestine arrangements being made with Egypt. Much was at stake so far as the Israeli government was concerned. Menachem Begin had come to power as a no compromise hard-liner, and his constituency in the country was none too happy with the idea that he had apparently gone soft and become a peacemaker, the more so if peace moves were to fail. Mr Begin was convinced that only deadly secret diplomacy offered a chance of success. The United States is not best known as a keeper of secrets, and any premature detailed revelations about under-cover Israeli-Egyptian contacts could only compromise their success. In Israel there also existed the suspicion that the Americans, anxious to improve their own relations with Egypt, might not be over-pleased at the idea of Israel developing a liaison with President Sadat which might change the balance.

For all these reasons secrecy was considered paramount. Mossad called in help from the special foreign relations department of the foreign ministry which has dealings with many countries where there are no Israeli embassies. It was responsible for establishing further contact with the Egyptian authorities. On this occasion, Vienna was the chosen place for the encounter with the former Egyptian delegate to the international atomic centre there, Mohammed Hassan Tohami. He had become vice-president and was also coordinator of the Egyptian secret service.

Moshe Dayan, the foreign minister, used the pretext of a visit to Brussels on 16 September 1977 for a meeting with General Alexander

Haig, the NATO supreme commander, to make a clandestine trip to Morocco. In the afternoon he was due to take a Sabena flight to New York. But although Dayan and his wife Rachel checked in at Brussels airport, Rachel alone arrived in New York. Before take-off from Brussels, a black Citroën 2CV drove up to the plane. General Dayan, disguised with sunglasses and a hat, jumped into it and drove to another runway where a Moroccan air force plane waited to take him to Tangier. There he met Tohami, who confirmed that Anwar Sadat was ready to go to Israel – on one condition, which was that Israel must agree to an eventual withdrawal from Sinai. Next day Dayan appeared briefly in Paris, and then returned to Tel Aviv before flying on to New York to complete the process of mystification.

Not until early November, when President Sadat publicly announced that he was ready to go to Jerusalem, did the CIA become aware of what had been going on. Ten days later, the Egyptian leader made his momentous journey to Israel and began a new era, if not of friendship, then at least of non-hostility, between Israel and Egypt. At first Mossad officers, accustomed to the idea that Egypt was the main enemy, had heavy doubts about Sadat the peacemaker, and were distrustful of his intrigues over the Palestinian question. In fact it was not long before, in the wake of the peace settlement, the Israeli service began taking advantage of it to establish amicable and fruitful links with the Egyptian secret service. Officers who for years had devoted most of their professional lives in trying to discover what the Moukhabarat was up to, and who were consumed by curiosity about life in the Arab world, suddenly experienced the pleasures of living in Cairo and working together with their former enemies.

Other Mossad men were active also in the United States. The man in their figurative sights was Andrew Young, US ambassador to the United Nations, picked upon as an ostentatious supporter of the Palestinian cause. It was always Israeli policy to discourage any possibility that America might recognize the PLO, and it seemed to them that Mr Young was moving in that direction. Yitzhak Hofi, head of Mossad, devised a plot to discredit Mr Young and with prime ministerial approval set it in hand. Israeli agents learned from two sources in 1979 that a meeting was being arranged to enable Mr Young to exchange ideas on the subject with Zehdi Labib, the Palestinian representative at the United Nations. This was being arranged to take place at a party given by the Kuwaiti UN representative, and Mossad was there in advance to bug the conversation.

Having recorded the exchanges, the Israelis fed information about it to *Newsweek*. Although Mr Young at first denied that the encounter had taken place, he was finally forced to admit that it had. As a result of this manoeuvre he lost his job, for it was considered that his indiscretion gave a kind of recognition to the PLO at a time when it was the policy of the administration not to do so. This was a classic piece of disinformation, which is one of Mossad's specialities, carefully planned to put an end to what Israel considered to be a dangerous flirtation between the Americans and the PLO. It could not be claimed that the operation was a complete success, for when it became public knowledge that the secret service men had been eavesdropping in New York speculation developed about who else the Israelis might be bugging. *Time* magazine claimed that the Israelis had gone even further than the KGB in illicit listening in Washington. The whole affair served to increase suspicion about the covert activities of a foreign service in the USA. Mossad reacted by denying any involvement in the Young affair. But American mistrust remained.

The same tendency on Israeli's part to suspect any of its allies of disloyalty at the slightest hint of discussions with the PLO also affected relations with the Federal Republic of Germany. The friendship between Israel and West Germany, both in the matter of straightforward diplomatic exchanges and in the relationship between secret services, had always been one of nuance. For Israelis of a certain age Germany remained the land of the holocaust, and despite the emergence of a democratic and liberal republic there, despite generous reparations and good-hearted moves of reconciliation, old suspicions died hard. What continued to offend and irk Israel was the apparent predilection of liberal Germans for favouring the Palestinian cause. Moshe Dayan was not the only notable figure to attack West Germany for recognizing the principle of self-rule for Palestine.

When German terrorists first appeared in Middle Eastern training camps in the 1970s, and international terror flourished as Baader-Meinhof jointly with Palestinian gangs spread their networks, Mossad, seeing that the support of German anti-terrorist services would become essential, seized the opportunity to develop police cooperation in Europe. Before long they had flooded the BKA and BfV with tip-offs about terrorists on the move, were giving frequent warnings about plans for hijacks, and were denouncing Arab agents in German terror groups.

Until President de Gaulle became critical of aggressive Israeli policies, the French alliance had been of great advantage to Mossad. Paris was the place chosen as its European headquarters. Based at the embassy in Rue Rabelais, just off the Champs Elysées, were the offices of regional controllers of both the collection department and the political action and liaison department. Before the Six Day War Mossad's resources were skilfully used in diplomatic attempts to

132

strengthen French support and approval. The OAS, the secret army which tried to overthrow President de Gaulle in order to display their determined opposition to his Algerian policy, themselves tried to win Israeli support based on their mutual mistrust of the Arabs. Mossad certainly had its connections with the OAS, but when that underground army began launching a series of attempts to assassinate the French president the secret service used its resources to thwart such plots. Even this help, however, failed to persuade President de Gaulle to return to the old alliance, and he raised objections to Mossad's use of his capital as an operational base.

The most troubling feature of Mossad's foreign connections concerns its relationship with the Soviet Union and the KGB. It is easy now, in the light of the events of the last two decades in Middle Eastern affairs, simply to assume that the USSR, supporter and arms provider of the Arab states most implacably opposed to Israel, is in the nature of things the enemy of Israel. The impression is strengthened by the undoubtedly harsh treatment and persecution of Jews by the Russians. Only with great difficulty were the Soviets persuaded to permit even limited emigration of Jews.

It is important to remember, however, that things did not always stand like that in recent history. The Russians were among the first to recognize the new state of Israel. They were aware that many of its prominent leaders had been born either in Russia or in the European states of the Russian empire. They were people who spoke the languages and understood the culture of eastern Europe, and at first the Kremlin believed that a socialist state of Israel might well turn into a most useful ally in the Middle East. The Russians made considerable efforts to infiltrate Israeli trade unions and left-wing political groups in the hopes of building an alliance. Of course, things did not turn out like that. But for a time it seemed reasonable to consider the possibility that an extreme left wing, or perhaps even a communist Israel, might spring from the dreams of the kibbutz and experiments in communal living. In the early days there was no shortage of Israeli communist believers. Some of them, indeed, were prepared to work for the KGB. Israel Beer, a close friend and confidant of David Ben-Gurion, provided cabinet papers for the Russians, and there was also the case of Professor Kurt Sitte, a nuclear physicist at the Haifa Institute of Technology exposed as a Soviet agent.

In the early 1960s the Soviet leadership made a U-turn in *realpolitik* and, mindful of the giant oil resources controlled by the Islamic nations, decided that its cause would be best advanced by supporting the Arab 'liberation' movements, instead of pinning its faith on the hope that Israel might in the future become a communist base in the area. In 1967, after the Six Day War, the Russians closed down their embassy in Tel Aviv and relations were severed. After that time, however, the two countries maintained contact by way of Mossad. Although this remains a subject shrouded in mystery there are indications that Mossad itself made connections with the Soviet state organs in its capacity as a purveyor of undercover diplomacy. The intelligence service was certainly involved in the process of trying to save fellow Jews in many foreign countries, so why should they not do so in the Soviet Union? There can be no doubt that the Institute bargained, for example, with Arabs so as to get diaspora coreligionists from Yemen and North Africa safely to the homeland, so it was reasonable to attempt the same kind of deals with the Soviets, even when they became increasingly closely identified with the Arabs.

A rare piece of evidence about Mossad-KGB relations came to light in the spring of 1989 with the publication of a book of memoirs entitled *The Vipers*. Its author was Aharon Moshel, a former Mossad agent now settled in retirement in West Germany where, according to his own account, he had worked at one time as a mole inside the neo-Nazi groups. Mr Moshel claims that he was recalled from holiday in 1963 and ordered to Beirut to make contact with Kim Philby, the British traitor identified as a double agent working for the KGB. Moshel's task was to warn Philby that British intelligence was about to arrest him and to offer help if he needed it.

Some clues about the reasoning which prompted the Institute to work in favour of the Russians rather than of the British at a time when MI6, the British secret service, was trying to get the traitor back to London, are offered in Aharon Moshel's account. From his base at the Commodore Hotel in West Beirut he made sorties to keep watch on Philby's apartment, and then called on him while he was alone there. 'I bring greetings from Kohlmann,' he had been instructed to say. This message was understood at once by Philby, and the explanation offered is that Philby's first wife was Lisl Kohlmann, an Austrian lady who was both Jewish and a communist. The ex-Mossad man himself asks the question, 'Did Philby perhaps secretly serve the interests of Israel too – was he in this bizarre way a double agent?'

In any case, the British spy refused the offer of help in smuggling him out of Lebanon which Mossad had so painstakingly transmitted. 'No,' he replied. 'You obviously know all about me and consequently I can well imagine who sent you. You may tell them that I shall not forget it. For the rest, I prefer to rely on my own friends.' Later on, Mossad went to the trouble of tracing out the escape route organized by the KGB when Philby fled from Beirut to the Soviet Union in January 1963. According to their information he simply took a taxi

134

to Damascus, then under the protection of pro-Soviet Kurdish rebels, and was smuggled through northern Iraq to the village of Dogubayazit, where he was taken over by KGB agents for the rest of the journey into the Soviet Union.

One interpretation of Mossad's interest in offering help to Kim Philby at a critical moment in his devious career is that he had some time earlier done them a favour, possibly acting as their channel to the Soviet state security organs. Psychologically the master traitor was greatly affected by dislike of his father St John Philby, also a secret agent, and a convinced romantic Arabist in the tradition of his friend T. E. Lawrence. The fact that St John Philby was also an extreme right-winger who voiced pro-Nazi and anti-semitic opinions strongly influenced Kim Philby in his conversion to Soviet communism. It is by no means impossible that the family quarrel might have prejudiced Kim in favour of Israel, to the extent that in order to spite his father he was ready to do favours for the hated Mossad. While he worked as a foreign correspondent in the Middle East, an area he knew extremely well, Kim Philby could easily have had opportunities to be in touch with the Israeli service.

Other indications of the KGB's ability to obtain secret information by way of Israeli secret service connections emerged in the wake of the Pollard affair, when American officials were assessing the harmful effects of his espionage for Israel within the US intelligence community. A spokesman for the US Justice Department claimed in 1988 that sensitive information provided by Jonathan Pollard, including weapons technology and strategic information about the defences of Turkey, Pakistan and the moderate Arab countries, including Saudi Arabia, had reached the Soviet organs. If that were so, the implication was that it must have been transmitted by a mole within Israeli intelligence.

The other explanation, favoured by American analysts, was that secret information had been offered to the Russians as part of a bargain to persuade them to release more Soviet Jews and allow them to emigrate. Certainly it may be imagined that Mossad would not worry too much about betraying the defence secrets of Arab states.

135

18. The CIA Alliance

Successive Mossad chiefs have pinned their faith on the development of strong intelligence links with friendly countries, and in particular with the United States. Over the years, arrangements both public and secret have ensured close cooperation between Mossad and its military relation, Aman, with a variety of US agencies including the CIA, the FBI, the Defence Intelligence Agency, the National Security Agency, the foreign technology division and the foreign science and technology centre. Nor do they neglect other countries capable of supplying their needs. The French counter-intelligence unit, the DST (Direction de la Surveillance du Territoire), gave the benefit of its experience in surveillance to Shin Beth as well as to Mossad.

On the American side the founder of this significant intelligence alliance was James Jesus Angleton, a lean and rangy introvert with a natural taste for the art of espionage. When he was working in Europe during the Second World War for the newly formed Office of Strategic Services – the forerunner of the CIA – he made contact with Jewish underground leaders in London. Later, while based in Rome, where he plotted to keep postwar Italy out of communist hands, he also worked with clandestine Jewish operators who were later to be among the first senior officers of the intelligence service of the new state of Israel. In 1945 the OSS was disbanded but, when it was replaced by the CIA, Angleton became a man of power in the new agency. He served as chief of the counter-intelligence staff, and it was in this capacity that he renewed contact with his former Israeli friends and became the pillar of close cooperation between the US and Israeli intelligence services. His passionate interest in counter-espionage was based on firm belief in

136

the great worldwide KGB plot, and he was convinced that Israel, many of whose citizens had first-hand experience of life under the Russian heel, would be valuable allies if he played his cards right.

His friendship with Mossad was amply repaid by the great break given to the CIA in April 1956. Mossad contrived to get its hands on documents from the Soviet Union with the exact text of Khrushchev's secret speech to the 20th Party Conference, in which the Kremlin boss for the first time revealed to the party leaders some of the details of Stalin's misdemeanours and crimes. For a time only digests of the speech were available in the West, and frantic attempts were made by every spy in the business to get more details. Allen Dulles, the head of the CIA, was particularly keen to have sight of the entire speech. Exactly how the Mossad network in Europe managed to procure the Khrushchev speech has never been revealed, but it was hinted that it had come their way through an Eastern bloc diplomat who had agreed to sell a copy. Of course, the temptation was for Mossad's boss, Isser Harel, to hand this rich propaganda prize to his own government so that it could startle the world by announcing a great coup. But eventually it was decided that the more rewarding course of action would be to pass the document on to the United States. It was a most useful bargaining counter, and from this deal the Israelis gained an arrangement which allowed them access to material which was only available through the CIA. Mossad had every reason to hope that this profitable two-way trade with the Americans might be expanded.

In 1957 Angleton created a special CIA liaison unit to deal with Mossad, which had responsibility for getting Middle East intelligence on behalf of both countries. As the cold war developed, the Americans were grateful to give help to Israel in return for valuable material provided by Mossad's material from the Soviet Union. Within a few years the two governments had made a formal agreement to exchange secrets. The CIA and the Federal Bureau of Investigation also undertook to supply the Israelis with top-secret equipment, including advanced computers for cryptanalysis, and to instruct a number of Israeli officers in their use.

But Angleton had made many enemies in the CIA, where his great power inspired jealousy, while younger men in the agency began to regard him as a bit of an eccentric leftover. One of his main rivals was William Colby, and when Colby became director of the agency in 1974 he relieved Angleton of his counter-intelligence command and dismissed him. The Israeli desk he had created was abolished, and responsibility for affairs in that country was handed to the regional directorate of the agency. For a while the CIA distanced itself from Mossad, even setting up its own independent operations on the West Bank.

As the oil crisis deepened and the US became more conscious of western economic dependency upon Middle East oil, the CIA found it necessary after 1975 to strengthen links with the Arab states. Saudi Arabia's friendship had to be cultivated because its oil resources were of such importance and because it was a rich market for the export of weapons and technology. Cairo was again becoming a focus of diplomatic activity as President Sadat, who had come to power with American help, adopted a more moderate line. The Americans began to hope for a peace settlement in the Middle East. To discourage further Arab attempts at making war against Israel, the Americans put about information confirming their view of the military superiority of that country. Information was allowed to circulate about Israeli nuclear weapons.

The Watergate scandal had its repercussions on Israeli thinking and led to suspicions about US security. Mossad, not much worried about the moral uproar it created, came to the realistic conclusion that the cosy arrangement with the CIA was threatened by the lack of confidentiality which had been revealed by public investigations into the comportment of the US intelligence services. As a precaution, Mossad became more cautious about taking the Americans into its confidence on the subject of secret operations and deals. Meir Amit explained it in these terms: 'After Watergate, the whole US secret service was dragged into the limelight. In our line of business you can only work with those who are prepared to guarantee a certain degree of secrecy. If we had passed information to the CIA in 1976, we might just as well have held a press conference.'

On an official visit to Washington in July 1977, Menachem Begin presented President Carter with a file of useful and important data which over the years had been passed to the CIA by Mossad. The new prime minister was very proud of this list of offerings, many of which he had only just learned about himself after coming in from the cold at the end of a long period in opposition. The old Mossad agent made this gesture in order to dramatize the extent of cooperation between the two secret services, and the hope was expressed that the cooling off in intelligence relations would not last for long. The Jewish lobby in the USA exerted its influence to make sure that Israel continued to enjoy strong support from the transatlantic ally. Besides that, the Israelis had a great deal to offer in the way of intelligence assets. Constantly in action against the surrounding Arab states, who were provided with the very latest military equipment made in the USSR, the Israeli army was in a position to offer detailed information gleaned from close examination of military items captured in battle. When I interviewed General Yitzhak Hofi at his headquarters just after the Yom Kippur

138

ceasefire, he threw on the table a Russian T-72 tank manual and jokingly asked, 'How would you like a copy of that?' When I replied that it was not much good to me, he said, 'I know a lot of people who would like to get their hands on it.' If the bargaining price was right, Israeli military intelligence was ready to give American technicians access to captured weapon systems. In return they were supplied with data analysis on performance, which the Americans with their superior electronic systems could provide.

After the 1967 Six Day War and again after the Yom Kippur campaign in 1973 Israel furnished the United States with examples of new Soviet missiles, both air-to-ground and ground-to-air. Anti-tank weapons and heavy artillery pieces were also shipped across the Atlantic for detailed tests and evaluation. American military planners were particularly grateful to get their hands on the T-72 tank used by Syria and Egypt in the 1973 war. They discovered, for example, that it had been fitted with special filters for defence against germ warfare. The volume of analysis later produced was put to good use in the development of US weapons and tactics.

Strings were attached to all the deals made between Israeli and American intelligence. Hard bargains were struck to ensure that when captured weapons were shipped to the United States Israeli experts had to go with them, ready to glean the fruits of detailed American research. Mossad harboured deep suspicions about the reliability of the intelligence services of some NATO countries and placed an embargo on America passing on certain sensitive data to her allies. At headquarters in Tel Aviv, the fear was that Soviet agents had penetrated the Western military establishment and might pass on to their Arab allies detailed information about the extent of Israeli knowledge of their equipment and tactics.

In 1983 the US administration began to fear that Israeli offers of deeper cooperation would trap America into long-term dependency on Israeli sources. Matters came to a head when Menachem Begin, then prime minister, offered to share high-grade military information gained in fighting the Syrian air force during the 1983 invasion of Lebanon. Begin claimed that an Israeli invention had enabled the defence forces to destroy Soviet-made surface-to-air missiles, and said that he was prepared to offer this secret weapon to the United States. Caspar Weinberger, the secretary of defence, feared that the deal would involve dangerous new commitments to supporting the Israeli cause; and it was claimed that the USA already possessed the knowledge to cope with the missiles anyway. But the flow of information soon resumed. As Syria showed signs of escalating its intervention in Lebanon to counteract the Israeli invasion and the situation there became more desperate, the National Security Agency, whose intelligence information from the Middle East is very high grade, recommended a 'tilt' towards Israel.

What Israel most needed was a supply of data which could only come from reconnaissance satellites operated by the Americans. Although Mossad and the other Israeli agencies are second to none in acquiring human intelligence about their neighbours in the Middle East, a small state such as Israel could not afford to provide its intelligence people with the expensive luxury of spies in the sky. In return for services rendered in other fields, the Israeli government succeeded in persuading William Casey, who took over as director of the CIA in 1981, to provide photographs and reconnaissance information from satellites in outer space. President Carter's intelligence chief, Admiral Stansfield Turner, had discontinued the earlier practice of letting the Israelis have access to such material. But by 1984 Major General Yehoshua Saguy, head of Aman, claimed that the CIA was providing such data, 'not only the information but the photographs themselves'. Israel also benefited from photographs and reconnaissance material obtained by high-altitude flights over the Middle East made from Cyprus by American SR-71 spy planes. They were supplied with the intention of reducing the risk of a fresh round in the Arab-Israeli wars by providing advance information about warlike preparations.

William Casey, the new man at the CIA, was, like James Angleton, a veteran of the OSS. He was a close friend of President Reagan, and a man in a good position to help his Israeli friends. In the Israeli intelligence community, they soon began to speak of the satellite information being provided by the USA as 'Casey's gift'. The trouble about providing Aman and Mossad with such material was that the Americans could never be quite sure to what use it might be put. It was one thing to help their Middle Eastern ally to defend itself against Arab aggression, but quite another to provide advance intelligence which enabled them to target such Arab countries in pre-emptive raids. This is what happened when American reconnaissance photographs were used by the Israeli air force in making its operational plans for the attack upon Iraq's nuclear reactor. As a result of that misuse of material becoming known the Americans tried to restrict access to their intelligence information and to make a clear distinction between defensive purposes, to protect the frontiers of Israel, and offensive purposes, to plan aggressive attacks. Although the USA was prepared to offer material about war preparations in hostile Arab states, it did not normally hand over material about the deployment of the armed forces of Jordan and Egypt. After all, they were allies of the Americans.

Ideally, the intelligence chiefs in Tel Aviv and Jerusalem would have liked a spy satellite of their own, launched by, and preferably paid for, by the Americans. That possibility having failed they often tried to persuade the American administration that they should at least have direct access to the special US satellite as it passed over the Middle East transmitting its findings.

One factor remained permanent in the relationship between Israeli and American intelligence, and that was that Mossad and its sister services always wanted more. It would be a mistake, however, to draw the conclusion that this was a totally one-sided business. In a number of ways America benefited, too. Mossad passed on various titbits about eastern Europe and the Soviet bloc. Jewish emigrés arriving annually in varying numbers from the Soviet Union were all debriefed on arrival in the promised land. Material derived from these Mossad interviews, although not sensational, was useful in helping to build an up-to-date picture of life in the communist superpower. Numerous examples have also come to light of Israeli cooperation in support of US covert operations in various parts of the world. Captured Soviet-made military equipment has been recycled to supply various anti-communist groups fighting guerrilla wars in countries as far apart as Afghanistan and Central America. Israel also constantly sought to strengthen her influence in Africa, and was able to provide helpful information on that continent to the North American ally.

It is in the nature of things that Mossad should be best informed about affairs in its own home region, the Middle East. There can be no doubt that Washington has often had cause to be grateful for timely warnings about forthcoming events in that troubled part of the world. In particular, Mossad's unrivalled knowledge of the Palestinian terrorist groups was placed at the disposal of American agencies combating terrorism. In 1985, when a Palestinian group seized the Italian cruise liner *Achille Lauro*, it was Mossad which reported the ship's position after the murder of an American passenger on board. Even more useful was the Institute's tip-off about the EgyptAir plane which was flying the pirates back to Tunis after they had left the liner. Seconds after the plane took off the Israelis supplied details of its call signs and route. American sources had lost track of the Palestinian terror group until that point, and it was the Mossad intelligence which enabled them to scramble fighter aircraft from the Sixth Fleet which forced the EgyptAir flight to land at a NATO base in Sicily and led to the arrest of the group's leader.

Every Western intelligence agency is indebted to Mossad for help in identifying the networks of Arab terrorists in the Middle East and in Europe. The success of Israeli agents in infiltrating the terror bands and analyzing their tactics inspired the work of British and French services as well as the American ones. To a great extent too the Israeli philosophy of how to deal with the terrorist threat has made its mark on foreign security and intelligence people. American thinking was influenced by the words as well as by the deeds of Mossad. This was demonstrated when George Shultz, then US secretary of state, made a public statement in June 1984 advocating the creation of specialized intelligence networks to help with military retaliation against terrorists.

A purely passive defence does not provide enough of a deterrent to terrorism and the states that sponsor it. It is time to think long, hard and seriously about more active means of defence – about defence through appropriate preventive or pre-emptive actions against terrorist groups before they strike. We will need to strengthen our capabilities in the area of intelligence and quick reaction. Human intelligence will be particularly important, since our societies demand that we know with reasonable clarity just what we are doing. Experience has taught us over the years that one of the best deterrents to terrorism is the certainty that swift and sure measures will be taken against those who engage in it.

That view, put forward at a conference arranged by the Jonathan Institute, which was established by Israel for the study of terrorism and named in honour of the hero of the Entebbe raid, mirrored the Israeli view on such matters. The strategy of Zionist decision makers in combating terrorism stresses the importance of reprisals based on first-class intelligence.

Precedents set by the Israelis led to dangerous side-effects when they became part of official American doctrine. The dealing which followed the hijacking of a TWA airliner to Beirut in 1986 is a case in point. American opinion was particularly incensed at news of the murder by the Hizbollah terrorists of a US navy diver who was a passenger on board the aircraft. Israel was involved in subsequent negotiations, because the hijackers had demanded the release of prisoners held in that country. Despite the hard line advocated publicly by both the Americans and the Israelis, negotiations did take place, and after the unfortunate passengers had been released prisoners were freed. It was not the first time that Israeli agents had bargained with terrorists. Although they condemn such practices in public, deals are arranged.

After the TWA affair, when attention focussed on the fate of American and British hostages held in Beirut by Hizbollah and other ultra

Shi'ite organizations, Terry Waite, the Archbishop of Canterbury's representative, attempted to make contact with the kidnappers and then he too fell victim to them. Oliver North, who was also in touch with Waite, was himself trying to get in touch with Iranians in Lebanon. In such moves they were following in the footsteps of Mossad agents who had trodden the path before them, though more effectively. It was because the American aims were less well defined and their experience of bargaining in the world of Islam less sure that they found themselves in trouble when negotiating with the Iranian revolutionaries.

Israeli intelligence set a bad example by taking part in secret arms dealing with Iran. Undercover arms salesmen began by selling 259 spare tyres for American-made jet fighters in 1980. In the following years they sold $60 million dollars' worth of arms. Only when one of their foreign chartered aircraft went missing on a flight from Cyprus to Tehran did it become known that this was just one of twelve planeloads of tank parts and ammunition from Israel to fuel Iran's war against Iraq. Such deals were only part of Mossad's clandestine commercial effort.

In many areas of the world, where the CIA moved out, Mossad jumped in. The Israelis did not allow themselves the luxury of moral pangs about the wickedness of dealing with dictators, opportunist generals or least-favoured regimes. So long as it was considered in the national interest to do deals with them, Mossad was happy enough to arrange the supply of weapons to anyone prepared to pay, with the further proviso that the deals remained secret.

For example, Israel ignored the UN boycott on arms to South Africa and delivered six warships to the Pretoria government. They also sold Chieftain and Centurion tanks as well as mortars and Gabriel rockets. Such deals were arranged through the Koor company in Tel Aviv and its subsidiaries, Tadiran, Iskoor and Telkoor. And until 1978 Meir Amit, the former head of Mossad, served as general manager of these huge conglomerates. In return Israel got uranium from South Africa, and it has even been claimed that permission was given to use test sites in the Kalahari Desert. Such deals displeased the Americans.

It became common practice for Israel to jump in and supply weapons to countries being boycotted by the Americans, as when they shipped Safir air-to-air missiles to Chile in 1976. When the USA, pursuing a policy of reconciliation with China, decided to stop supplies of offensive weapons to Taiwan in 1978, Israel sold them fifty Kfir fighter bombers. It was Mossad which helped to make the arrangements. In the same year, when President Carter abandoned support for Samosa in Nicaragua, Israel filled the gap and supplied him with Uzi automatic weapons and army trucks, thereby helping to prolong the civil war. By selling weapons to such countries, Israel, ignoring American protests,

143

created a sort of alliance of outcasts. During the 1970s arms exports tripled and arms dealing became one of the most important industrial activities in the country. Officers of Mossad and Lekem, the scientific information-gathering service, figured prominently among those who made the arrangements for such deals. This was simply one aspect of their extra-intelligence duties – the intelligence man as arms dealer.

Part VI
Mossad Goes Nuclear

19. *Lechaim* Lekem

After the KGB, Israeli intelligence ranks high among the national secret services which have devoted much effort to purloining industrial and technical secrets. It was in the 1960s that Shimon Peres, at that time defence minister, established an organization for the collection of scientific and technical intelligence. It developed from what was originally intended to be a nuclear intelligence body established under the leadership of Binyamin Blumberg, an experienced security man, who then became the first head of the innocently named bureau of scientific relations, generally known by the Hebrew acronym Lekem (*Leshkat Kesher Madao*). Officers seconded to the agency were ordered to collect scientific and technical data, particularly those aspects of it related to defence equipment and weapons systems. They were to use both open and hidden sources of information. Many went off to work in foreign countries as scientists or businessmen, while others were seconded as scientific attachés to the staff of Israeli embassies.

Most of the work of this bureau remains secret, but in some cases agents in the field were detected and their activities became known. A notable coup was the success in helping to provide technical information enabling Israel to build its own fighter aircraft. In the air battles of the Six Day War Israel lost 10 per cent of its jet fighters and many more were damaged. There was an urgent need to replace these losses and to get a supply of spare parts for maintenance and repair. This task was made difficult by a Western ban on exports of war material to the Middle East. In particular, President de Gaulle was anxious to register his disapproval of Israeli military adventures by cutting off supplies of Mirage fighter bombers and Mystère fighters, upon which the Israeli air force had relied heavily during the time when France was an eager ally. Although Israel had plans to build its own jet aircraft, they were not sufficiently advanced at that time to fill the gaps.

Attempts were made to get the French to change their mind by offering to provide them with military assessments of their aircraft in real air warfare, but President de Gaulle remained intractable. The next move was an approach to the Swiss government, which had purchased quantities of French warplanes for its own air force. An offer of a down payment of 150 million Swiss francs was made for delivery to Israel of spare parts for engines; but the Swiss turned down this offer because the terms of their purchase agreement with France expressly forbade the resale of aircraft parts.

Fair means had failed to get the tools of war, so less open ones were adopted and the services of Lekem, aided by Mossad, were called upon to obtain the technical information to enable Israel to build its own fighter plane. The agent of this plot was a businesslike amateur Swiss spy, Alfred Frauenknecht, who briskly delivered no less than two tons of blueprints and plans of Switzerland's version of the French-designed Mirage III jet fighter in weekly bundles weighing 110lb. His espionage on the grand scale enabled the Israelis to develop the Kfir fighter aircraft, which became sarcastically known as 'son of Mirage'.

A chief engineer in the fighter division of the Winterthur company Sluzer Brothers, Frauenknecht himself was the one to suggest, after he had been approached by Israeli agents asking him to furnish spare parts for the Mirage squadrons, that he was in a position to pass on the necessary plans of the aircraft instead. The curious feature of the Frauenknecht story is that, while he launched himself into espionage out of sympathy for the Israeli cause, he was not a Jew; he offered help to rid himself of the Teutonic guilt he felt about Nazi persecution of the Jews.

His clever plan for appropriating the blueprints began with a suggestion to his own company that they could save money and storage space by burning plans no longer in current use, once they had been photocopied. He personally took charge of arrangements for destroying them in the municipal incinerator, under the supervision of Swiss security officers. However, between the factory and the incinerator he and his cousin (who acted as driver) stopped for five minutes at a private garage he had hired and stocked with other waste blueprints purchased from the Swiss patent office. The Mirage plans were then stacked in the garage and the old papers were burned under the vigilant eyes of Swiss security, who never bothered to examine them very carefully.

The next stage of the operation involved a mysterious man known as Hans Strecker, transport manager of a company with warehouses at Kaiseraugst on the West German frontier. Strecker was originally introduced as a 'friend' of Colonel Nehemiah Kain, a Mossad agent working in Europe. His task was to collect the cartons of papers in the boot of Frauenknecht's Mercedes and take them into Germany to a small airfield from where they were flown by stages to Italy and then on to Israel. The operation continued undetected for a whole year, and was only revealed when people living near the warehouse mentioned to its owners, the Rotzinger brothers, that a strange man appeared there every Saturday. When the brothers went along to investigate and hailed the man whom they recognized as their employee, he sped off at once, leaving one carton behind, and was never seen again. When the Rotzingers examined the carton they were amazed to find that the papers in it were stamped, 'Top secret. Property of the Swiss military department'.

Swiss security investigated, and arrested Frauenknecht. The engineer, shrewdly aware of what troubles revelation of the Mirage affair would cause to relations between Switzerland and France, boldly offered a deal, saying that in return for his release he would guarantee to keep silent about the whole business and thus prevent a political crisis. The offer was rejected, and eighteen months later he came to trial. Frauenknecht made no attempt to deny that he had stolen the blueprints and handed them over to Israeli agents. Nor would he express any regret for his actions – declaring, indeed, that he had good reasons for deciding to aid Israel. The court convicted him in April 1971 of industrial espionage and violation of Swiss military security; the sentence was four and a half years' imprisonment. After his release in 1975, Frauenknecht visited Israel for the first time. He received no kind of official welcome in recognition of his important role in helping to provide Israel with the Kfir fighter which had proved so valuable in the Yom Kippur War; had the Israelis put out the flags to express their appreciation, they would have been forced to admit publicly that they were responsible for espionage operations carried out in the territory of neutral Switzerland. Although Israel would willingly have paid vastly more at the time for fighter planes, Alfred Frauenknecht asked only for $200,000 (£85,000 at the time) as a kind of insurance policy to make certain that, if he were discovered, his wife would be provided for.

In this affair Lekem proved its worth as an adjunct of the secret services, with which it cooperated closely. Although it may be taken for granted that it can claim many successes in gathering scientific and technological information, it managed to preserve a remarkable hull-down posture until the Pollard affair in America. That was probably because the service operated discreetly and with a fair amount of cooperation from Western defence industries. However, when one of its units working in the USA overstepped the mark a major public scandal did erupt. As a result of the row which followed Lekem was officially dissolved, but its work goes marching on. The ministry of defence, aided by colleagues from the science and technology ministry, continue their search for new and better weapons systems in collaboration with Mossad. Mossad itself has a long record of activity in espionage and special operations planned to improve the nation's defence capability. One important field of activity was bringing the military up-to-date with information about the latest weapons being supplied to the Arab powers by the Soviet Union.

Shortly after Meir Amit became head of Mossad, he received a specific request from General Mordechai Hod, commander of the air force. The general wanted the Institute to get for him a Mig-21 fighter, so that its performance could be properly evaluated. Eli Cohen had provided a photograph of the new aircraft but that did not satisfy the air force's curiosity, for at that time the Mig-21 was the most up-to-date and formidable of Russian jet fighters. The Russian warplane was in service in Egypt, Iraq and Syria and the air commanders in Israel were most anxious to have detailed information about its characteristics and capability. They knew neither its speed, armament, nor anything of its electronic counter-measures equipment, and knowledge of all these things was needed for successful prosecution of the air war. Under such pressure from the air force to supply the necessary information, Mossad headquarters contrived various elaborate plots to obtain a Mig. The specialists came to the conclusion that the best hope of success was to persuade an Arab pilot to defect, bringing his fighter with him.

The squadron leader chosen was an Iraqi officer, Munir Redfa, the son of a prosperous Maronite Christian family living in Baghdad and not entirely happy with life under the Iraqi regime. After long and careful approaches from Mossad agents who visited the Arab country in the guise of businessmen, Redfa agreed to fly out his Mig in return for half a million pounds and a guarantee that his wife and child, together with his entire family, including parents, grandparents, aunts and uncles, would first be smuggled abroad.

This latter demand made an immensely dangerous business even more complicated. Spurred on by the urgency of getting a Mig and to confirm his own position as undisputed master of Mossad, Meir Amit committed most of his clandestine teams. He also called in reinforcements from Aman, the military intelligence service. In order to evacuate Redfa's extended family it was necessary to have agents

150

in Kurdistan, to seek help from Kurdish rebels, and in Iran, where the family was to be taken by helicopter (an operation eventually carried out successfully). Further outside assistance was also needed and Amit himself flew to Washington in order to get support from the CIA, which was equally anxious to acquire detailed knowledge about the Mig-21. An American diplomat in Baghdad was persuaded to speak to Redfa and assure him that it was of vital importance for the whole Western alliance, as well as for Israel, to know the secrets of the Mig.

It was this argument which finally persuaded the young air force officer. In August 1966 he took off with full tanks from the air base near Mosul in northern Iraq on a training mission. Once airborne, he headed for Turkey, where US air force Phantoms waited to escort him to a covert CIA base. Having refuelled there, the Iraqi pilot flew out over the Mediterranean to rendezvous with Israeli fighters which escorted him to Israel. The operation was a classic of high-risk military espionage carried out with dash and vigour. It was precisely the kind of thing which gave Mossad its high reputation for doing things which other intelligence services would have hesitated even to try.

Veterans in the service still look back with pride to the high old days of the sixties when nothing seemed impossible, and adventure after adventure ended in triumph. Three years after the Mig capture, the Institute was again called upon to provide equipment for the IDF, this time for the navy, the most neglected branch of the armed forces, still making do with ancient warships left over from the Second World War. The navy needed fast missile-firing patrol boats and commissioned the building of eight such vessels in a West German yard. Under Arab pressure to stop supplying weapons, the Germans withdrew from the contract and the order to finish them off was transferred to shipbuilders in the French port of Cherbourg. Although in 1969 the French president was still marking his disapproval of Israeli policy by an arms embargo, the patrol boats escaped the ban on the grounds that they would not sail with military equipment.

A permit had already been issued for one of them to sail when an event took place in the Middle East which decided the French president to strengthen his resolve not to sell arms of any kind to Israel. On 28 December, Israeli commandos made a helicopter-borne reprisal raid upon Beirut airport and destroyed thirteen MEA airliners on the ground. The French government promptly ordered the detention of the warships at Cherbourg. One week later skeleton crews sneaked aboard three missile boats which were almost completed and in three busy hours prepared them for sailing, warmed up the engines and, flying the Star of David flag, headed out to sea. The five left behind awaiting completion were

151

put under tighter security and moved out of the naval dockyard.

Israel was still determined to get these vessels, so badly needed by
the navy. Accustomed to dangerous missions against the Palestinians
in Beirut, the military and some wilder elements of special operations
were quite ready to take on the French. There was even talk of grabbing
the remaining 'gunboats', as they were now called, by a *coup de main*.
Cooler counsels prevailed and Mossad, with the help of military intelligence, began formulating a more rational plot to be carried out by a
special unit working under the codename Operation Noah's Ark.

As a preliminary move Admiral Mordechai Limon, who headed
the purchasing mission in France, began talks about the complicated
question of compensation for non-completion of work on the warships.
This ensured that in the meantime Israeli technicians who had designed
the boats could stay on in Cherbourg until work was completed, ready
for their sale elsewhere. To convince the French authorities of their
intention to sell off the warships Mossad made complicated arrangements. Martin Siem, director of the Norwegian shipping company
Starboat, acting as a front man for the Israelis, arrived at Cherbourg
and declared that he was interested in buying the vessels as soon as
possible for use in oil exploration work. Unlikely though it seemed that
such obvious warships might be used in that role, the sale won approval from the appropriate French committee controlling the export of
war materials. Had they checked more carefully the authorities might
have discovered that Starboat, a 'Norwegian' company registered in
Panama, had been in fact set up by Maritime Fruit, Israel's biggest
shipping company.

The plan was for French and Norwegian sailors to take possession
of the ships on behalf of the new company. To complete the illusion
sixty Israeli sailors, vaguely Gallic or Nordic in appearance, had to be
rounded up and smuggled into Cherbourg ready to crew the boats for a
dash out into the Channel if the ploy succeeded. Herded like sheep by
Mossad and military intelligence people, young national servicemen
were transmitted to Cherbourg in small groups and lodged discreetly
in hotels there just before Christmas 1969. They must have been the
first quasi-secret agents in the history of espionage to arrive equipped
with slips of paper instructing them precisely where to go.

Christmas had been carefully chosen as a time when French vigilance
would be at its lowest ebb, and to give the reassuring impression that
the original Israelis, already familiar figures in the town, were in holiday mood also, a group of officers ostentatiously booked a large table
for dinner at the Café du Théâtre. Finally, all was ready. On Christmas
Day the five captains simultaneously started up their engines and the

152

'gunboats of Cherbourg' roared out into a Channel gale on the first stage of the voyage to Israel. On the way they were refuelled at sea by tankers of the Maritime Fruit Company stationed along the route. As Georges Pompidou, who replaced General de Gaulle as president of France, felt compelled to admit, 'We have been made to look complete fools because of the incredible casualness and intellectual complicity of our civil servants.' Here was a completely successful, non-violent Mossad operation in which it had outwitted the opposition by stealth and low cunning.

Within two days the Institute again displayed its versatility, this time by organizing a commando raid in Egypt. A special forces team under its direction landed at the Red Sea naval base of Ras Ghaleb and, after overcoming resistance from the guards, took to pieces a seven-ton state-of-the-art radar system. It was loaded on board the helicopters and flown back to Israel. The radar, designed to pick up at long range the movements of aircraft operating from Israeli bases in Sinai, had provided early warning coverage for the Egyptian defence system.

20. Rogue Operation

Under the astonished eyes of carloads of FBI watchers, Jonathan Jay Pollard drove his green Mustang through the gates of the Israeli embassy in Washington one afternoon in November 1984. With him were his wife and the family cat, Dusty. He shouted to the security guards, 'I am an Israeli spy.'

That was the beginning of the end of a most bizarre story in the history of Israeli espionage. It became an affair which shook to its roots the close relationship between the USA and Israel. Pollard was a 'walk-in' agent, a volunteer amateur spy. An American Jew, he was an intellectual fantasist who had already falsely boasted to friends that he was something high up in Mossad long before he had had any contact at all with Israeli intelligence. He had worked for various US naval intelligence agencies, and in 1979 he had been posted to Washington as an analyst in the US navy intelligence office.

This well-educated and capable man identified himself with the triumphs and sorrows of Israel, admired her heroes and wanted to do his bit for the country. Finally his chance came when an influential relation in New York spoke enthusiastically to him about his encounter with a real live Israeli hero, Colonel Aviem Sella, an ace pilot who had flown to Baghdad with the squadron which destroyed the Iraqi nuclear reactor. The colonel, who was on a fund-raising mission in the United States, had also spoken of his part in the air battles over Lebanon during the invasion of that country; in these operations the air force had practically wiped out the Syrian Mig fighter squadrons. Such tales of skill and daring inspired Pollard, who contrived an introduction to the dashing air force commander and promptly offered

154

to supply Israel with secret files to which he had access through his intelligence work.

Colonel Sella, a fighting airman with little experience of espionage operations, reported the offer to his country's intelligence agencies. Mossad already knew something about Pollard, and his name figured in their dossiers. Its people in Washington had their suspicions about him, no doubt on the grounds that he was a strange personality given to boasting, and for that reason they felt reluctant to take up his offer. Like all professionals in espionage, they were naturally suspicious about volunteers and feared that this one in particular might lead their agents into a trap set up by the CIA to discover whether Mossad was probing in friendly territory. A further reason for hesitation was that Mossad ground rules discouraged the recruitment of diaspora Jews because of the harmful effect that their discovery might have on their coreligionists.

The Institute's view was not shared by a segment of its fellow service Lekem, the bureau established to furnish the ministry of defence with scientific material, usually gathered openly, but obtained covertly when necessary. Lekem had representatives working in Israeli consulates in New York, Boston and Los Angeles. Joseph Yagur, a scientific attaché, was its man in the New York consulate; he was consulted about Pollard's approach and reported back to headquarters in Tel Aviv. This report attracted the attention of Rafael Eitan, now head of Lekem, a former deputy chief of operations with Mossad who after nearly twenty years' service with it had been eased out of that organization. Known in Israel as 'Rafi the Stinker', he was a close friend of Begin and General Ariel Sharon, a powerful figure in the councils of the ruling party Likud during Menachem Begin's premiership. In that time he was appointed as adviser on counter-terrorism in the prime minister's office. In his other capacity as boss of Lekem, Eitan was riding high because of recent successes in acquiring scientific data. Seeing the arrival on the scene of Pollard as an opportunity to display again his skills as a spy chief, Eitan used his influence in high places to get authorization for Colonel Sella to sound out the possible American source further at a private meeting.

When they did get together, Pollard renewed his offer to provide secret information and Colonel Sella gave him some basic instruction in the use of contact calls by way of public telephones and suggested a primitive code using letters of the Hebrew alphabet. Joseph Yagur from the New York consulate was to be Pollard's handler. But Rafael Eitan wanted to meet the new agent himself, and arranged for Jonathan Pollard and his wife to make a trip to Europe in 1984 where a first meeting took place in Paris. The trip was, of course, paid for by the Israelis who had also insisted, as all intelligence services do, on binding the spy more tightly to them by insisting that he should accept payment for his services. In case anyone noticed that the new friend was spending more money than usual, there was talk of a rich uncle in France. Reluctantly at first, Jonathan Pollard accepted payment of $30,000 a year to be paid into a Swiss bank account. His wife Anne soon began to take advantage of the family's new-found wealth to indulge in shopping expeditions.

Back in the United States Jonathan Pollard started taking out stacks of secret papers, many of them specifically ordered on instructions from Tel Aviv by title and document number. Without too much bother, he was able to extract papers which, he said, were important for his many tasks in naval intelligence, although at that time in his American role he was mainly concerned with terrorism and counter-terrorism. His Israeli masters, indeed, had to curb his enthusiasm by telling him not to bother about terrorist stuff. The controllers were avid for material about progress towards an Arab nuclear weapon and the location of factories in Iraq and Syria producing the materials for chemical warfare. Israel has always feared that Arab enemies might acquire the capability to launch nuclear and chemical weapons against them, a development they first began to dread when Colonel Nasser's Egypt recruited German scientists in the 1950s.

The Pollards made another trip to Europe and also visited Israel for more consultation with Rafael Eitan in July 1985. Two months later Jonathan procured from another US agency detailed information about the air defence systems of Libya, Tunisia and Algeria, data which the Israelis needed for the preparation of contingency plans for a retribution raid which might be necessary following a terrorist incident. He also supplied details about the movements of Soviet, French and US ships in the Mediterranean.

The occasion to make use of the fruits of his espionage arose fairly promptly in September, when Israel decided to take revenge for the Palestinian raid on Larnaca in Cyprus in which two Arab gunmen and a British recruit to Force 17 of the PLO seized an Israeli yacht in the marina there and murdered three Israeli citizens. A week later, eight F-16s of the Israeli air force flew a long-range mission across the Mediterranean to strike at Yasser Arafat's PLO headquarters at Hammam beach just outside Tunis, killing sixty people including Mohammed Natour, commander of Force 17. All the aircraft returned safely, and the success of their mission was partly due to information, gleaned by American agents and US satellite pictures pinpointing the HQ and their air defences, which had been provided by Jonathan Pollard.

The zealous agent in the United States redoubled his efforts to search out quantities of top-secret documents. He blatantly took out of the security area where he worked whole piles of material. The arrangement was that he then drove to an apartment block, leaving his hoard with Irit Erb, secretary to the scientific attaché at the Israeli embassy. She took them to a safe apartment in the same block rented secretly and equipped with special photocopy equipment capable of handling satellite photographs as well as other secret documents. Pollard collected the papers afterwards and returned them to source. Eventually Lekem had a whole team at work processing this harvest of secrets. And a new handler took him over – a mysterious personage named Uzi, whose true identity has never been revealed. He was described as an Israeli arms merchant in the USA who had sold weapons to Iran during the Irangate scandal.

By this time Jonathan Pollard was acting as a one-man agency for recycling the fruits of American intelligence gathering direct to Mossad. He had become reckless in his pursuit of secrets, and his movements began to attract the attention of a colleague who saw him leaving the office compound bearing obviously and specially marked sensitive communications documents. Jerry Agee, his boss, did not like Pollard very much and became suspicious. Checking through the quantities of files which Pollard had abstracted, he discovered that among them were papers on Soviet weapons systems and Arab military capabilities which seemed to have nothing to do with the work which Pollard was paid to do for the American navy. After a great deal of worry and circumspection, Agee decided in his own mind that the only explanation for Pollard's conduct was that he was spying for some other country. Eventually, he decided to inform security and the FBI. Using a concealed video camera they kept watch on Pollard in his office as he sorted out papers, checking them against what appeared to be a spy's shopping list, before confronting and questioning him. Not yet under arrest, he was allowed to telephone his wife to tell her he was delayed at the office. In the conversation he used the word 'cactus', which it turned out later was a prearranged code word to indicate that he was in trouble.

This was a critical moment in the whole business. That evening the Pollards had a date to dine with Colonel Sella who was again in Washington, this time with his wife. In a panic, Anne Pollard telephoned the colonel and had a brief meeting with him. Late at night Sella was suddenly confronted with an emergency. He had no diplomatic immunity and realized that he was now in danger of being arrested as a spy. There was only one thing to do – get out of the United States quickly. There were no more flights abroad out of Washington, so Sella and his wife

157

drove in a hired car to New York and took an early morning flight to London, using false passports.

Joseph Yagur at the consulate in New York had also been alerted, but there was little that he could do to help. In professional style, Mossad always had plans ready for the rescue of any of its agents in trouble. But this operation was being run by outsiders and by Lekem, which had apparently failed to make any arrangements to come to the aid of their man once he was in trouble. *Sauve qui peut* was the cry which went up among the Israeli diplomats involved in running Pollard, as Joseph Yagur, Irit Erb and Ilar Ravid, another Israeli scientific officer compromised in the affair, hastily left the country, diplomatic immunity or not.

Jonathan Pollard, unaware of these happenings, was also in a panic, although he had been assured that a grateful Israel, for love of which he had accomplished so much, would look after him. He had stalled his interrogators by assuring them that he had not spied against the USA and had no desire to harm America. They were reluctant to arrest him for lack of the kind of hard evidence which would be needed if he were to be charged and brought to trial, although he was kept under surveillance by a team of FBI men in cars. Not knowing what to do, he and his wife packed their bags, gathered up the cat and drove by a circuitous route towards the blue star flag which marked the Israeli embassy, and finally entered its drive, hard behind a diplomatic car. Under the surprised eyes of the FBI watchers, he began talking to a security guard. That official was under strict orders to tell Pollard simply: 'Get out.' Israel had no wish to be contaminated by the presence on embassy soil of a caught-out spy. And so Jonathan Pollard drove out again through the gates, where he was promptly arrested.

In Jerusalem, the panic was as great as that among the Israeli diplomats in the United States who had made a run for it. The first moves were designed to play for time as the Israeli intelligence community went into deep and silent cover. While a damage control operation was being mounted, nasty signs of mutual recrimination between the different secret services began to emerge. Mossad itself put the blame upon the amateurish management of the Pollard operation, and some of its people gave the impression that if the whole thing had been left to them this ugly situation would never have happened. In due course Jonathan Pollard had some sharp words of reproach for Rafael 'Rafi' Eitan. Later he told Wolf Blitzer of the *Jerusalem Post*, 'The quality of tradecraft exhibited by Rafi in this affair was less than poor – it was criminally irresponsible.' The Israeli foreign ministry spokesman, Aviem Pazner, declared that the government had no knowledge of Pollard. 'We don't have the slightest idea about this matter. We are checking,' was his comment.

In hurt and bewildered tones from Washington, President Reagan asked: 'Why are they doing it?' Shimon Peres, the prime minister, and his foreign minister, Yitzhak Shamir, finding themselves under fire from angry Jewish American leaders, signalled Mr Shulz at the state department that they too had been taken by surprise. They summoned the heads of various agencies to discover what had gone wrong. Mr Eitan came up with a number of strange excuses. The operation, he said, had been launched with the unlikely aim of finding out whether the USA was spying on Israel. He thought that no harm would be done, so long as there was no spying against the security interests of the United States. Rafael Eitan also disingenuously reported that he had assumed that Lekem was authorized to run the operation.

A panel consisting of Avraham Shalom of Shin Beth, Hanan Bar-On, deputy director general of the foreign ministry, and Ram Caspi, a Tel Aviv lawyer friend of Peres, began a hasty official enquiry. In November their report concluded that Pollard was part of a 'rogue intelligence gathering unit', of whose activities the government had been unaware. In Israel, the coalition cabinet formally accepted the enquiry's report and was forced to take overall responsibility for what was undoubtedly a most damaging episode in relations with the United States. The Israeli government also promised to cooperate with US law enforcement agencies and to return the papers which had been misappropriated. By no means did this satisfy the state department, which remained strongly critical of Israel for failing to provide the full and prompt cooperation they had promised in getting to the root of the matter, as formally requested. Mr Peres apologized to Mr Shulz, the secretary of state, and gave an undertaking that such things would not be allowed to happen again; he also said the Lekem unit would be dismantled.

During the long period in which Pollard awaited trial in the USA, a strong American legal delegation visited Israel to conduct investigations on the spot. Led by Abraham Sofaer, state department legal affairs adviser, its members began questioning Rafael Eitan, Yagur, Miss Erb, Ravid and other officials involved. The hearings took place at a country club near Tel Aviv. At this stage, although the part played by Colonel Aviem Sella was mentioned, the actual name did not emerge, for once his role in the affair was on the record it would be impossible to sustain the claim that the operation was unofficial. It was taken for granted that such a high-ranking and well-known officer could not conceivably have engaged in espionage of this importance without the fact becoming known, at least to the air force commander

159

and probably the chief of staff as well. Aviem Sella himself, having been sent abroad to get him out of the way, was not available for questioning. So frustrated was the American legal team in its efforts to uncover the truth that Abraham Sofaer threatened to go back home unless more information was provided.

The then director of the FBI, William Webster, whose officers were investigating the affair in America in preparation for Jonathan Pollard's trial, spoke of 'selective cooperation' by the Israelis. He already had evidence that Israel was lying about its espionage plot. Within a few months, the law enforcement people knew the full scale of the Pollard operation and had also discovered the extent of Colonel Sella's involvement. The Israeli government none the less continued to deny that the espionage affair had been approved by the highest authorities. As the official spokesmen put it: 'It was an unauthorized deviation from the clear-cut Israeli policy of not conducting any espionage in the United States or activities against the interests of the United States, given that the United States is a true friend of Israel.'

This attitude of apparent contrition was undermined by the fact that no sooner was Rafael Eitan dismissed from his positions as head of Lekem and special adviser on terrorism than he was appointed head of the government-owned company Israeli Chemicals. To American eyes this looked like a reward for services rendered. So did the promotion of Colonel Sella to be commander of Israel's second largest air base at Tel Nof, an establishment built with US aid. This was an act which further outraged American opinion. The colonel was forced to resign his new command 'for the sake of Israel and good relations with the US', as he put it, after American personnel had been instructed to boycott the base. Instead he was posted as head of the IDF staff college. On 3 March 1987 the American court indicted Colonel Sella in his absence on three charges of espionage. He was accused of conspiring to deliver information related to the national defence of the USA, causing documents to be delivered, and unlawfully receiving classified information.

Now the Israelis began to realize that they really had gone too far. Before the trial of Jonathan Pollard took place US defence secretary, Caspar Weinberger, in a sworn statement to the court whose contents were kept secret at the time, spoke of the 'significant harm caused to national security' by the defendant. He justified taking this action in these words: 'Because it may not be clear to the court that the defendant's activities have caused damage of the magnitude realized, I felt it necessary to provide an informed analysis to the court so that an appropriate sentence could be fashioned.' He pointed out that intelligence, even when it was disclosed to friendly countries, could still be damaging to United States interests because it might be used for unintended purposes. Such information could expose a larger picture of US capabilities and knowledge – or lack of knowledge – in some areas. In legitimate exchanges of confidential material there was a requirement to protect sources and methods of collection, either by human intelligence agents, or by electronic intercepts or photographic surveillance material. No such guarantees existed when material had been obtained illegally by spying. The defence secretary believed there was a risk that Americans and US combat forces 'could be endangered by successful exploitation of this data'. It had been admitted by Pollard that he had passed a mass of high-grade intelligence material to his Israeli masters; he had given them no fewer than eight hundred classified publications and a thousand classified messages.

A further danger was that, in using secret material for its own purposes, Israel might produce a harmful effect on American foreign policy. An example of this was the data stolen about PLO headquarters in Tunis and about North African radar air defences, which helped the Israeli air force to make its attack there – an action which naturally offended nations in North Africa friendly to the United States. A further disadvantage for the USA was that, because of Pollard, it had lost out in the normal exchange of intelligence with Israel; since Israel had got hold of secrets by foul means there was no reason for it to share information from its side in return. The affair was described as a major setback to US-Israeli intelligence sharing agreements. Jonathan Pollard was sentenced to life imprisonment and his wife Anne to five years as his accomplice.

What worried the Americans most was that documents given to Israel had revealed a good deal about their intelligence collection from identifiable human sources. Certain items of secret material which had fallen into Israeli hands might be traced back to agents in the field, some of whom were probably Arabs who might subsequently be exploited by Mossad and put at risk.

Apart from the obvious and immediate results of raising American hackles and deep suspicions about the widespread nature of Israeli espionage, the Pollard affair had longer-term consequences upon the relationship between Israel and Jews in the diaspora. American Jews were deeply shocked by the revelation that Lekem, by a 'rogue operation' or not, had deliberately stolen defence secrets from the United States. Other communities outside Israel reflected their alarm. Even among Zionists, blind support for the 'homeland' – which had been taken for granted – was now called into question. Since that time there has been stronger criticism of the actions of the Jerusalem government, especially after the beginning of the Arab uprising. Already when the

161

affair broke, doubts had been expressed about Israel's invasion of Lebanon and the involvement of security services in the massacres at Sabra and Chatila. Jews abroad were worried about the controversial issue of military support being given by Israel to South Africa, and yet another bone of contention was Israel's hard-line views on the immigration of Soviet Jews. The Jerusalem government insisted that such people had an obligation to settle in Israel, but this view was challenged by some Jewish leaders in the USA who insisted that they had a right to choose where they wanted to live once they left the Soviet Union.

When the Pollard affair first surfaced, William Safire, the *New York Times* columnist, wrote, 'Jewish Americans feel doubly betrayed. Most of us are offended first as Americans at seeing our foreign aid dollars used to buy US secrets. We are betrayed again by the easy exploitation of Mr Pollard's Zionism by Israeli spymasters blind to the immorality of an inducement to treason and the consequences of being caught.' In the American Jewish community, a majority considered that the security services were reckless and stupid to try to run a spy inside the American intelligence services. A criminal act had been committed against their government, and they felt indignant and apprehensive that their patriotic loyalty to the US administration had been needlessly called into question.

An opinion poll sponsored by CBS News and the *New York Times* in 1987 showed that most Americans believed that the Pollard business would not inflict lasting damage on relations. Among Jews questioned, a resounding majority replied that American Jews did not place the interests of Israel above those of the United States. Common interests between Israel and the USA ensured that the alliance and friendship was able to survive the setback. Even such a grave scandal could not alter the community of interest between two countries which share similar political, economic and strategic aims. But that did not prevent an atmosphere of distrust and suspicion from continuing for some time.

American intelligence officials spoke of other Israeli intelligence operations in the United States and recalled cases where non-Jewish American citizens, prompted by their pro-Israeli sentiments, had passed on secret information. John Davitt, a former head of the justice department's internal security, went so far as to say that 'Israeli intelligence services were more active than anyone but the KGB. . . . They were targeted on the United States about half the time and on Arab countries about half the time.'

In the aftermath of the Pollard affair, the Israelis indulged in yet another bout of introspection about the secret services; this in turn led to demands for further investigation. The fact that all the armed services had given their own shopping lists to Pollard meant that many people must have known what was going on. If, as was claimed, Mossad was not running this spy, it must be assumed that the service had displayed less than its customary efficiency by failing to discover what another branch of the service, namely Lekem, was up to.

Two government reports in 1987 condemned the lack of leadership, supervision and management control exercised by Israeli politicians over their secret services. One reason for that was undoubtedly the political arrangements made so that Yitzhak Shamir of Likud and Shimon Peres and his party alternated in power. Coalition government led to weak government and confusion. As Mr Peres said, 'In effect we are sitting in the same government while conducting an election campaign against each other.' In such conditions it was not surprising that the intelligence services were tempted to take things into their own hands in mounting rogue operations which they considered were in the best interest of the country. A number of prominent Israelis expressed anxiety about the lack of control over the state organs. One of them was Professor Yitzhak Zamir, a leading legal expert and former attorney general, who warned: 'Terrible things have happened recently because of lack of political supervision over the activities of the security services. They must never be allowed to happen again, because they cause as much damage to Israel as they do to themselves.'

21. Dimona

The old troopers of Mossad were forced to adapt themselves quickly to enter a strange world once the Israeli leaders became determined to take the state into the nuclear age. It soon turned out that, unfamiliar though the subject was, the methods required were very similar to the ones at which secret agents were already adept. Before Israel could begin establishing its first nuclear plant, the necessary raw material for an atomic industry had to be acquired illegally and Mossad moved into the business of importing uranium by deception on the grand scale. Its agents, used to transporting illicit arms, did not hesitate to employ the same old knavish tricks to evade the efforts of international agencies whose task was to prevent the spread of nuclear weapons through control over uranium supplies. Radioactive material for military purposes was reserved exclusively for the use of those nations in the West who were members of the nuclear club – the USA, Britain and France. On the other side of the fence, both the Soviet Union and China were members of the same club and, up to a point, shared the Western desire to prevent lesser powers from getting their hands on the devastating weapon. But the supreme military advantage of having nuclear capability was as obvious to Israel as it was to some countries in the Islamic world – and Israel was determined to get there first. So the government began plotting to acquire quantities of the uranium needed for the eventual production of weapons.

The foundations for Israel's nuclear programme were laid immediately after independence. Chaim Weizmann, the first president and himself a distinguished biochemist, encouraged Israeli scientists into the field by setting up a special nuclear physics department at the

164

country's main scientific establishment which was named in his honour. It seemed desirable to him and to the founders of the state that a nuclear reactor should be built. The most suitable place for its location was the Negev Desert, where deposits of uranium had already been discovered. The creation of the establishment at Dimona was initially justified by talk about the need for a new energy source in a land not blessed with conventional power resources. Nuclear power, it was claimed, could fuel desalinization plants to irrigate farmland.

A formal decision to develop nuclear weapons was taken in 1955 and progress towards achieving this end gained momentum after the Six Day War, when the USA cut off arms supplies while the Soviet Union went on furnishing weapons to the Arab states. David Ben-Gurion, the prime minister, declared his conviction 'that the state of Israel needs a defence research programme of its own so that we shall never again be as lambs to the slaughter'.

The scientist chosen to start the project was Ernst David Bergmann, who had worked under Albert Einstein. As scientific adviser to the defence ministry, Bergmann had the task of recruiting Jewish scientists to help with the project. In 1957 steps were taken to begin building one or two nuclear plants, and to use installations at Dimona to develop a nuclear bomb.

It was Shimon Peres, then one of Ben-Gurion's bright young men, who after persistent lobbying persuaded the French government to provide outside help in construction of a nuclear reactor at Dimona. In 1956 he had constantly been meeting ministers in Guy Mollet's socialist government as they planned the Suez operation. Having established close relations he then broached the subject of nuclear aid.

In return for Israeli help with the Suez plot Bourges Maunoury, the defence minister, finally agreed. After he replaced Guy Mollet as prime minister and shortly before his fall, Bourges Maunoury and his foreign minister signed a top secret document agreeing to supply Israel with a powerful 24-megawatt reactor and the know-how and uranium to go with it. The Israeli signatories were Peres and Asher Ben-Natan, an old intelligence operator representing the ministry of defence. The arrangement was made so discreetly that only nine people knew of it. After General de Gaulle came to power in 1958 the programme came under threat. The new President could see no good reason why Israel should have a nuclear reactor at all and extracted a promise from David Ben-Gurion two years later that it would be used only for peaceful purposes.

The Dimona operation was one of total clandestinity. Shimon Peres set up a special nuclear intelligence agency. Mossad and Shin Beth jointly maintained watertight security control over the whole area in the Negev. So paranoid about the possibility of an attack upon the plant were they that on one occasion the military commander took the agonizing decision to shoot down an Israeli air force Mirage returning damaged from a raid, because it was heading into Dimona air space and could not be positively identified as friendly.

Despite Israeli precautions, the Americans could not be prevented from getting to know what was going on and were alarmed at the prospect of nuclear weapons spreading to the Middle East. The secret of the establishment at Dimona was first penetrated when in 1960 an American U-2 spy plane photographed it from high altitude. The Russians too were aware of these developments. None the less, the government persisted in claiming that the building under construction was a textile plant. Even the Knesset was told that the desert nuclear reactor was intended for research purposes, and not to produce nuclear weapons.

Plans to obtain alternative supplies of uranium were drawn up at a meeting attended by Bergmann and Isser Harel, at that time head of Mossad. Dr Zalman Shapiro, a Zionist Jew who had worked as a research chemist on the original wartime Manhattan Project set up in the US by the Americans and British to build the first atomic bomb, was chosen as the scientist adviser in the USA to help get things moving, and in 1957 he set up Numec, the nuclear materials and equipment corporation, a firm financed with Israeli money. Although the CIA was anxious about the ease with which classified documents at the corporation's headquarters in Pennsylvania were made available to foreigners, and suspected that on his frequent visits to Israel Dr Shapiro was dealing in sensitive information, there was little that they could do about it. The Atomic Energy Commission did investigate the apparent disappearance from the plant of 206lb of enriched uranium. Its report concluded, 'Although it cannot be stated with certainty that theft or diversion did *not* take place, the survey found no evidence to suggest these possibilities.' By the time that Numec eventually ceased to operate, the CIA estimated that more than 200lb of uranium had disappeared from it in ten years. Some of it had simply been hijacked and taken to Israel. The corporation was fined $1 million.

After the 1967 war American regulations safeguarding uranium supplies were tightened, making it much more difficult for the Israelis to acquire the stuff. The war also produced a dramatic change in the attitude of President de Gaulle. France had been the only country willing to provide military assistance to Israel after the Suez affair. That was because, so long as the Algerian conflict continued, the two countries were natural allies, with Arab states as their common opponent. Once that conflict ended, General de Gaulle saw Israel and the close friendship which had been in existence between the two countries as a hindrance to his plans for reconciliation with the Arab world. In his memoirs, the General claimed that he had effectively stopped nuclear cooperation. But François Perrin, the French high commissioner for atomic energy, publicly admitted that in 1957 France agreed to build a reactor for producing uranium, and said, 'We considered we could give the secrets to Israel provided they kept them to themselves.'

Senior commanders like General Moshe Dayan remained convinced that a stock of nuclear weapons was absolutely essential for defence. So, when France renegued on the original deal, Meir Amit, who had by then replaced Isser Harel as head of Mossad, assumed responsibility for using all the resources of the service to find ways of acquiring the raw material and obtaining information about the latest developments in nuclear physics, even if that involved circumventing international controls designed to prevent the proliferation of nuclear weapons. The aim was to get enough uranium to make twenty bombs. The expert services of Mossad were stretched to the full, to make sure that the Dimona enterprise would get its raw material. Some of their methods were outlined in the American magazine *Rolling Stone*. Howard Kohn and Barbara Newman reported that the Institute had formed a special unit with the task of procuring uranium wherever it might be found. To this end they had established a dummy company in Europe. The journalists also retailed stories that an Israeli team, armed with tear gas canisters, attacked and hijacked trucks loaded with uranium on French country roads.

As in the American operation, so in Europe; a dummy company was indeed set up by Mossad. This time it was run by a former German air force pilot named Herbert Schulzen who was a partner in Asmara Chemie, a small and unsuccessful chemical company at Wiesbaden. He was told by an Israeli agent named Elijah Sakharov that he was in search of bleaching agents. Codenamed 'The Nazi Pilot' because he had served in the Luftwaffe in the Second World War, Schulzen was invited to convalesce in Israel after an operation and Mossad arranged to put business his way. At a price, he readily agreed to allow his company to be used as a front for the purchase of uranium.

In March 1968 Schulzen made an approach to Société Générale des Minéraux, a Belgian company with stocks of uranium oxide imported from the mines of Zaire. He told Denis Dewez, deputy head of the company's uranium division, that the material was needed for use as a catalyst in the production of petrochemicals, and for that purpose it would have to be transported to Casablanca in Morocco. Although Dewez had misgivings about the offer because he had never heard about this kind of catalyst, the contract was finally signed at Schulzen's home in Wiesbaden; payment of 8.5 million Deutschmarks was made through a Swiss bank. Dewez expressed surprise at discovering that the German company was such a small-scale affair.

What Mossad failed to appreciate was that, in order to ship the uranium to Morocco legally, authorization would need to be obtained from Euratom, the EEC agency which controlled the movement of all radioactive material. A row broke out within the special Mossad unit about this lack of attention to detail, and one senior controller was at once transferred to other duties. A new plan was hastily improvised which involved taking the uranium to Italy where Francesco Serterio, the owner of Saica, a hard-up Milanese company, was persuaded to process it, despite the fact that his factory had never before handled such material. Indeed, he had to buy special equipment.

The plot was to transport the Belgian raw material by sea to Italy, ostensibly so that it could be processed there. Such a move was legal because both Belgium and Italy were Common Market countries. The only snag was that for part of the voyage the ship would be sailing outside EEC waters. Mossad gambled on the fact that nobody from the atomic control authorities would check out the companies or notice the transgression. Their guess was correct; no inspectors came.

A Liberian-registered freighter, the *Scheersberg A*, 1062 tonnes, was purchased in Hamburg for a cash payment of £160,000. The buyer was a Turk named Burham Yarisal. The hastily set-up company operating it was registered as Biscayne Traders, whose chairman turned out to be a Danish-born Israeli agent named Dan Aerbel. In October this ship, under the command of Captain Percy Barrow, described on his master's certificate as a thirty-five-year-old Londoner but in fact a Mossad agent like the rest of his crew, sailed the ship on a test run to Naples. The only difficulty encountered was an awkward question from Herr Felix Oboussier, a West German official working for Euratom, who wanted to know whether uranium really could be used by the Italian company as a catalyst. He was assured that it could. By the end of the month the team was able to signal that all was ready for launching Operation Plombat.

The word 'Plombat' was painted on each of the 560 barrels containing the uranium when it was loaded aboard the *Scheersberg A*, under the supervision of Schulzen. On 15 November the ship sailed from Antwerp bound for the Italian port of Genoa. But it never arrived there. Instead it headed eastwards across the Mediterranean to rendezvous two weeks later with an Israeli tanker off the coast of Cyprus. There the Plombat barrels were transferred at sea and shipped on to the Israeli port of Haifa for onward transport to Dimona. Within fourteen months of the cabinet decision to order the illegal procurement by Mossad of the uranium needed to manufacture the atom bomb Operation Plombat had been successfully completed.

It was not until December that the *Scheersberg A* was seen again, arriving in the Turkish port of Iskenderun. The final two weeks of the voyage had not been recorded in the ship's log. Of Captain Barrow and his crew there was no sign, and when a search was made in international shipping records it emerged that the captain was a fictitious person invented for the operation. Three Israeli authors wrote what they claimed was an accurate though fictional account (accurate through leaked information; fictional so as not to embarrass sources) of this adventure in *Operation Uranium Ship*. It took Euratom, the European atomic control organization, seven months to find evidence that the cargo had actually disappeared. Police enquiries failed to discover what had really happened, and the companies involved refused to make any statement. Finally, the European Commission decided to close the dossier on this affair and to allow it to remain secret so as to avoid further embarrassment.

Mossad commanders were well content with the success of their operation. Dan Aerbel, the agent who had done so much to make the plan work, was promoted and posted to Norway. Having been brought up in Denmark, he was one of the few Mossad agents who felt at home in Scandinavia and was therefore selected in 1971 to join the team hunting Ali Hassan Salameh, the man believed responsible for organizing the Munich massacre. That operation ended as a fiasco, when the hit team killed the wrong man in Norway. Among the agents arrested after this failed operation was none other than Dan Aerbel, and it was that fact which led to the public exposure of his earlier role in the Plombat affair.

Although the Mossad recruiters were unaware of the fact, Aerbel suffered from claustrophobia, having spent some time hidden in a cellar to escape persecution during the Second World War. For that reason he proved to be an excessively cooperative witness when questioned by the Norwegian police after spending a night in a cell. To the mystification of the Norwegians he confessed, 'I owned the *Scheersberg A*.' The puzzled intelligence interrogator pursued this matter; eventually Aerbel explained, 'It carried the uranium to Israel', and piece by piece the story emerged. Mossad made use of the *Scheersberg A* on a second occasion in 1969, when its teams stole the five French gunboats from Cherbourg. The refitted ship, which was in the ownership of Biscayne Traders Shipping Corporation whose proprietor was Dan Aerbel, met the gunboats and refuelled them at sea off the Spanish port of Corunna.

Mossad took the credit for providing the scientists at Dimona with enough smuggled uranium to fuel the bomb-making plant. Eventually the state was able to dispense with secret service help, once the physicists had discovered a new process for enriching uranium on the spot.

The policy of successive governments was to deny that Israel possessed atomic weapons, but in 1969 prime minister Golda Meir, when asked in Washington by President Nixon whether Israel possessed any dangerous toys, felt able to respond, 'We do.' The truth of that reply was further confirmed by the military crisis in the Yom Kippur War when the combined forces of Egypt and Syria seemed on the point of overwhelming Israel. General Yitzhak Hofi, commander on the northern front, strongly doubted his army's ability to hold out much longer against the Syrian onslaught on the Golan Heights and raised the question of going nuclear. Moshe Dayan also believed that the time had come to consider using the ultimate weapon. Thirteen atomic devices stored in tunnels under the Negev Desert were prepared for action. During a tense period of twenty-four hours, while the cabinet pondered the gravity of the decision before them, atomic weapons were loaded aboard Phantom and Kfir jets. This move became known both to America and to the Soviet Union when their spy satellites picked up the preparations for nuclear war. Soviet reaction came in the form of a threat to ship nuclear warheads to Egypt for use with the Soviet-made missiles in service there. Counter-threats from the USA led to a nuclear stand-off of the superpowers. The situation stabilized, but Israel's secret was out in the open.

22. Zap Isis and Osiris!

Seen from an Israeli perspective, Mossad succeeded in its patriotic duty by helping to provide the materials from which the scientists could create nuclear weapons for the defence of the country. After the nuclear crisis of autumn 1973 there was no longer any doubt left that *in extremis* the Israelis would use the ultimate weapon in a final move to save the country from Arab conquest. Israeli intelligence was also enmeshed by the nuclear problem at other levels. The service which had helped to make Israel a nuclear power also had the more aggressive task of preventing nuclear weapons from becoming available to the Arab powers. Nobody knew better than Mossad how the international rules could be bent so that an ambitious state might acquire uranium and the reactors necessary for processing it. What the service had achieved for its own country, it was then called upon to prevent from being accomplished by underhand Arab forces. It was generally considered that the so-called Islamic bomb would threaten the very existence of Israel and clearly it was the duty of Mossad and Aman to prevent the menace from becoming a reality. Together with Shin Beth they also bore responsibility for protecting the nation's own nuclear research secrets from foreign spies.

Pakistan, whose scientists had the necessary technical and scientific ability to build nuclear weapons, was watched with great suspicion. It was known that nuclear research was going ahead on the Indian sub-continent. The suspicion was that money for the project was being provided by the Arab oil-producing states. The threat also came from other Islamic quarters. Muammar Gaddafi publicly made known his determination to obtain nuclear weapons, either by buying them, which

171

he had tried to do on several occasions, or by contributing funds so that they might be constructed by some friendly power.

The immediate threat came from Iraq. It was in the 1970s that a distinct possibility emerged that this powerful military state, ruled by President Saddam Hussein, would soon become the first Arab country to get its own nuclear arm. From France the Iraqis bought a 70-megawatt Osiris reactor, which at that time was one of the most advanced experimental models in the world. A second reactor named Isis was also to be delivered, ready for building at a site near Baghdad. The total cost was $275 million, and included in the bargain was delivery of 12kg of uranium enriched to 93 per cent – weapon-grade fuel which could be used to produce three or four nuclear devices. The agreement signed in 1976 committed Iraq in return to sell quantities of oil to France and to buy French conventional armaments. Indeed, it was the need to ensure oil supplies after the great fuel crisis provoked by the Yom Kippur War which spurred on the French government of Jacques Chirac to agree to the deal.

President Giscard d'Estaing went out of his way to declare, 'During negotiations I have personally taken the opportunity to ensure that nuclear weapons are not introduced in the Middle East.' Despite French and Iraqi denials that the Baghdad nuclear installations were intended to produce weapons, Israel was certain that President Saddam Hussein intended Iraq to become the first Arab nuclear power, an achievement which would further his ambitions to become top dog in the Middle East. If he succeeded in making and stockpiling bombs, they would be invaluable for ultimate weapon blackmail or, worse still, they would give Iraq the power to launch nuclear war, either against Israel or even against Iran, the other enemy to the east.

It was a development very worrying for Israel, for if this Arab nation had its own atomic weapons any Israeli threat to use her own bombs as a final option would become much less convincing. Mossad and the foreign ministry kept close watch over the Baghdad nuclear project. Field agents and diplomats became in a sense poachers turned game-keepers. They knew the game from the other side, having contrived themselves to purchase nuclear materials and smuggle them to Israel in order to construct their own secret weapon down in the desert at Dimona. This experience gave them an edge in planning to prevent their Arab neighbours from succeeding in the same way.

In France there were scientists and technicians who themselves had been involved in nuclear cooperation with Israel at a time when France considered itself a staunch ally, before President de Gaulle changed his mind and withdrew his cooperation. Detailed information about the new French deal with Iraq became available to Mossad's technical

172

teams. From the start, its men in Baghdad had accurate information about progress being made at the installations fourteen miles from the Iraqi capital. Penetration of the Arab establishment had long been a primary task of the intelligence service, and it was especially well connected in Baghdad. The political will was there to prevent President Saddam Hussein at all costs from realizing his ambition to force his way into the nuclear club.

In the spring of 1979 the French company CNIM, Constructions Navales et Industrielles de la Méditérranée at La Seyne, near Toulon, finally completed work on the cores for two nuclear reactors ordered by Iraq. Originally named after the ancient Egyptian gods Isis and Osiris, they had been renamed Tamuz 1 and Tamuz 2. This change was ordered by Saddam Hussein in a fit of spite when he denounced President Sadat and all things Egyptian because of his peacemaking with Israel. The equipment had been crated and was made ready for shipment to Iraq. The fact that the containers were ready for export and kept locked in workshop number three in a dockside building by the port was supposed to be a closely guarded secret, known only to a select group of French technicians and physicists. But strong security did not prevent Mossad from obtaining detailed information from a contact inside the factory. They learned that during the night of 8 April the reactor parts were to be loaded on trucks and driven to Marseilles, where a ship waited to transport them to Iraq. To forestall this, a team penetrated the factory two days earlier and, using plastic explosives, blew up essential parts of the nuclear equipment. Naturally, the Israeli secret service refrained from claiming a victory, but subsequent French police reports left no doubt that Mossad was responsible. One agent who had by then left the service later revealed that the job was called Operation Biglift.

Police investigators traced a three-man Israeli team which flew from Paris to Hyères, the nearest airport to Toulon, two days before the explosion. They arrived on a late flight on 4 April, and presented French identity papers when they checked in individually at three separate hotels and paid in advance. At Toulon railway station they were picked up by a Renault 12 and driven to a rented villa outside the town to join four other men who had arrived earlier. The following day the trio from Paris made a reconnaissance of the factory at La Seyne, and noted that the guard made a round at midnight and another at 3 a.m. After final preparations for the raid had been worked out, the entire group of seven made their way in two trucks to the waterfront warehouses. There was a wall to be scaled, with the aid of breeze blocks brought along for the purpose, and the alarm system needed to be put out of action. Once that was done, the next part of the raiders' task

173

was made easy by the fact that they had with them a duplicate key to the shed where the vital material was stored.

Investigators on the spot discovered that attempts had been made to dismantle equipment before it was blown up. This led to the belief that the sabotage team originally had orders to steal essential parts of the reactor cores and take them away for shipment to Israel; that explained why they had chosen to go to the dockyard in trucks rather than in cars. The chances are that the original plan had to be abandoned because the saboteurs did not have enough time to take the equipment to pieces and remove it. Instead, they switched to an emergency fall-back plan which was to use plastic explosives in the time bombs brought for the purpose to destroy parts of the so-called beehives on the spot. The team took good care to concern itself only with Iraqi material, and avoided damaging reactor components intended for Belgium and West Germany.

After the raid three of the Israeli team left by sea as crew members aboard a ship bound for Haifa. The remaining four agents stayed in France for several months before returning home. One of their tasks was to leave a false trail so as to distract the attention of the French police. This was done by making anonymous telephone calls claiming that the sabotage was the work of the 'French Ecological Group', a totally unknown environmental protest group against all things nuclear.

Both of the reactors for Baghdad were badly damaged in the attack, and the estimate was that Saddam Hussein's programme would be delayed by two years as a result. Because the French government seized upon the opportunity afforded by this delaying attack to try to persuade the Iraqis to accept another model of reactor, capable of working on lower-grade uranium instead of weapons-grade material, some suspicion was voiced that the French themselves had blasted the workshop. Yet the raid bore all the hallmarks of a carefully contrived Mossad operation and there can be no doubt that the destruction of the reactor cores was greatly to the advantage of Israel.

That raid slowed down progress of work on the nuclear infrastructure in Baghdad. The next development was cloaked in another mystery. In the summer of 1980 Paris police found the body of Professor Yahia el-Meshad, a forty-eight-year-old Egyptian nuclear scientist, in his room at the Hotel Méridien near the Arc de Triomphe. He had been bludgeoned and stabbed to death. The reason for his killing appeared to be that the scientist, who had trained in the USA and Moscow, was working under contract to the Iraqi nuclear authority. He had come to France to attend French atomic agency conferences in the suburb of Fontenoy-aux-Roses. News of his death was kept secret for four days on orders from the French foreign ministry. The only comment from Israel on this affair came in a broadcast, baldly stating that the death of the professor, 'one of the small circle of Arab physicists with advanced nuclear know-how', would set back progress on 'Iraqi production of nuclear weapons by two years'. The dossier was closed, and nobody was ever arrested for this crime – but suspicion fell naturally upon Mossad agents.

Still the government of Menachem Begin was not satisfied that every possible step had been taken to prevent the creation of an Islamic nuclear weapon. Ze'ev Schiff, an influential Israeli military correspondent, wrote at the time in *Ha'aretz*, 'Israel must make every possible effort in order to delay and stop Arab progress in this area.' He concluded that efforts 'should be expressed both in the political realm and in other areas'.

The obvious determination to prevent Iraq achieving a nuclear weapon made it inevitable that Israeli plots were suspected in a series of incidents. In the autumn of 1980, two Phantom jets fired rockets at the Tamuz research centre near Baghdad. They were said to have Iranian markings, but that did not prevent the spread of stories that the incident was a warning by the Israeli air force, flying under false colours, planned to frighten away French scientists who were working there. Small-scale commando raids were also made which strengthened the belief that the intelligence service was trying its hand at sabotage operations. It was certainly true that Mossad agents were most active in Iraq spying upon the nuclear installations on the ground.

There were clear indications that Mossad had made careful preparations when, the following year, a strike force of fifteen Israeli F16s protected by F15s zoomed in to make a low-level bombing raid upon the reactor complex at Daura on the banks of the River Tigris. It was the first air attack ever to be made upon a nuclear installation, and its success demonstrated how well the pilots had been briefed about their target. Major General David Ivri, chief of the air force, claimed that every bomb found its target. The timing of this long-range raid was based on information provided by Mossad agents that the reactor was within three months of becoming operational. It had been considered essential to make the attack before that happened and so avoid nuclear fall-out so close to the city of Baghdad. An official government statement plainly stated, 'From sources whose reliability is beyond doubt, we learnt that this reactor – despite its camouflage – is designed to produce atomic bombs. The target for such bombs would be Israel.'

The Institute had provided not only detailed plans of the installation's layout, but also intelligence about air defences which enabled the jets to make the attack without loss. To carry out the raid was a delicate business, for French technicians and scientists were at work there and the Israelis were obviously anxious that they should not suffer casualties. Studies had been made of their working schedules. 'What we did was defend ourselves,' said Menachem Begin. 'We warned the French; we told them not to continue to supply the Iraqis with this equipment.' The prime minister justified the decision to carry out the strike by saying that his information made it clear that the Iraqis could have produced four or five bombs. 'For the last two years I have been living a nightmare,' he declared. Israelis were united in believing that it was Mossad which had helped to save them from that nightmare.

23. Public Spy

The spy stories most enjoyed by Israelis, who have a natural taste for yarns of that kind, are the ones with happy endings in which the *dénouement* is another brilliant success for the Institute. Less popular are those which draw attention to the fact that Israel itself is spied upon and that the intelligence services do not always get their man before the mischief is done. So there was little rejoicing in March 1988 when a Jerusalem court finally found Mordechai Vanunu guilty of aggravated espionage. The charges proven against this thirty-two-year-old citizen born in Morocco were of treason and of collecting secret information about the Dimona Nuclear Centre in the Negev Desert, where he worked for nine years as a technician. Vanunu was a peculiar kind of spy. The recipient of his espionage gleanings was, not a rival intelligence service, but the London newspaper the *Sunday Times* which in 1986 published for all to read the confidential information provided by him. The paper boldly proclaimed that it revealed 'The Secrets of Israel's Nuclear Arsenal'.

The sentence of eighteen years in prison passed upon Vanunu seemed at first sight a harsh penalty for what was in essence a leak to a newspaper. But the Israelis have always been particularly secretive about their possession, not officially recognized, of the ultimate weapon, and they did not see things in that light. Clandestine production of nuclear weapons is, in the nature of things, a most sensitive subject. Vanunu's story went into convincing detail about Israel's nuclear capability. The source was a man who had worked in the heart of the defence installation and who, moreover, had taken photographs of part of the set-up to prove his point.

177

According to his account, the French engineers who originally constructed the Dimona plant in 1957 dug a 25-metre-deep crater in the sand in which they buried a unit which came to be known as Machon 2. There they installed 'the technology de Gaulle claimed that he had denied to Israel'. Vanunu asserted that beneath the crudely constructed two-storey building on the edge of the Negev Desert was concealed an underground edifice going down six subterranean levels. The components of nuclear weapons were produced in this place and machined into warlike parts. This authoritative-sounding account also gave a detailed stage-by-stage description of the plutonium extraction processes carried out in Dimona using the radioactive raw material smuggled into Israel by Mossad.

Fascinating and authentic though the descriptions undoubtedly were, the most politically significant revelation was Vanunu's claim that Israel, disposing of a stockpile of about a hundred devices, had become a 'major nuclear power ranking sixth in the atomic league table after the US, Soviet Union, Britain, France and China'. It possessed the components and the ability to build atomic, neutron or hydrogen bombs. Far from being a 'nuclear pygmy', as had been assumed, the country had built up a powerful armoury. Vanunu alleged that scientists were at work on a new design programme codenamed Operation Hump, and that on Level Four there was equipment to produce thermonuclear weapons.

It caused great alarm to the coalition government of Israel to read the country's best-kept secrets publicly displayed in the columns of a newspaper when, after some hesitation, the *Sunday Times* finally published the story. At the time Vanunu was in London being questioned by various experts brought in by the paper to confirm that the information was not just a hoax. Among those who took a close look at Vanunu's papers and photographs was Theodore Taylor, a former head of the Pentagon atomic weapons test programme. He declared that there should no longer be any doubt that for at least a decade Israel had been a fully fledged nuclear weapons state. The programme was more advanced than any previous report had suggested. He estimated from the evidence provided that the country had the capability to produce ten nuclear weapons a year.

Mordechai Vanunu had left Israel to make an expedition to the Far East, in order to 'find himself', as he explained to friends, and then fetched up in Australia where he was baptized as a Christian. Through church activities he met a Colombian freelance journalist and told him all about Dimona. This individual, Oscar Guerrero, offered to sell the story to the press. His boasting and contact making alerted Mossad, probably by way of the Australian secret service, and by the time Vanunu was called to London its people were keeping track of his movements.

Within a few days of the publication of the Dimona revelations Vanunu disappeared from London, and soon stories were put about that he had been kidnapped by Mossad. The Rev. John McKnight, an Australian clergyman who had helped with his spiritual problems, flew to Israel to try and discover what had happened. The London newspaper, whose own security for their 'walk-in' source had clearly not been as watertight as they constantly urged that British security ought to be, was embarrassed.

Official wrath in Israel turned naturally upon the security services. Something was clearly wrong with arrangements at Dimona if a technician and a signatory of the Official Secrets Act had managed to wander about top-secret parts of the installation, taking forbidden photographs with a camera he ought to have been prevented from introducing into the atomic plant in the first place. Undetected, he had also managed to copy details and diagrams from secret booklets. In January 1986, when he flew to Australia, he had smuggled out with him handwritten notes, as well as fifty-seven photographs taken inside Dimona. Here was the real mystery. How had he managed to elude the guards who, it had always been assumed, were especially diligent in protecting the holy of holies of Israeli defence secrets?

The first reaction was to condemn the security service for grotesque incompetence in failing to detect Vanunu's activities before further harm could be done. Careful vetting of the kind in which the Israelis are highly experienced ought to have demonstrated that here was an unreliable technician who had publicly aired his doubts and worries about nuclear proliferation. Vanunu himself admitted that he had been questioned three times about his left-wing tendencies. Furthermore, taking the material with him, he had managed to elude the amazingly strict controls at Israeli ports and airports put in place to combat terrorists. It hardly seemed possible that anyone could leave Tel Aviv airport without being thoroughly searched. Despite such difficulties the spy got through.

It was not surprising, then, that experienced Israel-watchers began wondering about the possibility that the whole affair had been contrived by Mossad with the aim of confirming that the country possessed a formidable stock of nuclear weapons by way of a warning to Arab countries against daring to launch another war. This was a theme which was returned to again as the Vanunu affair developed.

First in line for criticism was Shin Beth, the general security service responsible for guarding secrets at Dimona. Quickly it was blamed by members of the Knesset for failing to spot a traitor. There

179

were immediate calls for a purge in the service, and a senior security official was promptly dismissed. As Vanunu's life story came to light, it turned out that he had often drawn attention to himself – by becoming a Christian, by becoming a communist, by giving his support to the PLO – all pretty eye-catching acts in Israel. It further emerged that he was a surly person of unstable character. How had he ever got through the vetting procedures for those employed in the nuclear development centre?

Attention then focussed upon what had become of Vanunu after his sudden disappearance from the Mountbatten Hotel where he had been staying in London. From Washington came a *Newsweek* story that Shimon Peres, while still prime minister, had ordered Mossad to fetch him back to Israel. The reaction of the coalition government – as it had been in the business of Irangate and amid accusations that the country had sold arms to Ayatollah Khomeini – was to lie. 'We do not know anything about this matter,' declared the spokesman at the PM's office. Practically everyone in Israel knew that the unhappy Vanunu was by that time held incommunicado in a prison cell somewhere in Israel. The government, said Yitzhak Shamir, the next coalition leader, rather tetchily, 'will say what it finds fit to say'.

This did not greatly please the British government, because there was now more than a strong suspicion that Mossad had indeed kidnapped the traitor in London and spirited him away back home. Disinformation was put about that he might have been taken on the high seas, without any explanation being provided as to why he should have taken a sea trip at all. Requests from the British government for clarification about how Vanunu had disappeared from Britain were at first met with silence. Eventually the Jerusalem government assured the British ambassador, William Squire, that no British law had been broken in recovering Vanunu, although no further details were officially provided about the circumstances. Nor was there any explanation about why the Israelis had failed to take the straightforward step of seeking the arrest and extradition of a man wanted for a serious misdemeanour.

In any case the government of Israel was determined to take action against the Jewish spy who in their view had betrayed the state, and the head of Mossad was ordered to devise a way of getting him back to Israel for trial – the only proviso being that whatever plan was chosen should not unduly embarrass the British government. For Israel had no wish to irritate Mrs Thatcher, who was held in high esteem at the time for her strong and prompt action in severing diplomatic relations with Syria after the trial of Hindawi, the man caught trying to get a bomb aboard a London–Tel Aviv flight of El Al. This ruled out any idea of trying to smuggle the nuclear technologist out of the UK in a crate of diplomatic baggage.

First, they had to capture their man. When Mordechai Vanunu arrived in London under the auspices of the *Sunday Times* the long arm of Mossad was already reaching out towards him. Left to his own devices and wandering moodily about the streets of the capital examining his conscience, which he later said had prompted him to uncover nuclear secrets, he fell in 'by chance' with an attractive woman named Cindy. She was in fact a Mossad agent, and the meeting had been artfully contrived to take advantage of Vanunu's strange, listless personality. After several meetings, she suggested that he might like to fly to Italy with her to consummate the affair developing between them in her sister's apartment in Rome. The fact that Vanunu was lured out of Britain made it possible for Israel to assert with some truth that he had not been 'kidnapped' on British soil and for Mrs Thatcher to accept the denial.

Exactly what happened then remained shrouded in mystery for some time. But eventually the Israelis announced that they were holding Vanunu 'under lawful detention' and intended to bring him to trial. He had in fact been seized with the help of the Mossad temptress and smuggled back home aboard an Israeli ship sailing from Italy. The manner of his abduction might never have come to light had it not been for the fact that, when Vanunu was originally charged, he managed to transmit a message to reporters waiting outside the Jerusalem District Court. He had scrawled upon the palm of his hand three lines in English. As he held up his hand to the window of the van they were able to read: 'Vanunu M WAS HIJACK en IN ROME ITL 30.9.86 21.00 Came to Rome BY BA FLY 504'. This garble was interpreted as meaning that he had been hijacked in Rome on 30 September 1986 at 2100 hours, and had arrived in Rome on British Airways flight 504 from London. When pictures of Vanunu's hand were printed in Israeli newspapers the military censor blacked out the message.

Either because there was no more hand space available, or because Vanunu did not know what happened after Rome, he gave no indication about how he was taken to Israel. No further information came to light as the trial proceeded in camera. But Meir Vanunu, who had eventually visited his brother in prison, produced new information passed to him by Mordechai, who claimed that two secret servicemen had attacked him in the flat where Cindy had taken him in Rome. While they held him down, she injected him with a powerful anaesthetic. Eventually, he was taken from Italy chained in the hold of a cargo ship. 'He did not arrive in Israel until 7 October, one week after the abduction.' He was taken ashore

181

tied to a stretcher and thrown into a cell where they held him for two days.

Although the story was generally accepted, Domenico Sica, the Italian public prosecutor appointed to enquire into the happenings in Rome and who questioned Meir Vanunu personally, was less convinced by some of the details. He pointed out that a third-floor flat in the centre of a populous part of Rome was 'the most unsuitable and dangerous place from which to carry an unconscious body'. He further commented, 'it is obvious that a group of specialists would never have committed such an error.' The Italian official also expressed surprise that Vanunu had written such a coherent message in English on the palm of his hand without the collaboration of someone else. But what impressed him most was the series of pictures taken by Vanunu which demonstrated the whole process of the making of a nuclear warhead. Such evidence convinced Signor Sica that the photographs could only have been taken within a top-security establishment with the help of those in charge. His conclusion was that this bizarre episode was 'a well-organized disinformation operation'.

What did become perfectly clear was that Vanunu had not returned willingly to face trial and that Mossad had been involved in nasty activity on British soil, and in an even more doubtful operation conducted in Italy. Nor were the Institute's methods very polished. The impression given was that they had put together a crash plan without their customary subtlety and care. One indication of this was suggested by the poor fieldcraft of their woman agent, Cindy, who was quickly identified in London as Cheryl Ben-Tov, an American-born Israeli married to a man named Ofer, with whom she lived in Netanya. A small and fairly attractive woman, she was sent by Mossad to London where she contrived to meet Vanunu in Leicester Square. She stayed at the Eccleston Hotel and used the cover name Cindy Hanin, describing herself as a trainee beautician from Florida. She made the bad mistake of assuming the name and occupation of a close relative, which made it possible to trace her true identity. It also revealed that Mossad had failed to train her well enough to avoid leaving such embarrassing clues lying around.

The whole Vanunu affair was a source of serious embarrassment to Mossad and to the Israeli intelligence community in general. One branch had failed to detect the presence at Dimona of a neurotic and disaffected technician, and another had clumsily and hurriedly put together a plan to retrieve that error by grabbing the man on friendly European territory, but only after his secrets had been published. No one emerged with much credit from the episode, and once again Israeli secret service activity had become public. It also created serious diplomatic incidents in Britain and in Italy. As ever, the favourite Israeli phrase of understatement came into use to describe a disaster; Yitzhak Shamir, who took over as prime minister from Shimon Peres, said it was a 'serious mishap'. The only way in which the Vanunu affair might be put down as a success for Israeli intelligence would be if it were accepted that Vanunu had been exploited by Mossad in order to achieve the aim of convincing the enemies of Israel of the country's nuclear strength, without the embarrassment of having to answer to the Americans for their boasts.

Although opinion in Israel was content enough with the conviction of Mordechai Vanunu, a number of foreign scientists and lawyers expressed disapproval by defending his decision to speak out, which was justified by the claim that, inspired by his horror of nuclear weapons, he had acted for ideological reasons. He was even put forward as a candidate for the Nobel Peace Prize, the only spy ever to be suggested for such an honour. So strange had been the handling of the whole business that after the trial suspicions grew about the motives of the Israeli government. Perhaps they really had used Vanunu deliberately in order to let it be known how powerful was their nuclear armoury. This theory was cautiously voiced by Frank Barnaby in his book *The Invisible Bomb*. He was a physicist and professor of peace studies, and one of those called in to question Vanunu to assess his information before newspaper publication. Professor Barnaby asserted that Mossad discovered what Vanunu was up to and decided to give him a chance to tell his story. In this version of events, both the abduction and the secret trial served to add authenticity to Vanunu's information. He wrote, 'I am not suggesting for one moment that Vanunu was a willing tool of Mossad. . . . But it is entirely possible that unwittingly he was allowed to serve a purpose – to tell the world about Israel's nuclear-weapon activities.'

The point was that Israeli leaders could not make public a triumphant announcement about their formidable stock of nuclear weapons, yet they were satisfied to let it be known to their enemies that such stock existed. In a state where so many operations normally take place in the furtive atmosphere of secrecy that would be entirely acceptable to a political leadership afflicted with a secret service mentality. Officially the government stuck to the tired old formula by declaring that Israel would never be the first power to introduce nuclear weapons into the Middle East. But they were reasonably content that Vanunu had made it plain that the country had powerful nuclear war potential.

183

Part VII
London End

24. An African in the Diplomatic Bag

The first in a series of recent affairs which brought a clash of interest between Mossad and the British government developed out of Israel's machinations in Africa. For many years it had been one of the aims of the Jerusalem government to strengthen its links with the independent countries there. This was partly prompted by the desire to impress third world opinion, often favourable to the nationalist aspirations of Palestinians, and to secure support in the United Nations when Israel came under pressure. Any move which could win allies and friendly votes at the UN, and thereby reduce the isolation of Israel, was welcomed by the foreign ministry, even though it sometimes meant consorting with such unsavoury regimes as that of Idi Amin, the brutal dictator of Uganda. Mossad indeed played its part in the conspiracy which overthrew Milton Obote, the previous and equally malign incumbent, and brought Idi Amin to power. Also, it was of interest to counter the thrustful policies of Islam throughout the continent, for countries practising that faith were ever hostile towards Zionism. Muammar Gaddafi, the Libyan trouble-maker, always anxious to spread his influence as an African leader, had also been busy in Africa promoting his interests, which were alien to those of Israel.

In its relations with Black Africa every Israeli government faced a double task which involved a delicate balancing act. Jews from South Africa were among the most active supporters of the new state of Israel and some 8500 citizens, mostly well-educated and well-connected, emigrated to Israel. Strong financial support was also forthcoming in the early days, and later Israel was able to repay past favours by supplying South Africa with weapons and military expertise. This military aid became especially valuable when Western governments began to impose a boycott on South Africa to express their disapproval of apartheid. It was not surprising that strong links also developed between Mossad and BOSS, the South African bureau of state security. Indeed, it has been claimed that a good deal of the success of the security services in South Africa is due to the help received from Mossad teams specializing in counter-intelligence operations and in interrogation techniques.

A CIA analysis of Israeli foreign intelligence and security services makes this comment:

Israeli liaison in Africa has varied considerably from country to country, depending on the exigencies of the situation. Israeli intelligence activities in Africa have usually been carried out under the cover of police training, arms sales to national military forces and aid and development programmes. The Arab nations, in conjunction with the Organization of African Unity, have brought great pressure on most African nations to break all formal ties with Israel. Despite the break in diplomatic relations between Israel and many African nations, the Israelis still maintain good intelligence liaison with the Kenyan service. In central Africa the Israelis are still active in Zaire. In West Africa, the Israelis trained the Liberian security service and police. They also helped to establish the Ghanaian military intelligence service. In southern Africa, the Israelis have a relationship with South African intelligence and security services.

The American document demonstrated the two-headed nature of Mossad activities in the African continent. The Institute had established an excellent intelligence-gathering network in the black African states which gave it the power to exert covert influence there, and in the process it acquired a great deal of precious information of value to its ally South Africa. In 1976 the two countries made an intelligence swapping agreement which has been of great benefit to both partners. So far as South Africa was concerned, one important windfall came as a result of the Israeli invasion of Lebanon in 1982. In the headquarters bunkers of the PLO establishment there, huge quantities of documents were seized which revealed many secrets about the international terrorist networks operated with the aid of the Palestinians. Included in the haul, which took years to analyze, was a store of valuable detailed information about the help given by Palestinian groups to the ANC,

188

the African National Congress, the main enemy of the South African government. This material was passed on to the South African bureau of state security.

Despite close cooperation with the country labelled as the enemy of all black African countries, Israeli diplomats and intelligence men were remarkably successful in their friendly overtures to those same states. The secret of their success was the reputation for military prowess built by Israel in its continual wars with the Arabs. For anxious rulers of unstable governments, protected by armies always standing by for the chance of a coup d'état, the prospect of help from proficient outside advisers and trainers with a reputation for efficiency was irresistible. Idi Amin was fiendishly proud of wearing paratrooper wings awarded to him by the Israelis, even though he never took a jumping course. In a dozen African republics Mossad was able to establish itself on the heels of military and economic advisers who arrived to lend a 'non-imperialist' hand to the new states. A formidable intelligence network was built up and friends were in position to give assistance – as, for example, when Mossad needed local support to help the army mount its long-range rescue of the hostages aboard the Air France flight hijacked to Entebbe in the heart of Africa.

The grand design to win influence throughout Africa was interrupted by the 1967 war, which publicly displayed how closely Israel was linked to South Africa. Weapons and money were pumped in to help Israel in her moment of need, and several hundred Jews from South Africa travelled north to join the armed forces. After the Yom Kippur War of 1973 the Arab states, full of new confidence because of the rising value of their oil, themselves began a diplomatic offensive in Africa, offering aid programmes and cheap fuel. As a result, a number of states turned against their former friend, a notable example being Tanzania.

After that war, twenty-five African governments broke off diplomatic relations with Israel, although concerted efforts were subsequently made by the Israelis to regain their favour. A case in point was Nigeria, doubly important in Israeli eyes as an oil supplier and as one of the better-off African states. Here was a potential market for Israeli weapons and armaments. More than two thousand Israelis were at one time working in Nigeria, for although diplomatic relations were severed, economic and other ties with that country remained intact; they helped to build schools and hotels as well as military installations, and also provided military training.

In 1984 political events in Nigeria provided Israeli intelligence with an opportunity to gain favour in the eyes of the freshly installed Lagos government. On New Year's Day of that year Major General Muhammed Buhari seized power in a coup d'état, overthrowing

189

President Shagari and declaring that the army could not stand by and watch while the country drifted towards a dangerous state of political and economic collapse. One of the leading supporters of the old regime and brother-in-law of the president was Umaru Dikko, a former transport minister, who, it was widely believed in Nigeria, had made a fortune while in office. He had also run the electoral campaign of the man now overthrown by the military. Whatever the truth of the allegations against him, Dikko was at once listed by the new regime as a man wanted for economic crimes – in fact the most wanted man. He did not wait to argue and within a few days of the coup he was reported to be in London, a haven he reached after slipping out of his own country and making a circuitous flight to Europe.

A few months later on a July morning just after noon, Umaru Dikko strolled from his opulent house in Porchester Terrace in west London on the way to meet a friend for lunch. Two armed black men set upon him, forced him into a yellow van and sped away. The only witness was Elizabeth Hayes, his private secretary, who heard a commotion followed by a scream and promptly called the police. It was obvious to her that he had been kidnapped.

Commander William Hucklesby, commander of the Scotland Yard anti-terrorist unit, was called and within half an hour he alerted special branch men at ports and airports. Their attention concentrated on Stansted Airport, thirty miles from London, a place much used by transport aircraft. As a Boeing 727 of Nigerian Airways bound for Lagos was readied for take-off police cars roared down the runway and pulled up in front of it. A sharp-eyed customs officer, Charles Morrow, had been suspicious about two large wooden crates loaded on board. Labelled to go to the ministry of external affairs, Lagos, as diplomatic baggage, they were covered by diplomatic privilege and the British authorities were not empowered to open them. However, there was a loophole in that the customs men claimed that they were incorrectly marked and on this pretext the cases were unloaded into a hangar; because suspicious noises could be heard coming from them, the police felt convinced that they contained human beings. Fearing that whoever was inside might be armed, they had the crates hoisted on a fork lift to await the arrival of a Nigerian diplomat whose presence was deemed necessary before the wooden crates were opened.

When eventually they were broken into, officers discovered in the first one Umaru Dikko, trussed and unconscious in a drug-induced coma. Sitting alongside him in the four-feet-square space was another man armed with a syringe and a supply of drugs designed to keep his companion sedated throughout the long flight to Nigeria. The unfortunate Dikko had an endotracheal tube in the throat to enable him

190

to breathe, and he was crouched, handcuffed and gagged, in a pool of his own vomit. Another tube led from his arm to a plastic bottle clamped to one of the inside walls. He did not recover consciousness for twenty-four hours. In the second piece of diplomatic luggage police found two more men, neither of them bound nor unconscious; they were both Israelis, Alexander Barak and Felix Abithol.

The man with the syringe turned out to be Dr Lev-Arie Shapiro, a senior hospital consultant and Israeli army reservist living in Peta-Tikvah. All three Israeli citizens were at once arrested and charged with kidnapping and administering a number of drugs which had almost killed Dikko. So also was a Nigerian diplomat, Major Mohammed Yusufu, who was in fact an agent of the Nigerian security organization. It was obvious that an abortive plot had been afoot to smuggle the former minister home to Nigeria and expose him at a show trial as an economic saboteur, because he was accused of corruption while in office. Evidence showed that the national security organization, Nigeria's secret service, had mounted the operation, and that it had received a helping operational hand from Mossad. Major Yusufu had spent months planning the operation under the pretext of making a film, and he was the one who first made contact with Alexander Barak, himself an Israeli intelligence operative.

The folk memory of Mossad was perhaps stirred by recollections of an earlier incident which involved the clandestine transport of a man as diplomatic baggage. The Israeli intelligence service itself had taken steps in 1964 to rescue a young Israeli of Moroccan origin whom the Egyptian secret service was attempting to smuggle back to Cairo in a trunk. Mordechai Louk was a rare deserter from the IDF, bored with national service and eventually recruited by the Egyptians to spy on Israelis in Europe. He made rather a hash of it and indeed was a fine example of how not to be a spy, and for that reason fell foul of his new masters, who put him in a trunk at Rome airport for shipment as diplomatic baggage back to Cairo. Israeli agents tipped off the Italian police, who freed him at the airport. He returned to a prison sentence in Israel, making suitable apologies for his behaviour.

In the Dikko affair the kidnap crates were custom-built to designs prepared by Major Yusufu and Alexander Barak. They cost £550 and were delivered to the welfare section of the Nigerian embassy in Bayswater, near to Dikko's house. While that was being done Barak went back to Israel and, with the help of a former senior officer of Mossad, alerted the team they had recruited to be ready to fly to London.

Those responsible for the Dikko affair appeared in the subsequent trial at the Old Bailey, the central criminal court, in February 1985. The three Israelis and the Nigerian pleaded guilty. By so doing they were able to make use of the provision in English law which allowed them to choose not to face cross examination by the prosecution. For the same reason the prosecution simply presented the Crown case against them without detailed revelations emerging, as they would certainly have done if the case had been contested.

Alexander Barak maintained in evidence that he had been acting on behalf of a group of Nigerian businessmen who decided they wanted to bring Dikko back to his home country. Yet his defence counsel, George Carman, QC, told the court, 'Perhaps the most plausible explanation is that the Israeli intelligence network was never far removed from this entire operation.' Certainly it was Barak who recruited Dr Shapiro, a senior anaesthetist and director of the intensive care unit at Hasharon Hospital in Tel Aviv. Originally he offered to pay $1000, which the doctor refused, saying that he would only help the scheme along out of his sense of patriotism as a good Israeli citizen. Barak, the middleman, also said that he was under the impression that Dr Shapiro thought that he was working for Mossad. He had chosen to recruit Israelis for the mission because they were the only people he could trust to carry it out.

Dr Shapiro, who had accepted $2000 to buy specialist medical equipment in London, confirmed that he had only taken part in the kidnapping because he thought he was doing a job for Mossad. Friends of his in Israel confirmed that the doctor was not the kind of man who would knowingly have given help to mercenary kidnappers, and would certainly not have acted as he did unless inspired by higher motives. Born in the Soviet Union, Dr Shapiro had emigrated with his aged parents to Israel, where his career had been advanced thanks to his friendship with an important and influential Israeli – who, indeed, had persuaded him eventually to help with the abduction plot. The prosecution, led by the barrister Roy Amlot, tactfully chose not to bring forward any evidence of the involvement of the Israeli intelligence service. Because the accused were not cross-questioned in court few details about the Israeli connection actually emerged. None the less, in his judicial summing-up Mr Justice McCowan made plain his opinion when he told the jury that the finger of involvement almost certainly pointed at Mossad. The court sentenced Alexander Barak, the twenty-seven-year-old organizer of the plot, to fourteen years in prison, and the other two Israelis received a sentence of ten years each. The Nigerian got twelve years.

The reason behind this operation was that Israel believed it could improve commercial and political relationships with Nigeria by lending a hand to the authorities there in kidnapping Dikko to face trial and punishment at home. It was not the first action of this type sponsored by Mossad. In 1965 General Mohammed Oufkir, the Moroccan minister of the interior and a friend of King Hassan, asked Meir Amit, the Mossad boss, for help in a similar situation. The King was exasperated by the left-wing and republican activities of Mehdi Ben Barka, an opposition leader living in exile and cutting rather a dash in third world politics, and had hinted to his interior minister that the world would be well rid of such a troublemaker.

Although Morocco, as an Arab monarchy, was in principle implacably opposed to the state of Israel, quite cordial relations based upon mutual self-interest existed between the two countries. King Hassan lived in fear of revolution in his country sponsored by Gamal Abdel Nasser, the Egyptian president, and had negotiated with Mossad for protection. With the help of Shin Beth, the service had trained a special security team for the King. It was composed of Moroccan Jews who after emigration to Israel had been specially trained and equipped by Mossad experts. Help was also given in the establishment of a Moroccan security and spy service. In return for this assistance Israel obtained a useful point of access into the Arab world and King Hassan guaranteed the safety of the Jewish minority living in his country.

In these circumstances the ministerial request for help and guidance in the matter of Ben Barka did not come as a surprise. Even so, Mossad was far from enthusiastic at being used as an organization of professional assassins. They agreed to give help only in organizing the kidnap of the Moroccan politician, which involved luring him from Switzerland across the border into France in cooperation with a faction of the French intelligence service, the SDECE (Service de Documentation Extérieure et Contre-Espionage). Once that had been done Mossad adopted a Pontius Pilate attitude over what might happen to the unfortunate Ben Barka.

He was in fact grabbed by a French plain clothes police officer aided by an intelligence stringer as he left the Brasserie Lipp, a fashionable Paris restaurant in St Germain des Prés frequented by politicians and intellectuals. His abductors took him to the country home of a French gangster at Fontenay-le-Vicomte; there he was done to death and his body buried.

There was no suggestion that Israelis had taken part in the murder, but the wrath of President de Gaulle was upon them. Furious that members of the French intelligence service were involved in what he regarded as a ludicrous banana republic kind of plot, he purged his own service as the scandal broke and then turned upon Israel. The Israeli involvement was kept secret in France, but the president was determined to punish Mossad for illegal activities in French territory

193

by ordering Israel to close down its operations in Paris and to withdraw its spies from what had been their principal base in Europe. He never forgave Israel for its part in this affair and his hostility cost the country dear in terms of a strict ban on military aid.

At home, too, Meir Amit found himself in desperate trouble for having sanctioned this seedy, unpleasant and immoral affair. The Eshkol government was informed of the details and called in the former head of Mossad, Isser Harel, to investigate as intelligence coordinator. Once more in an intelligence scandal the drama centred upon who had given the order – a question which again was never satisfactorily answered. The main recommendation was that Meir Amit should resign at once. When he failed to do so it was Isser Harel who abandoned his final intelligence appointment.

Despite the grave international consequences of the Mossad-Ben Barka affair, the Israeli intelligence people got away unpunished for a monstrous act. Two decades later the service was still prepared to transgress against British law, as it had done against French law in 1965, by once again lending a hand with a kidnap attempt on foreign soil. To win friends in Africa it helped Nigerian intelligence, with which it had close connections, to commit unlawful acts in Britain. The British did not go out of their way in public to stress the obvious offence against international law of which Mossad was guilty, and the trial was a low-key affair. Yet the government did express its indignation at the kidnapping of a former minister of an African member of state of the Commonwealth in the centre of London. The incident also caused further trouble for the British government because the Nigerian administration, angry at having been caught out using hired foreigners to carry out a criminal act in London, threatened reprisals if the man they wanted to put on trial was not returned to Lagos.

In British intelligence circles the blame was put squarely upon Mossad for helping, albeit not in a very competent kind of way, to bring the incident about. The Israeli excuse that the men involved were just freelances was not accepted, and MI5 remembered that the same cover story had been used to wriggle away from responsibility for the Ben Barka affair in France. The Sowan plot was just one of several incidents provoked by Mossad's arrogant behaviour in the United Kingdom.

194

25. Death of a Cartoonist

The next affair had its origins in the European odyssey of a Palestinian named Major Abdul-Rahim Mustapha. By the late 1980s the PLO had become so formalized in its structure that its terrorist agents in the field flaunted military ranks. It is one of the fascinating features of irregular military forces that before long they acquire a taste for the formal trappings of a regular army by giving themselves ranks, badges and flags. Such an example of the new model officers of what the PLO considered to be its élite special forces unit – with the designation Force 17 – was Major Abdul-Rahim Mustapha. When he began flitting in and out of Britain – with Mossad, unknown to him, hot upon his trail – that was the beginning of a diplomatic incident which became known as the Sowan affair. At the centre of it were the London movements of Ismael Sowan, an Arab agent in the service of Mossad, arrested by the British police and eventually sentenced to prison for possessing arms and ammunition. His biography revealed a good deal about the complicated hostile relationship between the Israeli secret service and the PLO.

On the other side of the coin the life story of Major Mustapha, a typical officer recruit to the PLO unit, provided a guide through the recent history of the Palestinians. In 1970 he became a member of Fatah and, after finishing academic studies, emerged as a subaltern just as he might have done in a regular army. But the kind of operations he was sent to accomplish in Europe were neither regular nor, strictly speaking, military. His first mission was to help in an attempt against an Israeli aircraft in West Germany in 1970. Later he had further training at the Pakistan Military Academy and in 1980 was appointed to command a

Force 17 operational group for covert action and special operations. After the Israeli invasion of Lebanon he was evacuated to Tunis and then posted to London. In 1985 the PLO transferred him back to Beirut to one of the units which had been re-established there. In one of the many clashes between Palestinians and the Shi'ite militia of Amal he was captured and spent four months in prison in Syria. On release to Cyprus he returned to London in 1985.

Force 17, the unit in which Major Mustapha served, had its origins in the ten-man security guard formed in 1970 to protect Yasser Arafat from attempts on his life, mostly by compatriots in rival organizations. The name derived from the telephone extension number of the guard office at the old PLO headquarters in Beirut. Its commander was Ali Hasan Salameh, a man killed by Mossad because of the conviction that he had organized the kidnapping of Israeli athletes at the Munich Olympic Games. At that time the PLO terrorist unit went under the name of Black September. In Lebanon the leader's bodyguard expanded hugely into a special forces unit of a thousand men. When the PLO was forced to withdraw to Tunis the command remoulded Force 17 into a tightly knit, well-trained commando unit of hand-picked men of assured loyalty who would protect the leader. At the same time Force 17 was restructured for offensive operations. Leaders were awarded military ranks and titles, and new recruits who were brought in to establish cells in Europe, as well as in the Middle East, were carefully vetted to prevent Mossad infiltration. The PLO was only too conscious of the fact that Mossad had thoroughly penetrated its command in Beirut and was now taking measures to try to prevent the same thing happening in Tunis.

Yasser Arafat needed personal protection against the open hostility of such men as Abu Nidal, the boss of his own fringe group which he claimed was the authentic Fatah of the armed struggle. Abu Nidal threatened to kill his old master after Arafat had sentenced him to death for offences against the movement. Nor was Abu Nidal the only dissident chief who wanted to get rid of Arafat. A number of leaders of the diehard groups of the Palestinian movement denounced the chairman, deserted from his forces, and took themselves to Damascus under the protection of President Hafez al-Assad of Syria.

The PLO declared in 1987 that it had stopped 'external' operations, that is to say terrorism outside Israel itself. But as Jehosophat Harkabi, former head of Israeli military intelligence, put it, 'They did still engage in covert attacks from time to time, especially among themselves.' The trap for Arafat was that to justify his leadership he had to be seen to be capable of military action, even while he was trying to figure principally as a peacemaker. To get a consensus in the Arab world he was forced to play it both ways, for only a leader with proven ability to make war dares to try his hand at making peace in the Middle East. The same principle applies to Israeli leaders too.

Force 17 demonstrated its new aggressive policy by attempting to place a bomb in the Syrian embassy in Madrid. Spanish police arrested two suspected members of the force as they prepared the bomb. This attempt demonstrated that Arabs considered to be unfriendly to the PLO were included among the targets, as well as Israelis.

The new unit worked closely with another offensive operations group, the western sector office, whose role was to specialize in action within Israel and which therefore did not come under the Arafat rule banning external terrorism. Their spheres of action sometimes overlapped. Operating at first from Jordan, the western sector was placed under the command of Khalil al-Wazir, a veteran PLO leader, who used the war name Abu Jihad, second only to Yasser Arafat in the hierarchy. When the chairman began mending fences with other Arab leaders after the PLO's 1982 expulsion from Beirut, especially with King Hussein of Jordan, he concentrated on diplomacy. Protracted negotiations were planned to secure some kind of arrangement by which the Palestinians would obtain homeland space on the occupied West Bank and in Gaza. But even while this process continued, and the more so when it failed to achieve results, it was considered necessary for the PLO to be seen to be active in the armed struggle as well.

The task of the western sector office was to use its men for carrying out raids in Israel, and the problem for its Chinese-trained commander, Khalil al-Wazir, was that his headquarters in Tunis were sixteen hundred miles from the potential battlefield. Jordan was unwilling to allow the use of its territory as a base for operations against Israel, and tight security within that country made plotting difficult and dangerous. Instead, Abu Jihad chose to try raiding from the sea, using Cyprus as a staging post. In April 1985 one group of his men, trained in Algeria, embarked aboard the freighter *Atavirus*, equipped with small assault craft with which they would land on the Israeli coastline. But the ship was intercepted by Israeli patrol boats and sunk before the enterprise got going. Abu Jihad took the blame and there was recrimination that his western sector had been infiltrated by Mossad spies. It was at this point that Force 17 tried its hand with similar tactics, but again the Israeli navy succeeded in detecting the raid. It seized the motor yacht *Casselredit* off southern Lebanon and arrested the eight guerrillas aboard, together with Faisal Abu Shahr, deputy commander of Force 17. A few days later yet another yacht with PLO men aboard, the *Ganda*, outward bound from Cyprus, was also intercepted by Israeli gunboats.

197

Back at PLO headquarters in Tunis the leaders came to the conclusion yet again that they were being outsmarted by Mossad, and that the failure of seaborne operations must be put down to Israeli spies keeping watch from Cyprus over their plans. On the Jewish Day of Atonement, a three-man squad from Force 17 boarded an Israeli yacht in the marina at Larnaca, shooting an Israeli woman and taking prisoner her husband and another man. At first they demanded the release of captured comrades in return for the prisoners' lives, then they shot both men dead with bullets in the head. Israel convincingly insisted that the yacht people were simply tourists.

Whether or not the PLO hit team had selected the right target, there could be no doubt that Mossad agents were active in Cyprus, an island which has become, as regards plotting and espionage, a geographical centre comparable to that of Switzerland during the Second World War. On the one side is a swollen PLO representative's office, and on the other a capable Israeli embassy which offers facilities for its intelligence service to use the island as a listening post within easy distance of the Arab world. When Shimon Peres, the then prime minister, was justifying the revenge air strike upon PLO headquarters near Tunis he confidently declared that Israel had sure intelligence that it was indeed Force 17 which had murdered the three Israelis in Cyprus. One curiosity of the Larnaca yacht affair was that the squad of Arab killers was led by a blond Englishman from North Shields who had joined the PLO on impulse three years earlier and had been recruited by Force 17, presumably for operations where it would be easier for such an obvious Anglo-Saxon to work than for an Arab. He is now serving a life sentence in Nicosia.

While these events were taking place in the Mediterranean the PLO also had its teams at work in Europe. One of them was led by Major Mustapha, an officer who was in the Mossad dossiers. Repeating its old tactics, tried and tested in Lebanon, the service actively gained knowledge of his activities through the use of fellow Arabs recruited for the purpose.

The Mossad agent keeping track of Major Mustapha was an ambitious young Jordanian named Ismael Sowan. He came from a village between Bethlehem and Jerusalem where he was born in 1960, seven years before the Israelis conquered the eastern part of the capital city. He was recruited by the Israeli intelligence service while still a teenager, when, like many other young Arabs who found themselves unexpectedly living under Israeli government, he was the victim of conflicting loyalties. It seems likely that, as an ambitious Arab said to be both greedy and crafty who wanted to become a science student, he was happy enough to sign on with Mossad in return for money to pay for his education and his travels abroad. After his eventual arrest in Britain he claimed, no doubt for form's sake, that threats had been made against his family if he refused to join. But his parents, who formally disowned him in a statement published in an Arab newspaper, made no mention of this allegation. 'All the village knew that Ismael was working for the Israeli intelligence,' said his brother Ibrahim. 'They were very angry.'

After training in intelligence fieldcraft Sowan went to Beirut in 1977 by way of Jordan, for it was relatively easy for Arabs from Israel and from the occupied territories to make their way legally across the Allenby Bridge over the River Jordan. Once in Lebanon, and no doubt on Israeli instructions, he joined the PLO. That organization gave him a course of military training, and even sent him on a mission to Jerusalem, without knowing that he was already working for the Israelis. The first task given to him by the Israelis in his new career was to help to decoy an arms smuggler; most moles in the Israeli service were at the time being used to find out as much as possible about the Palestinian leadership and their operational plans. Sowan's other task was to discover the whereabouts of its stocks of weapons. After five years in Lebanon he was ordered to Paris by his PLO masters, ostensibly to learn French. He later gave evidence that Israeli agents there met him regularly in cafés and at other live drops and paid him monthly in cash. His case officer at the Israeli embassy at 3 Rue Rabelais, near the Champs Elysées, was a man known to him simply as Adam. The Paris embassy had long been used by Mossad as its control centre for operations in Europe.

The next stage in Sowan's career as a spy took him to London in 1984 where he acquired an apartment, paid for by the Israelis, in the suitably anonymous district of Maida Vale. Mossad was also paying him £600 a month for his services. His professional aim was to complete a degree course in engineering at Bath. Not long after his arrival in London he made his way, like many other questing Arab students, to the office in central London which the PLO shared with the Arab League. Like the others he said he was in search of money to continue his education. A Palestinian official claimed after the trial that Ismael Sowan had been given the address of the education section and was told not to come back to the main office. That sounded like an excuse.

It was a stroke of good fortune that the first man Sowan met was Mustapha, the Force 17 man who had temporarily taken responsibility for security at the office. The two men already knew each other from encounters in Beirut in the old days. This same Mustapha was the officer more grandly known at PLO headquarters as Major Abdul-Rahim Mustapha. The two men became friendly, as no doubt the

Mossad case officer had intended they should, and began to see a lot of each other. As Sowan's defence counsel, David Cocks, put it, 'He mixed with the PLO. He was working for the Israeli intelligence services. He was in a horrible, dangerous and alarming situation.' The friendship with Mustapha continued even when Sowan enrolled as an engineering student at Bath.

Mustapha told his new friend and fellow PLO supporter about life in Force 17 and about his exploits, among which was an attempt to hijack an Israeli aircraft in West Germany in 1970. He also boasted of other battle honours in Jordan, Cyprus and Spain. Although Sowan later described him as 'a fox, a very intelligent man', there was no reason for secrecy between two Palestinians in a foreign country. Anyway, Mustapha's photograph had already appeared in an illustrated book recounting the history of Force 17 which was freely circulating among Palestinians; in it he is pictured standing on an armoured vehicle in Lebanon, which is probably what drew the attention of Mossad in the first place.

Mustapha and Sowan, the Mossad agent in London, were on such intimate terms that when Sowan married an English girl named Carmel Greensmith Mustapha was his best man and signed the marriage certificate. Eventually in mid-1986 Sowan moved to Hull to take up a post as a researcher at Humberside College of Further Education, and from that time onwards he saw less of the man from Force 17. Indeed at this point he tried, according to his version of the story, to sever his connections with Mossad in order to get on with his academic career. 'But you do not resign from that sort of job,' said his defending barrister.

The Palestinian pair did not meet again until the following year when Mustapha was about to leave the country. He was being expelled by the British authorities at a time when, because of financial trouble, he also had to close down the garage he was running at Leigh-on-Sea in Essex. He needed somewhere to store his arms cache, as he had disposed of the house he had lived in before that. Mustapha paid several visits to his friend in Hull, saying that he wanted to leave a number of suitcases for safe keeping. According to Sowan's defence in court, he did not know that they contained explosives, weapons and ammunition; but that seems an unlikely story. In any event Sowan went to London intending to report the return of Mustapha to someone at the Israeli embassy, but claimed that when he got there he found it was closed for the weekend. If he was speaking the truth that shows either that he was not a very diligent agent, or that his controller had not briefed him very well. What seems more likely is that this was a cover story, intended to hide the fact that Mossad knew at this stage about the arms store and did not want to tell the British authorities about it. Sowan flew to Israel on 14 July 1987 and admitted that once there he brought the Israelis up to date about Mustapha's activities. For reasons of its own Mossad did not want to share that information with anyone else.

Indeed the affair might have remained secret had it not been for a violent event in London that month. On that day a cartoonist named Ali al-Adhami was shot dead by a team of assassins near the offices of the Arab newspaper *Al Qabas* in Ives Street, Chelsea. Who on earth, it might be asked, would kill a cartoonist? It was a question that Scotland Yard began trying to answer by looking at his drawings. There was a sarcastic one showing a body proclaiming that it had died laughing at a newspaper report of elections in the PLO. In another, a man said in the caption, 'They would kill me if I said I was in the PLO and they would also kill me if I said I was not in it.' Several times al-Adhami had been warned that his work, which often showed Yasser Arafat leading a jet-set life of luxury greatly in contrast with the sufferings of his people in the Middle East, was irritating the leadership. In the light of that information it seemed at least possible that an offended and humourless Palestinian hit team might have taken it into its head to murder the Arab funny man.

From France came a tip-off about Mustapha of Force 17, whose name appeared on the wanted list in Paris. In fact, according to the television programme *World in Action* the information was passed on directly on the orders of Charles Pasqua, then French minister of the interior. The anti-terrorist team in London began looking for traces of Mustapha as the man suspected of organizing the murder of Ali al-Adhami. They also sought out people connected with him and discovered that, using a number of different passports, he had slipped in and out of the country for years organizing PLO operations; he was one of the most wanted men in Europe. For the last three years he had lived quietly in Romford, Essex, commuting to work in London as a security guard at the Palestinian office. As part of his cover, he ran the garage at Leigh-on-Sea. The police further discovered that he was a friend of Ismael Sowan and established that on three occasions Mustapha had been to Hull in Yorkshire where Sowan lived. Mustapha's movements in a red Volkswagen Polo were easily traced, because he used an Access card to buy petrol and his car number was written on it by several filling stations. That established the connection with Sowan, whose house was then searched. In it the police found a huge hoard of weapons packed into six suitcases. In the PLO armoury, concealed in a bathroom cupboard at Westbourne Avenue, Hull, were stocks of Semtex explosive, grenades and Kalashnikov assault rifles of the kind favoured for terrorist enterprises. There was enough material there for a sustained terrorist campaign, and Mustapha's fingerprints were on it.

But by the time that this discovery was made, after the return of Sowan from his holiday in Israel, Major Mustapha was gone. The day after the murder of al-Adhami the Palestinian tried and failed to take a flight from Heathrow to Cyprus. Instead he hired a car, drove to Manchester, and from there flew to the Mediterranean island, taking a circuitous route by way of Belgrade. Major Mustapha escaped arrest and remained operational after rejoining Force 17 headquarters in North Africa, ready for further duties. The blame for that failure rested upon Mossad for failing to provide the information which would have led to his capture earlier. By its silence, the same organization became responsible for the arrest and punishment of its own agent, Ismael Sowan, the man left holding the PLO's secret hoard of terrorist material. At the Old Bailey trial he was sentenced to eleven years' imprisonment on conviction for possessing arms and ammunition.

26. The Whitehall Reproach

The whole conduct of Mossad's operations involving Sowan and Major Mustapha provided further evidence of the bad and tactless behaviour of Mossad agents active in Britain. Once again it was the over-eagerness of the Institute's men in their kind of *sans frontières* pursuit of Arab terrorists which got them into trouble. Investigations by the anti-terrorist unit of Scotland Yard, directed by Commander John Churchill-Coleman, into the murder in London of the Arab cartoonist produced disquieting, though intriguing, discoveries about the tactics of Israel's secret service in foreign countries.

They were not responsible for the murder. But when their secret operations were uncovered a tremendous row broke out, with Mossad being accused of acting deceitfully and dangerously in that they had failed to pass on information, of which their man Sowan was the source, to the British authorities. The PLO weapons hoard which he knew about might well have been used at that stage by Arab terrorists raiding in Britain. For Mossad alone knew that the suspected PLO terrorist Major Mustapha, who was wanted on an international arrest warrant and had already been expelled as a dangerous suspect from the UK on an earlier occasion, was again on the loose in Britain after making a clandestine re-entry. That was why the British government reacted with such vigorous protests to Israel.

Mossad could hardly have been expected to unveil all the details of its undercover operation. It dared not risk the life of Sowan or of Bashar Samara, another of its agents in close touch with the PLO cell in Britain. But once the agents had discovered the whereabouts of a large store of PLO explosives and weapons in a friendly country, they were none the less under an obligation to reveal these facts to the authorities. This they did not do; nor did they report the presence in London of a man as dangerous as Mustapha, at a time when Scotland Yard was still ignorant of the fact that he had returned. Moreover, the Israeli case officer sent his men to break in and enter Mustapha's home and remove papers from it, again without informing either British intelligence people or the police.

So that there could be no mistake about the depth of British anger, Arie Regev, an attaché at the Israel embassy, was told that his presence was no longer welcome because of activities incompatible with his diplomatic status. British intelligence found out that he had controlled Ismael Sowan and the other Mossad agent, Bashar Samara, who was by origin a Druze with Israeli citizenship. Another Israeli diplomat, Jacob Barad, was excluded from re-entering Britain while he was still away on leave. The Israeli embassy put out an indignant statement declaring: 'We regret that Her Majesty's Government saw fit to take measures of the kind adopted. Israel did not act against British interests. The struggle against terrorism was its one and only motive.' Once again, Israel was voicing the familiar justifications for its undiplomatic behaviour – 'so long as we are fighting against terrorists, anything goes', and 'we are not doing you any harm, anyway'. The rather defensive attitude of Israel at that time led to the belief that its diplomatic conscience was still by no means entirely clear. To Mrs Thatcher's accusation of Israeli deceit, prime minister Shamir replied in a newspaper interview, 'I will only say that I think there is a misunderstanding. It is regrettable.'

The cause of Mossad's unwillingness to share information with a trusted allied service sprang from over-confidence. Having placed agents so close to Major Mustapha, and knowing where his arms store was located, the natural inclination of the controller was to keep the operation running and the arms cache under surveillance. By so doing he hoped to trace out Mustapha's connection with other Force 17 people and its cells in Europe. Mossad is an institution not over-burdened with anxiety about Arabs murdering Arabs, as in the case of the unfortunate cartoonist who was killed on the London streets. The main concern was to keep their operation secure and private while they searched for further game among Palestinians connected with terrorism, either as enemies or as friends.

It might even have been the ultimate intention to capture or kill Mustapha, or his contacts. After the Munich affair in 1972, Mossad mounted a deliberate campaign of 'taking out' all those leaders deemed to be guilty. In that they had gone too far, and orders were subsequently issued forbidding the murder of suspected terrorist leaders, except in special circumstances. It now seemed to Western intelligence officers that the policy had again changed. It was a belief reinforced by the murder in Tunis in 1988, which was attributed to Israeli intelligence, of Khalil al-Wazir, generally considered to be the likely choice as an eventual successor to Yasser Arafat.

In London, and simultaneously with diplomatic action against the Israelis, the Foreign Office ordered out Zaki al-Hawa, a PLO official who acted as spokesman for its representative in London. He also was known to be a member of Force 17. This gesture was intended as a warning to the Palestinians against planning acts of terrorism in London, for they were the leading suspects in the murder investigation into the death of the cartoonist. It also served to irritate Israel, which resented the gesture in that its embassy was being treated on the same footing as the office of the Palestinian representative, which did not even enjoy full diplomatic status.

When it first became known that clandestine operations were being carried out in the UK by Mossad agents, Mrs Thatcher herself wrote a confidential letter of protest to prime minister Yitzhak Shamir. She warned that, unless its officers behaved themselves in future, Mossad could be removed from the list of friendly intelligence agencies entitled to liaise with Whitehall and its agents, and might be refused help from that quarter. Until then Mossad, together with the secret services of such trusted allies as Australia, Canada and the United States, had been classed as a friendly intelligence agency. The preferential status hitherto given to Israel was demonstrated by the fact that the name of the expelled diplomat, Mr Regev, did not appear in the list of accredited Israeli diplomats in London; this confirmed that Mossad agents attached to the embassy were allowed to preserve their anonymity. Even those not enjoying diplomatic status were favoured by the authorities. After the Sowan affair came the firm warning that further misbehaviour might force Britain to classify Mossad with the KGB and other notably unfriendly secret services whose activities were strongly discouraged.

It was a threat which gave some pleasure to British intelligence officers, who sometimes consider that Mossad is inclined to get too big for its boots. Intelligence services always gain a certain satisfaction from seeing rivals, even when they are friendly members of the intelligence community, being caught out. But it seemed unlikely that in the long term relations between the two countries' services would suffer too much. The fact was that each needed the help of the other from time to time. Certainly Britain was only too keen to tap into Mossad's files on the subject of, for example, links between the Arab terrorist groups and the IRA. Similarly Israel was glad to have a friend in Europe like Mrs Thatcher staunch enough to take a tough line on terrorism and who scorned to negotiate with hijackers and hostage takers.

For all that, relations between the two countries were undoubtedly soured by the Sowan affair, further complicated by fierce Israeli criticism of the huge arms deal announced in that summer of 1988: British firms had contracted to sell to Saudi Arabia quantities of Tornado jet fighters, warships and defence infrastructure. The British stepped in after the Americans had been prevented from making a deal by Congressional opposition sponsored by the Jewish lobby. It was a blow made more bitter by the fact that since 1982 Britain had embargoed the sale of arms to Israel. Yitzhak Shamir went so far as to accuse the British government of 'an irresponsible pursuit of economic interests at the expense of principles'.

It was an accusation which irritated ministers in London and prompted them to call for a full report from the security service on clandestine Israeli operations in Britain. This revealed that although Israel had given the British to understand that, after Mrs Thatcher's warning, they would wind up their networks in Britain, the embassy in Kensington was still running at least one undercover unit, and five agents remained operational in the capital. They too were officially requested to leave. At the same time it was made clear to Mossad that in future the activities of its people would only be tolerated in Britain, on the strict understanding that they kept the authorities fully informed.

Yehuda Azner, the Israeli ambassador, accused the foreign office of deliberately leaking information about Mossad's goings on. And he asked Sir Patrick Wright, permanent under-secretary at the foreign office, to put an end to such leaks, which he claimed were damaging relations between the two countries. None the less there were Israeli politicians, who suggested that such moves were simply part of a Mossad campaign to get itself off the hook. One newspaper demanded an enquiry into the whole affair on the grounds that, if things were not set to rights, then Israeli intelligence would lose access in London to what it described as 'a first-rate water-hole for any intelligence group with Middle East interests'.

An unnamed official quoted by the newspaper *Yevioth Ahronoth* declared, 'In terms of negative repercussions, this is a smaller version of the Pollard case.' The comparison was not entirely valid. Jonathan Pollard, caught spying for Israel in the USA, was run, not by Mossad, but by a rogue intelligence section controlled by the cabinet office. In the Sowan case the arrogant over-confidence of intelligence controllers led them to go on operating their field men after their activities had become public knowledge, and from that dangerous political and diplomatic consequences were likely to result.

It is well understood by friendly governments that Mossad scores its most spectacular successes against terrorists by managing to insert agents within the Palestinian movements. But trouble was bound to arise when they used in Europe the same crude infiltration tactics which had been so successfully employed in Beirut when the PLO headquarters was located there. At that time it was relatively simple for Israeli case officers to manage the men and women in close touch with their targets. One unforeseen consequence of the military success of the Israeli army in the 1982 invasion of Lebanon, which drove the PLO away into further exile, was to make spying operations more difficult: PLO units fanned out through Europe as well as in the Arab world.

In the summer of 1988 while the London clash was at its height Mossad reverted to its old ways by organizing the assassination of the PLO leader held responsible for the seaborne raids, and for the establishment of a new network in Europe. The death of Khalil al-Wazir, in a blast of machine gun bullets in his villa at the organization's Tunis headquarters, robbed the PLO of one of its most senior men. He was the commander of its armed forces and the leader who at long range took control of the Arab *intifada*. So far as hard-line Israelis were concerned that would have been reason enough to merit a death warrant; he was an obvious potential victim for Israeli covert action. One of the 'Big Abus' and a founder member of Fatah, the operational side of the organisation, al-Wazir, because of his diffident manner, was known as the 'silent man'. A capable and widely travelled organizer, he used the war-name Abu Jihad (Father of the Holy War) and masterminded guerrilla operations against what he always called 'occupied Palestine'.

Usually the Institute's killing methods are more individualist than was the commando-style raid in Tunis which ended the career of Abu Jihad. On numerous occasions they either blew up their enemies or mounted small 'surgical' operations. But sometimes, as was the case with the earlier raid upon Palestinian headquarters in Beirut, military units rather than Mossad action squads were used. When the secret service required firepower, it used a specialist counter-terror army unit, Sayaret Matkal.

27. Breaking Taboos

To answer the question, what is amiss with Israel's secret service? it is necessary first to examine the more fundamental question, what has gone wrong with Israel? The scandals, confusions and blunders which afflicted Shin Beth, Aman and Mossad itself were maladies of a kind to which all secret and security services fall victim from time to time. There is no such thing as a record of guaranteed continual success in the espionage and security trade. No clandestine service in a democracy is immune from such happenings, as the record of the United States and Britain all too plainly demonstrates. The rise and fall of Mossad over a period of forty years mirrors the history of Israel from a beginning afire with optimism and enthusiasm to the disabused gloom of a state which now displays all the symptoms familiar to an individual in a mid-life crisis.

For that state of affairs the policies of Israeli leaders, as they wrestled with the insoluble problems created by the very fact of Israel's existence as an independent state in the Middle East, are largely to blame. The noble Zionist dream of a return to the home-land of millions of Jews scattered through the world, to create a new Jerusalem for the oppressed in the promised land, was confronted by the fact that other people were already in possession of most of that territory. The 656,000 Arabs who fled from Palestine, or who were terrorized and turned out of it when part of it became Israel, were no more willing to lose their homes for ever than had been the Jews at the time of the dispersal. Oblivious to the sufferings of refugees the Arab powers kept them in the border camps, pointing like a multi-barrelled weapon at the heart of Israel. For political reasons

208

they refused even to consider the idea of resettling the dispossessed. So the people problem refused to go away.

In the squalid camps of the Arab states the refugees waited for vengeance and multiplied, so that by the 1980s there were more refugees than there had been forty years earlier. The Arab population of the West Bank, Gaza and East Jerusalem totalled more than a million and a half. Early in the twenty-first century, as the Arab birth rate outstrips that of Israelis, Jews will become a minority even in greater Israel itself.

In a debate in the House of Commons in 1939 the then British colonial secretary, Malcolm Macdonald, baldly declared, 'There is no solution to the problem of Palestine. It is a question of right against right.' His words seem equally true today and many people, including myself, descant on the phrase when asked the perpetual Middle East question – Are you for the Israelis or the Arabs? – by answering 'Both.'

During the truce which followed the 1948 war of independence Arabs from the camps began fighting back with raids across the borders, and it was in face of that threat that the new Israel, visualized by the pioneers as a collectivist and pacifist paradise sponsored by the Almighty, was transformed into a militarist Sparta, protected by an increasingly complicated system of internal security. At first, when it seemed that the threat to the new state was a military one posed by the armies of Egypt, Syria, Iraq and Jordan, the Goliath nature of the menace inspired the unconquerable spirit of David. There is no more uplifting and invigorating call to action than to be a hero facing terrible odds, especially when that hero wins. The Israelis rose to the occasion and basked in the admiration of the outside world as their gallant armies threw back the massed ranks of their enemies time after time, and established military supremacy.

Sadly for them, it was the celebrated victory in 1967, the capture of Jerusalem, the whole of Sinai and the whole West Bank of the Jordan, that inspired Palestinian nationalism and produced the menacing plague of terrorism. And it was the war against terrorism which lured Israel into the invasion of Lebanon and involved the IDF and the intelligence services in the morale-sapping operations of a dirty conflict which terminated in the massacres of the Chatila and Sabra, for which they could not escape responsibility. Those events, which still scar the modern history of Israel, led to national doubts and disunity. A lack of self-confidence manifested itself even in the army, whose strength and seeming invincibility had always been a powerful element in unifying the nation. The same lowering of morale was detectable in a war-weary Mossad.

Reservists returning from service in Lebanon were disabused and demoralized, barely recognizable as soldiers from the same army which had come back from other wars as conquering heroes. Discipline seemed lax. In the post-Lebanon period officers and men were actually court-martialled after an incident when a unit failed, through dilatory behaviour, to fight back against terrorists attacking their camp. For the first time young men tried to dodge the draft and avoid the military service which their elders had been so proud to perform. A further ugly sign of the Vietnam complex was that soldiers brought back from Lebanon the drug habit.

As elections failed to produce a satisfactory working majority, the Labour party and Likud agreed to alternate in power. This meant that government was conducted in a perpetual atmosphere of political and electoral strife. Another consequence was apparent in the civil service and in the command structure of the army and the intelligence services. Because Israel had been run virtually as a one-party state in the time of the Labour ascendancy from 1948 until 1977, a system had developed by which there was little distinction between party politicians and the civil service establishment. A defence ministry bureaucrat, Shimon Peres, became prime minister. A party man, Moshe Dayan, became a general. Generals became spymasters, party men became anti-terrorist advisers. After 1977, partly as a result of the intelligence and military shortcomings which almost led to an Arab victory in the Yom Kippur War, the Likud party under Menachem Begin came to power. At that point its supporters made their claims to the fruits of political victory with posts in the establishment, civil and military, formerly occupied by Labour people. And when the two parties began taking it in turn to rule this created further confusion among senior civil service executives with divided political loyalties.

In this atmosphere it became increasingly difficult to run state institutions, including the secret and security services, with their customary efficiency. In the 1980s firm control and direction seemed to be lacking in Mossad operations. Mossad and its fellow services offended the Americans by running the Pollard operation. They infuriated Mrs Thatcher and the British government in the Dikko and Sowan affairs by their unorthodox and uncooperative behaviour. Then, when Western governments, convinced that Yasser Arafat and his PLO really would abandon terrorism in return for land concessions so that their people could live independently in their homeland, Yitzhak Shamir's administration resisted every effort towards a peace settlement. Mossad just fought on in the old style. Undaunted by its error in failing to foresee the dire consequences of trying to redraw the map of the Middle East in alliance with the Lebanese Christians, it was taken by surprise by the Arab uprising which, beginning in 1987 on the occupied West Bank and in Gaza, quickly spread into Israel proper.

After the weary years of the great battle against bomb and bullet terrorism, the security forces seemed to have little idea how to cope with spontaneous demonstrations by groups of young Arab nationalists who simply chanted and threw stones. The military society of Israel had prepared its young people to fight as soldiers in a just war, but few Israelis want to be policemen because of the association with police persecution in the past in Russia and eastern Europe. Instead of riot police the Israelis used conscript soldiers for internal security duties, and, like all soldiers trained for real war, whenever they got into trouble they shot their way out. A senior staff officer recently expressed his worries about what he called 'the low moral standard of soldiers in the territories' and spoke of the need for iron discipline. A young reservist officer publicly told Mr Shamir on a tour of inspection that he and his men were ashamed of what they had to do in action against the young Palestinians.

The Arab death toll has risen to more than five hundred and more than thirty Israelis have been killed; as fear of the Arabs spread, Jewish ultras began taking the law into their own hands, setting upon Arabs, beating them and killing them. Yet the *intifada* still rolled on, and the supreme irony was that the stone-throwing kids of the Arab towns won more support for the Palestinian cause in the outside world than all the terrorist deeds of all the Palestine liberation movements put together. How to master the uprising was a subject which divided Israelis as they had never been divided before. In the summer of 1989 Yitzhak Shamir himself was mobbed by extremists who called him 'Traitor'. As Israeli fanatics began taking the law into their own hands to attack Arabs indiscriminately under the horrified eyes of liberal compatriots, fears were again voiced of the old spectre of civil war among the Jews, described by the prime minister as 'the most dangerous thing that could happen'.

In a mood of self-pity and doubt brought on by all these recent events, Israelis became bolder and more critical in their attitude towards the authorities. Israel had always been a liberal democracy inhabited by argumentative people, which sometimes makes the place seem like one huge debating society. But national security remained sacrosanct and there used to be general agreement that some things were best done with deep discretion. But even the most secret of institutions no longer escaped criticism. Many things have changed in Israel since Mossad was a name never even to be mentioned in

211

print, and in 1988 an attempt by the chief military censor to forbid publication of an article with sharp words to say about the secret service and its bosses was over-ruled by the high court of justice. It was the first time that the censor's decision on such a subject had been successfully challenged. Written by Aluf Ben at a time when a new head of Mossad was being chosen, the article in question eventually appeared in the Tel Aviv weekly *Ha'ir* and cast doubt upon the competence of the outgoing head of Mossad, whom it described as 'a mediocrity'. The court agreed that the name of the Mossad chief ought not to be published, although it rejected the argument that criticism of the leadership of the secret service would cause it grievous harm. The chief military censor, Yitzhak Shani, had argued that even a published description of the Mossad chief would make it easier for hostile organizations to identify him and place his life in danger.

The important principle which the three judges asserted was that the press had a right and indeed a duty to criticize holders of public office. Their judgement laid down that every effort should be made to minimize the possibility that security considerations would harm freedom of speech, which was one of the fundamental values that the security apparatus was meant to protect. It went on: 'The way to achieve a balance between security and freedom of speech is to maintain freedom of speech and to apply restrictions only when there is absolute certainty of a real threat to the country's security, and when no alternative is available.' Commenting on the judges' pronouncement, the *Jerusalem Post* described it as 'an historic ruling'. It is remarkable that for four decades it has been left to the military censor to weigh in the balance how far free expression may be limited in the cause of security. His powers derive from the emergency defence regulations imported directly into the Israeli system from the British former controllers of Palestine. Those regulations were exceptional measures decreed in the United Kingdom on the outbreak of the Second World War, drafted specifically to cope with a national emergency.

The first result of the setback for censorship was that Mossad, taboo-protected for forty years, 'came out' and became the subject of public controversy. Newspaper readers enjoyed the forbidden delights of reading daily about fresh charges and counter-charges by unnamed sources holding forth on Mossad's shortcomings, a subject previously relished only by the knowing few. Nahum Adnonni, the outgoing *Memuneh* himself, was quoted, though still not by name, in the Israeli paper *Hadashot* as saying, 'I am concerned about the fate of Mossad, which has been subjected to mudslinging. The harm caused to Mossad as a result of recent reports angers me more than the harm being caused to me.'

The high court's opinion will no doubt have a long-term effect upon what may be published by the Israeli press and will change the manner in which censorship is carried out. But there is little enough sign that Mossad intends to raise the hem of its cloak of secrecy an inch more than it is compelled to. The influential newspaper *Maariv* commented, 'Now that the high court has made it possible to ask questions about Mossad in public, there are lots that need to be asked.' The writer of the editorial suggested that maybe the time had come for a judicial commission of objective public figures – the great and the good – to investigate the service. There have already been searching enquiries into the behaviour of military intelligence as a result of its errors of judgement before the Yom Kippur War. Shin Beth too came under the spotlight of public investigation after its disgraceful behaviour in the affair of Bus 300. Although Mossad's conduct in its contacts with Lebanese Phalangists, before and during the camps massacre, was probed during the investigation into Aman's part in all that, it has never been thoroughly examined by outside authorities. Nor does it seem likely that *glasnost* is about to break loose at Mossad headquarters, although at least some of the taboos have been broken.

The problem of how to make secret services politically accountable is one faced by every democratic society. The Americans have gone some way in ensuring control over the CIA; the British still wrestle with how to oversee MI5 and MI6, and despite numerous demands for parliamentary control the secret service's secrets are known only to the prime minister and a select few. A parliamentary sub-committee does already exist in Israel with limited powers of enquiry. Aharon Yariv, a member of it, has said publicly that on occasion the intelligence services did come up with detailed answers to questions put. He considered that the committee got a decent overview and was able to exert some influence. The real difficulty was that members without specialist knowledge of intelligence matters found it hard to know what questions to ask. For that reason they have little chance of establishing control over the organs of intelligence.

Part of the Israeli heritage, which it shares with third world countries which like Israel became independent by means of terror and resistance campaigns, is that it started life as an ex-colony whose leaders were more intent on achieving security than on considering how to establish democratic control over their essential secret services. No Israeli government has yet publicly defined the executive

213

controls over the intelligence community, which remains something of a state within a state.

When the *Ha'ir* article was finally published in January 1989 Yitzhak Shamir, the prime minister, was in the process of making the final choice between two candidates for the headship of Mossad. The chosen one also had to be acceptable to Shimon Peres, the alternative prime minister, and the choice was between an outsider who might be expected to revivify the service and a man from inside the service favoured by the Likud party. When it comes to selecting a new high priest of secrecy, every country faces the same kind of choice. Rival factions favour either the new broom from outside, or the old hand who knows where the bodies are buried. Liberal opinion in Israel hoped that if a politically aware executive from outside the service was allowed to take charge it would help their campaign to make the secret service more accountable to Parliament. In line with normal Israeli practice no announcement was made about the final choice, and the name of the new chief remains confidential.

The outgoing director who had served for six years, Nahum Adnonni, was the deputy who took over in September 1982 from Yitzhak Hofi whose reputation had been scarred by his involvement in the troubles which followed the invasion of Lebanon. General Hofi completed his term of office and Brigadier Aluf Yekutiel Adam had been designated as his successor. But this army officer, who earlier had a brief period of service with Mossad, was killed in action in Lebanon. Shortly after Adnonni took command, the Kahan commission, set up to enquire into the massacres at the Sabra and Chatila camps, questioned him about the role of Mossad and military intelligence in that affair although he had not personally been involved in it.

Within the service he was known as a bureaucrat rather than an action man, who began his career in the Shin Beth security service before transferring to Mossad in the 1950s. Colleagues said that they would never have expected this officer, whose most notable experience was as a liaison man with foreign intelligence services, to get to the top; when he was appointed deputy to Yitzhak Hofi, that was thought to be as far as he would get. Aluf Ben, the young journalist who wrote the *Ha'ir* article and was apparently well briefed by Mossad gossips, reported that Adnonni 'behaves almost like a European' and is a broad-minded, lively talker who enjoys the good life, though a hard worker in the office and a strong disciplinarian. Another Israeli publication reported that, because of his sartorial elegance, his colleagues called him 'Mr Gucci'.

Ron Ben-Yishai, a distinguished military commentator, expressed the belief that the *Ha'ir* story was leaked by Mossad officials eager to force out their boss and take his job. He claimed that competitors for the director's job made use of the media: 'To those for whom the manipulation of human beings is their profession, it is not hard to make use of a young and outraged reporter.' He said the blame for Mossad's troubles rested not only with Adnonni but also with political leaders who exercised insufficient control.

Anxiety has been expressed by influential Israelis about the appointment of mediocre people to senior posts within the service. The country seemed to be running short of the outstanding tough and cosmopolitan swashbuckler intellectuals who staffed Mossad in the early days. Brought up in exhilarating times of great danger, the origi-nals were ready to seize the initiative and to take risks. In times less dramatic younger recruits, many of whom have a more comfortable background, tend to be less reckless and more office-minded. The combination of cautious people and stronger hierarchical control has led to operational shortcomings. Former Mossad people assert there is less flexibility in coordination and control of clandestine operations. Although a good deal of the blame for recent failures has been placed upon the director, it has to be said that responsibility must also rest upon the political leadership. Responsibility for the efficiency of Mossad ultimately rests with the prime minister. Indeed suggestions have been made that the time has come to revive the 'X-committee', a small cabinet group which until the mid-1970s from time to time reviewed the conduct of sensitive operations.

Insiders criticized Adnonni on the grounds that he was a quiet-lifer anxious to avoid complications, and claimed that during his time in office Mossad was left just ticking over. It was in that period that the service lost power to influence events, as other agencies moved into its territory. Lekem conducted its own operation in the United States by running Pollard, and when he was exposed Mossad claimed that it had nothing to do with the operation. The suspicion was that Adnonni, knowing that Rafael Eitan, the man in charge, was a friend of the prime minister's, chose not to get involved in any way. The arms for Iran affair was run not by Mossad but by David Kimche, a former deputy director, using some of the Institute's men but without the close collaboration of its director. The other non-Mossad official heavily involved was the ex-journalist Amiram Nir, the prime min-isterial adviser on anti-terrorism. So great was the enmity between the director and Nir that Adnonni excluded him from inner council meetings.

The period between 1982 and 1989 was a pretty uncertain time for those at the top of the Israeli intelligence pyramid. After Lebanon Yehoshua Saguy, the head of military intelligence, was dismissed;

after Pollard the government was compelled to retire Rafael Eitan from Lekem, and Avraham Shalom lost his post at the head of Shin Beth in the backwash of the Bus 300 affair. The only intelligence chief to survive these perilous times and complete his term of office was Mr Adnonni; and that, no doubt, accounted for the hostility to him within the service, where they looked upon him as a trimmer who knew when to keep a hull-down position.

Whatever the truth of such charges, it is certain that Mossad no longer enjoys its former heroic status as a miracle-working intelligence organization. Its failures and misbehaviour in foreign countries can no longer be concealed. When the Mossad team ventured into Latin America to kidnap Eichmann, its exploits excited admiration. But when its squad went to Europe and clumsily kidnapped a nuclear informer Mordechai Vanunu by employing the squalid trick of a sex trap by Cindy, admiration turned to disgust. It suffered more humiliation when its agents in London were turned out by the British government. One of the accusations made by the Israeli press in discussing the scandal was that Mossad admitted it was to blame after a number of British passports forged by Mossad had been discovered in a West German telephone box. Mossad seems to have a taste for using British passports.

Even in Israel, where pride in the triumphs, and gratitude for the undoubted devotion, of the intelligence services have traditionally protected the agencies from public criticism, suspicions are now being voiced that all is not well. The Israelis are an intelligent and questioning people. Until recently they gave the benefit of the doubt to the intelligence men. But lately allegations, based on gossip, have been made of corruption and profligacy within the Institute. A TV film even dared to assert that faulty direction and too much pressure from headquarters may have led to the arrest in Syria of the most heroic of Israeli agents, Eli Cohen.

Mossad's present-day successes remain hidden under the law of secrecy, while its blunders are exposed. But in Israel's present situation, when the immediate threat comes from Palestinian street demonstrations which provoke the vengeance of Israeli extremists, rather than from the Arab armies, it is difficult to see how the secret service can again achieve glittering triumphs of the kind which made its reputation in more heroic times. The old order changes, yielding place to new, as the dreams, dear to the hearts of Menachem Begin and Yitzhak Shamir, of establishing Greater Israel are fading fast. In such times the aims of Israel's secret services become more confused. Their officers may be required to follow the path of the extremist General Ariel Sharon who has publicly demanded the 'elimination'

216

of Yasser Arafat and the archpriests of Palestinian terror. But it may just be that Mossad's next great task will be one of clandestine diplomacy. Distasteful though it may seem to some of the old guard, the alternative is to make the initial undercover contacts with the old enemy Yasser Arafat and the PLO, in the cause of settling the ancient quarrel, in which task military rule, abetted by secret service manoeuvres, has so singularly failed.

Appendix
Heads of Israeli Intelligence

Mossad Chiefs

Reuben Shiloach	1951–2
Isser Harel	1952–63
Meir Amit	1963–8
Zwicka Zamir	1968–74
Yitzhak Hofi	1974–82
Nahum Adnonni	1982–9

Aman Chiefs

Isser Be'eri	1948–9
Chaim Hertzog	1949–50
Benjamin Gibli	1950–5
Yehosophat Harkabi	1955–9
Chaim Hertzog	1959–62
Meir Amit	1962–3
Aharon Yariv	1964–72
Eli Zeira	1972–4
Shlomo Gazit	1974–8
Yehoshua Saguy	1979–83
Ehud Barak	1983–5
Amnon Shahak	1986–

Heads of Shin Beth

Isser Harel	1948–63

Amos Manor	1963
Yosef Harmelin	1964–74
Avraham Ahituv	1974–81
Avraham Shalom	1981–6
Yosef Harmelin	1986–8

Heads of Lekem

Binyamin Blumberg	1957–81
Raphael Eitan	1981–6

Further Reading

Bar-Zohar, Michael   *Spies in the Promised Land* (London: Davis Poynter, 1972)

Barnaby, Frank   *The Invisible Bomb* (London: I.B. Tauris, 1989)

Copeland, Miles   *The Game of Nations* (New York: Simon and Schuster, 1976)

Davenport, Elaine; Eddy Paul; Gillman, Peter   *The Plombat Affair* (London: Futura, 1978)

Dayan, Moshe   *Story of my Life* (London: Weidenfeld & Nicolson, 1976)

Deacon, Richard   *The Israeli Secret Service* (London: Hamish Hamilton, 1977)

Derogy, Jacques & Carmel, Hesi   *The Untold History of Israel* (New York: Grove Press, 1979)

Eisenberg, Dennis; Landau, Eli & Portugali, Menahem   *Operation Uranium Ship* (London: Corgi, 1978)

Golan, Aviezer & Pinkas, Danny   *Codename: The Pearl* (London: Allen Lane, 1980)

Hirst, David   *The Gun and the Olive Branch* (London: Faber, 1977)

Laqueur, Walter   *World of Secrets* (London: Weidenfeld & Nicolson, 1985)

Moshel, Aharon   *The Vipers* (Hamburg: Facta Oblita, 1989)

221

Posner, Steve	*Israel Undercover* (New York: Syracuse University Press, 1987)
Steven, Stewart	*The Spymasters of Israel* (London: Hodder & Stoughton, 1980)
Taheri, Amir	*Nest of Spies* (London: Hutchinson, 1988)

Index

223

225

226

Oboussier, Felix, 168
occupied territories: Arabs in, 24, 119, 124, 161, 209
Office of Strategic Services, 136, 140
oil weapon, 71, 97, 133, 138, 172, 189
Olshan, Judge Yitzhak, 42
Olympic Games (1972), 5, 23, 78–9, 83–4, 85, 86, 91, 169, 196, 204
On the Psychology of Military Incompetence (Dixon), 96
Organisation de l'Armée Secrète, 133
Organization of African Unity, 188
Organization of Petroleum-Exporting Countries, 97
Osiris, 171–6
Osman, Gen. Fouad, 43
Oufkir, Gen. Mohammed, 193

Pakistan, 135; nuclear weapons, 171; Military Academy, 195
Palestine Liberation Army, 105
Palestine Liberation Organization, 7, 79, 82, 180, 210, 217; abandons terrorism (1987), 7, 196, 197; and Jordan, 8, 73, 76, 81, 82, 83, 89, 104; and Lebanon, 8, 81, 82, 86–7, 103, 105–6, 110, 196, 197, 207; and Tunisia, 33, 156, 161, 198, 207; created (1963), 70–1; traitors, 74; Larnaca raid, 89–90, 156, 198; Mossad and Aman underestimate, 96; self-confidence, 97; and USA, 131–2; Force 17, 156, 195–6, 197, 198, 200, 201, 202, 204; international terrorism, 188; and ANC, 188–9; military ranks, 195; Madrid bomb, 197; and Cyprus, 198; in Britain, 203, 205. *See also* Fatah
Palestine Police, 11
Palestinians, 131; in occupied territories, 3, 7–8; in Europe, 33; birth rate, 71; Soviet guns for, 71; training camps, 73; and terrorism, 103; truce (1981), 105; clashes with Shi'ites, 196
Paris, 86, 90, 131, 173, 174, 193–4; Israeli embassy, 88, 132, 199; PFLP in, 127, 128
Pasqua, Charles, 201

Pazner, Aviem, 158–9
Peace for Galilee, Operation 105–9
Pearl, *see* Kishak-Cohen, Shulamit
Peres, Shimon, 37, 121, 122, 163, 210; and Iran, 113, 116; and Lekem, 147; and Pollard, 159; and nuclear programme, 165; and Vanunu, 180, 183; and Hamman raid, 198; and Mossad, 214
Perrin, François, 167
Peta-Tikvah, 191
Phalange, 104, 105, 106, 107–8, 213
Philby, Kim, 134–5
Pilz, Prof. Wolfgang, 55, 56
Plombat, Operation, 168–9
Pollard, Anne, 154, 155, 156, 157, 161
Pollard, Jonathan Jay, 9, 21–2, 24, 116, 135, 149, 154–63, 206, 210, 215, 216
Pompidou, Georges, 153
Popular Front for the Liberation of Palestine, 71, 77, 82, 83, 85; in Aden, 82; in Lebanon, 86–7; Entebbe hijack (1976), 98; plot to kill Sadat, 127–31
Posner, Steve: *Israel Undercover*, 90
profile dossiers, 66
Project 333, 55

Queen Elizabeth II, 127
Quibya, 32, 37
Quick, 86

Rabin, Yitzhak, 99, 128, 129
Rahman, Col. Abdel, 54
Ran, 15
Raphael, Sylvia, 8, 88–90
Ras al-Shak, 79
Ras Ghaleb, 153
Ravid, Ilar, 158, 159
Reagan, Ronald, 112–16, 140, 159
Recovery, Operation, 115
Red Army Faction, 85
Red Crescent, 76
Red Cross, 80
Red Sea, 153
Redfa, Munir, 150–1
refugees: Jewish 10, 12, 15, 27, 74–5; Palestinian, 45, 70, 75, 76, 83, 89, 106, 208

Regev, Arie, 204, 205
Rekhesh, 12
rescue missions, 4, 5, 98, 158
Reshud, 17
Reuter, Thomas, 98
Ritchie, Rhona, 119
Rolling Stone, 167
Rome, 86, 136, 181, 182, 191
Rommel, Erwin, 54
Ron, Dina, 50
Rotzinger brothers, 149

Sa'adi, Dr Victor, 40
Sabra camp, 107–8, 209, 213, 214
Sadat, Anwar, 138; Arab plot to
  assassinate, 79, 127–31; Yom Kippur
  War, 92–9; and Gaddafi, 127–8;
  meets Begin, 130–1, 173
Safire, William, 162
Saguy, Maj.-Gen. Yehoshua, 108, 109,
  140, 215–16
Saica, 168
Sakharov, Elijah, 167
Salameh, Ali Hassan, 79, 85, 87–8,
  90–1, 169, 196
Salameh, Georgina, 90
Samara, Bashar, 203, 204
Samosa, President, 143
Sandinistas, 83
satellites, 141
Saudi Arabia, 135, 138
Savak, 114
Sayaret Matkal, 87–8, 207
Scheersberg A, 168–9
Schiff, Ze'ev, 175
Schultz, Brigitta, 98
Schulzen, Herbert, 167–8
Schwartz, Diana, *see* al-Asan, Dina
Schwimmer, Al, 114, 115
Secret Intelligence Service, 3, 6, 11
Seidenwerg, Avraham, 40–1, 43–4
Sella, Col. Aviem, 154–5, 157–8,
  159–60
Serterio, Francesco, 168
Service de Documentation Extérieure
  et Contre-Espionage, 193
Shabak, *see* Shin Beth
Shacham, Brig. Michael, 32
Shagari, President, 190

Shah of Persia, 82, 112, 114;
  overthrown, 104
Shahr, Faisal Abu, 197
Shai, 12, 13
Shalom, Avraham, 121, 122, 159, 216
Shamir, Yitzhak, 11, 121, 163, 180, 210,
  216; and Pollard, 159; and Vanunu,
  183; and Margaret Thatcher, 204,
  205, 206; and British arms embargo
  (1982), 206; and *intifada*, 211
Shani, Yitzhak, 212, 214
Shapiro Dr Lev-Arie, 191–2
Shapiro, Dr Zalman, 166
Sharett, Moshe, 37, 46
Sharif, Bassam Abu, 85
Sharm-el-Sheikh, 68–9
Sharon, Ariel, 8, 32, 155, 216–17;
  Yom Kippur War, 93; and Lebanon
  invasion (1982), 105, 106, 108–9; and
  Sabra and Chatila, 108; and arms for
  Iran, 113; and Shin Beth, 122
Shi'ites, 106, 110, 111, 143, 196
Shiloach, Reuben, 16–17, 18
Shin Beth, 4, 117–24, 214; relations with
  other security services, 6; reputation,
  8; and *intifada*, 8; founded, 13, 15;
  role, 17, 18, 117; failures and
  scandals, 19, 120–3, 179–80, 208, 213;
  and Aman, 20; and Mossad, 20; and
  occupied territories, 24; and Beer,
  51–2, 118; and terrorism, 72, 103;
  informers, 73; Kilowatt group, 81–2;
  and Lebanon, 105; and El Al, 117;
  informers, 117, 119; interrogations,
  117, 123; and Begin, 117; expansion,
  118; Non-Arab Department, 118; and
  Sharon, 122; and foreign intelligence
  agencies, 136–44; and nuclear programme, 165–6, 171–6; and Morocco,
  193
shtinkerim, 31
Shultz, George, 142, 157
Sica, Domenico, 182
Sicily, 141
Sidon, 76, 79, 80
Siem, Martin, 152
signals, *see* electronic warfare
Sinai, 33, 38; missile bases, 55; Six-Day
  War (1967), 66–7; UN buffer force,

232

Sinai, *contd*
  UN buffer force, *cont.* 68; Yom
  Kippur War (1973), 92–9; Israeli
  occupation, 127, 131, 153, 209
Sitte, Prof. Kirt, 118, 133
Six-Day War (1967), 29, 32, 58, 59,
  61, 65, 66, 70–1, 75, 81, 92, 93,
  124, 132, 134, 139, 165, 166, 189,
  209; Israeli contrivance, 66–7, 68; air
  battles, 147
Sluzer Brothers, 148
Société Générale des Minéraux, 167
Sofaer, Abraham, 159–60
South Africa, 143, 162, 187–8, 189
South Yemen, 27, 82
Sowan, Ibrahim, 199
Sowan, Ismael, 194, 195, 198–202,
  203–4, 205, 206, 210
Spain, 200
Special Air Service, 32, 86
Special Operations Executive, 11
spy satellites, 141
spy ships, 21, 67
Spymasters of Israel, The (Steven), 15,
  94
Squire, William, 180
Stadelheim prisons, 85
Stalin, Joseph, 6, 137
Stansted airport, 190
Starboat, 152
Stern, 20–1
Stern Gang, 19
Steven, Stewart: *Spymasters of Israel*,
  15, 94
Strecker, Hans, 149
Sudan, 27
Suez Canal, 92, 93, 94; crisis (1956),
  38–9, 43, 47–8, 49, 165, 166
suicide bombs, 111
Sunday Times, The, 177–83
Suzanna, Operation, 39, 60
Switzerland, 56, 77, 193, 198; Kilowatt
  group, 81; and Israel, 148–9; and
  France, 149
Syria, 196, 209, 216; captures Israeli
  commandos, 38; coup, 38; and
  fedayeen, 45; Mossad in, 59–62; arms
  from USSR, 60, 61, 139, 150; Jordan
  project, 68; failure to destroy Israel,

71; Yom Kippur War (1973), 92–9,
  170; intelligence service, 104, 107,
  119, 123; and Israeli invasion of
  Lebanon (1982), 105; air force, 105,
  139, 154; nuclear programme, 156;
  and Britain, 180

Taabes, Kamil Amin, *see* Cohen, Eli
Tabriz, 115
Tadiran, 143
Taheri, Amir: *Nest of Spies*, 115
Taiwan, 143
Tal, Wasfi, 83
Tamuz 1 and 2, *see*, Isis *and* Osiris
Tamuz Research Centre, 175
Tangier, 131
Tanzania, 189
Taylor, Theodore, 178
Tehran, 25
Tel Aviv, 4, 143; intelligence HQ, 13,
  18, 21; British embassy, 31, 119; US
  embassy, 31; Ben-Gurion airport, 72,
  78, 179; Russian embassy, 134
Tel Nof, 160
Telkoor, 143
terrorism, 7, 70–80, 209
Thatcher, Margaret, 112, 180, 181, 204,
  205, 206, 210
Thompson, Brig., 113
Tigris, River, 175
Time, 132
Tobruk, 130
Tohami, Mohammed Hassan, 130–1
Toubianski, Capt. Meir, 14
Toulon, 173
Trans-World Airlines, 142
Trident, 114
Tunis, 141, 156, 196, 205; PLO base,
  161, 198, 207
Tunisia, 156
Turkey, 83, 114, 135, 151
Turner, Adm. Stansfield, 140
Tyre, 76, 79

U-2 spy plane, 166
Uganda, 98, 187
Umhashida, 33
Union of Soviet Socialist Republics:
  Jews in, 15, 27, 118, 133, 141, 162;